IN PRAISE OF NONSENSE

Kant and Bluebeard

MERIDIAN

Crossing Aesthetics

Werner Hamacher
& David E. Wellbery
Editors

Translated by
Henry Pickford

Stanford
University
Press

Stanford
California
1999

IN PRAISE OF NONSENSE

Kant and Bluebeard

Winfried Menninghaus

In Praise of Nonsense: Kant and Bluebeard
was originally published in German
in 1995 under the title
Lob des Unsinns: Über Kant, Tieck und Blaubart

Stanford University Press
Stanford, California

Printed in the United States of America

CIP data appear at the end of the book

Contents

IN PRAISE OF NONSENSE

Kant and Bluebeard

§ 1 Introduction: Nonsense, Victorian Nonsense, Romantic Nonsense

Thesis

"All the richness of imagination," Kant cautions in the *Critique of Judgement*, "in its lawless freedom produces nothing but nonsense."[1] Nonsense, then, does not befall the imagination like a foreign pathogen; rather, it is the very law of imagination's own "lawlessness." Kant therefore prescribes a rigid antidote: even in the field of the aesthetic, understanding must "severely clip the wings" of imagination and "sacrifice [. . .] some" of it. This politics of curtailment echoes the critique of the stormy genius well known since the 1770s. The "ideal" liaison between beauty and imagination, however, cannot be broken solely from the side of genius's excessiveness and unreason. In the 1790s nonsense escapes—for a brief moment in the history of Romantic literature, extending from its beginning in 1795 to its denouement in 1797,—the Kantian imperative that it be "disciplined" and sets off in another direction. It finds refuge in the aesthetics of ornament, arabesque, and fairytale, and acquires the character of a hyperbolically artistic form rather than of a natural power prior to all culture. Novalis inaugurates the ideal of "poems [. . .] without any sense or coherence;"[2] similarly, Tieck demands license for a "book without any coherence," full of "contradictory nonsense" and "spectacles about nothing."[3] "To introduce a new nonsense,"[4] seems to be the entire purpose of some literary productions. These citations introduce the central thesis of the present study: *there exists an early Romantic poetics of nonsense.* No-sense and non-sense [*Ohne-Sinn und Un-Sinn*] should be recognized as categories of the Romantic project in its earliest phase.

According to Kant, imagination in its pure form—which by the same token is its *vitium*—produces "tumultuous derangements" that shatter the "coherence which is necessary for the very possibility of experience."[5] On the other hand, as the "faculty of intuitions"[6] and of "presentation,"[7] imagination is precisely the guarantor, indeed, the producer of all reality: without intuitions and without signs all of our concepts would be empty and thus without "reality."[8] Fichte, who along with Kant was a main source for early Romantic thought, established this as a central theorem in his 1794 *Wissenschaftslehre*: "All reality—understandably, of course, *for us,* as in a system of transcendental philosophy it can only be understood—is produced merely through the power of imagination."[9] On this basis, there are two avenues open to the Romantic poetics of nonsense. It can bring the imagination's creative powers into opposition with imagination's function of constituting reality. Inversely, this poetics can see in the displacement of meaningful contexts an "indication of reality":[10] reality "in itself," which is otherwise unavailable, infiltrates the structures of the symbolic order, thus creating a phantom of the *Real.* The complexity of Ludwig Tieck's championing of nonsense lies in its attempt to negotiate both of these polar trajectories of imagination at the same time.

Around 1800, according to the diagnosis of Friedrich A. Kittler, the cultural "discourse network" was refitted and reoriented on a variety of registers toward "sense"[11] as a power of meaning that permeates and orders all details of a discursive event into a totality. The distinction between the *material surface* of a discursive event and the *depth* of its meaning, accompanied by the preference for the intelligible pole of this opposition, became the characteristic framework for numerous social practices. These entailed a transformation in pedagogy and practices of promoting literacy as well as a reform in reading and study, in universities and in the bureaucracy. In academic teaching, the institutionalization of hermeneutics as the new vanguard science responded to this comprehensive revolution in the discursive network of writing and reading. This network's new practices and its underlying assumptions surpassed the academic science of hermeneutics in its breadth, while at the same time undercutting its subtle problematizations. (Only in this less subtle sense does the following study speak of "sense," "understanding," and "hermeneutic.") The poetics of nonsense arises within the horizon of this discursive system, in the border area between late Enlightenment and earliest Romanticism. In Foucault's sense, this poetics can be read as one of the diverse "points of resistance" that are "present everywhere in the power network," as countermovements that do not simply exist outside the new sense-paradigm, and yet are not merely its parasitic "underside."[12] Long before today's "humanities," literature itself, at least in one of its genres, questioned the innocence of understanding and challenged the central fictions of the hermeneutical field.[13] At least for a short period of time, a playful, even provocative suspension of the sense paradigm became the center of a genre theory as well as of a new literary rewriting of this genre. The name of this genre is the *fairy tale.*[14]

Systematic and Historical Relationship Between Sense and Nonsense

"Sense" is, in Nietzsche's words, "necessarily [. . .] a sense of relation and perspective." It can never be attributed to any phenomenon per se but is rather an effect of "interpreting."[15] "Nonsense" too indicates something that is thoroughly relative: all utterances, actions, and facts that at a certain time and in a certain context are adjudged *not* to correspond to a certain idea of "sense."[16] The borders between "meaningful" and "not meaningful" are transitory and unstable; they must be continually reconfirmed and are constantly being displaced. This ongoing (re)determination of borderlines is required for every articulation of "sense" or "meaning."

The liminal region, the margin where sense and nonsense collide and pass into each other, is the *definiens* not only of nonsense but also of sense. Gilles Deleuze therefore formulated his *Logique du sens* by means of an interpretation of the prototypical nonsense books of Lewis Carroll.[17] Nonsense does not merely imply, like any oppositional concept, that its contrary also exists. Rather, its Other always recurs within its own field. "Sense," however, tends to posit itself as an absolute in its own field and in this ideological self-sufficiency it tends to efface the reminder of its being dependent on the difference between sense and nonsense. Walter Blumenfeld rightly noted that "nonsense is always related to sense (indeed, linguistically), as nothing is related to something, [but usually] not vice versa."[18] This asymmetry of an apparently symmetrical polarity shows not only that nonsense is parasitically dependent upon sense but also that it is a phenomenon that eminently articulates the *entire* difference between sense and nonsense.

The appeal to the border between sense and nonsense in general has a twofold character. Firstly, it enacts "a kind of taboo behavior."[19] It identifies that which we cannot understand or meaningfully contextualize within a given framework and banishes it into the realm of the anomalous, the deviant, and the unreal.[20] Wherever this excluded Other that threatens the integrity of an interpretational scheme is presented positively, monstrous forms and shapes are begotten that can fall into the grotesque and the absurd.[21] Through a reflexive turn, however, the excluded nonsense can accrue the opposite value. If everything that we consider to be real and meaningful is in fact merely an effect of our own interpretive schemes, then that which evades those schemes can become for us the "authentic" and absolutely real in its transcendental givenness and unavailability.[22] Indeed, it can even become from a religious perspective a proof of God's existence (*credo quia absurdum*).[23]

Demarcating the border between sense and nonsense makes interpretative frames reflexive and therefore serves as a catalyst for exploring the very parameters of learning: "To engage in nonsense, one must already have the ability to learn about learning; nonsense not only engages this ability, nonsense itself may be seen as an exploration of the parameters of contexts of learning [. . .] Nonsense is not simply a safe place to work out a response to the world of common sense, as it might be in simple reversals and inversions, it is also a field where one can critique the interpretive procedures used in manufacturing that world, and, with increasing self-consciousness, a critique of the interpretive procedures by which nonsense itself has come to be."[24] According to Walter Blumenfeld, it is "actually considered to be an indication of intelligence if someone has the capability to intentionally produce indubitable nonsense. Experiments to develop intelligence tests on the basis of this assumption are being prepared, and look promising."[25] From here, interesting prospects unfold for an anthropology of nonsense (which will not be further pursued in the present work): on account of its close connection to learning, intelligence, language, and laughter—hence to qualities that are generally regarded as defining *homo sapiens*—the faculty of voluntarily producing nonsense is actually a distinguishing characteristic of the human being. Up until now at least, no other beings have been discovered that possess this capability.

The extent to which the distinction between sense and nonsense is subject to historical change is proven primarily by the dynamism of worldviews: what today is taken for granted was yesterday condemned as nonsense. Even the asemantic play of language with its phonetic material allows very diverse classifications. If the baroque's phonetic playfulness is measured against the standard of the communication of meaningful sentences, it immediately falls under the category of nonsense. On the other hand, if it is related to baroque "theories" of sound and of the language of nature, such phonetic whimsy acquires a meaning and a function all its own. The same is true for counting rhymes (such as "eeny meeny miney mo"): even the most nonsensical ones are meaningful in the context of the counting exercise. Sense in this case, however, does not mean the specifically hermeneutical, comprehensive meaning of an individual text but rather the ability to perform a particular function within a given purposive context. With the varied coexistence of several, mutually irreducible levels of sense and nonsense one need not wait for Freud to speak of a "sense in nonsense."[26]

For literary history and poetics, an even more radical historicity of the discourse on "nonsense" is essential. Not only is the ordering of linguistic phenomena along the distinction of "sense" and "nonsense" historically contingent; the institution and the application of the distinction itself mark an eminent date in literary history. In fact, the distinction is no more than 200 years old and essentially belongs to the "discourse network 1800" that Friedrich A. Kittler traced from the perspective of the hermeneutical dictum of meaning (or "sense"). Kittler did not, however, consider its counterpart (in both senses of the word), namely "nonsense." For more than two thousand years poetics, buttressed by rhetoric, has inquired into whether or not literature is beautiful, sublime, sentimental, overpowering, cathartic, pacific, soothing, or entertaining; whether or not literature fulfills certain *virtutes dicendi* in diction, phrase, and verse; and whether or not it attains canonical models. With the end of the rhetorical paradigm and the emergence of the hermeneutical paradigm, however, *one* claim above all is made upon literature: to be *infinitely meaningful.* Only with this claim does the correlative concept of nonsense become a relevant category of poetics. The system of literature first had to make the topic of "sense" its project as well as its criterion of quality before a counterpart could be created: a discrete genre that explicitly institutes the concept of nonsense as its proper name.[27]

Nonsense as a positive category in poetics is not, as is generally assumed, a Victorian invention. It goes back, in fact, to early Romanticism where nonsense did not develop into a specific genre; nor did it have the same semantics and theoretical function as in Victorianism. Scholarship on Romanticism is largely ignorant of the fact that nonsense is a Romantic category at all and, moreover, an important one, nor does it recognize that such a category made it possible to describe fundamental innovations in Romantic literature. Indeed, no less a figure than Arno Schmidt himself drew attention to the phenomenon; but his portrait of Tieck[28] went strangely unnoticed by the academic guild.[29] The scholarship on

Edward Lear and Lewis Carroll reveals a different picture: it occasionally hints at a Romantic heritage in Victorian nonsense.[30]

Nonsense Poetry in the narrow sense can be characterized by a series of succinct procedures on the level of word, clause, sequence of clauses, and verse line: through devices such as phonetic substitution and inversion, addition or removal of phonemes, asemantic word combination, literalizations and decontextualizatons, the choice of specific rhyming pairs, unmotivated application and repetition of fixed schemata. The fairy tale and the Romantic fairytale arabesque, the subjects of this study, hardly offer any parallels to these techniques in their construction of word, clause, and verse. As a rule, they leave the phonetic material intact as well as the syntagmatic structures of everyday language.[31] Nonetheless, the fairy tale and the fairytale arabesque also anticipate, though indirectly, the linguistic techniques of Nonsense Poetry. The latter's phonetic and semantic "tricks" have their analog, and in part their prefiguration, in the Romantic nonsense arabesque at higher levels of textual patterns: in the demotivation, the inversion and empty repetition of traditional units of plot, and their narrative concatenation; and in the provocative indifference and even defiance of their narrative plot and of their figures of representation in complying with readers' expectations of sense and meaning.

The various linguistic techniques of Nonsense Poetry are not its exclusive possession nor are they obligatory in particular combinations or even as single devices. Therefore, these techniques by themselves cannot suffice for the creation of nonsense effects. Wim Tigges consequently looked for a distinctive type of communication that first and foremost makes inversions, serializations, and so forth into forms of nonsense.[32] His definition, certainly the most satisfactory to date for explaining the "canonical" Nonsense Poetry, is as follows:

> In order to be successful, nonsense must at the same time invite the reader to interpretation and avoid the suggestion that there is a deeper meaning which can be obtained by considering connotations or associations, because these lead to nothing [. . .] Nonsense therefore is a genre of narrative literature which balances a multiplicity of meaning

> with a simultaneous absence of meaning [. . .] The greater the distance or tension between what is presented, the expectations that are evoked, and the frustration of these expectations, the more nonsensical the effect will be.[33]

According to this definition, nonsense would have no effect at all and in fact would not even be perceived *as* nonsense were it not always already situated within the field of sense. It is therefore never simply the Other of the hermeneutical field but rather occupies an eccentric position to it and within it: as a provocative or playful exploration of its limit and as an impediment and intermittent suspension of its proper functioning. Nonsense is a way in which "the non-hermeneutical" (Gumbrecht) still appears *within* the horizon of the hermeneutical field; as a hybrid of inside and outside, it articulates the field's limitations. The Romantic discourse *about* nonsense in the literature *of* nonsense evidently also produces sense effects and hence the very negation of what such literature seems to be about. But even this "sense in nonsense" does not per se destroy the balance Tigges requires because it is immediately differentiated into contrary extremes and thereby submits to the "nonsense structure" of self-contradiction. Its poles are as follows: nonsense as the negative meaninglessness of existence (and so tending toward the absurd); nonsense as the positive promise of a "free" untrammeled poetry; and—not least of all—nonsense as the "real" that in Friedrich Schlegel's words is provided only "sparingly and drop by drop,"[34] in apparently realistic and completely motivated narratives. These elements of a Romantic poetics of nonsense—in order not to "sublate" themselves and in order *not* to be dispatched out of the border area of nonsense—can be presented in the mode of arabesque only at the cost of being unavoidably at cross-purposes with their own concept.

Within the polemical and ambivalent relation to the power of "sense," the poetics of literary nonsense pursues its effects with intention and calculation. Even when literary nonsense claims to short-circuit the control of conscious reason, this act depends on a conscious sanction, a deliberate license. Thus, literary nonsense effects are as distinct from involuntary nonsense as they are from

Derrida's dissemination of sense, which is always imminent and indeed ultimately omnipresent, overshadowing as well as undermining every intentionality. One could say that literary nonsense practices what for deconstruction to a certain extent is impossible as well as unnecessary: a deliberate dissemination. Nonsense does not "subvert" logos *tout court*, but rather has an historically specific opponent in view and remains bound in a "love-hate" relationship with the imperatives of that opponent.

Lewis Carroll called his books "fairy-tales."[35] Studies of Nonsense Poetry therefore habitually refer to "fairy-tale world," "fairy-tale chaos," "fairy-tale play,"[36] to the "fairy-tale quality"[37] of nonsense, and to "nonsense fairy tales."[38] However, these studies do not discuss in any detail the relationship between the fairy tale and nonsense. Often, vague reference is made to childhood as their common denominator and hence to something that as a privileged correlate of the fairy tale is an invention of the 18th and 19th century. At other times *Alice's Adventures in Wonderland* is seen as a fairy tale *inverted* into nonsense. The theory of the fairy tale and its Romantic reverberations, however, allow for an understanding of the suspension of "sense" as an integral element of the very genre of the fairy tale. Nonsense Poetry in this respect, then, does indeed continue several tendencies of the fairy tale and its Romantic rewriting.[39] By articulating the relationships between nonsense, the theory of the fairy tale, and Romantic poetics, the present study explores a constellation that hitherto appeared only as a vanishing point in studies on Nonsense Poetry and as a presupposed background;[40] this is a constellation that has hardly been a desideratum at all in the scholarship on Romanticism and the fairy tale itself.

Types of Nonsense

Walter Blumenfeld has distinguished five types of nonsense. *Semantic* nonsense—for example, the sentence "this round circle is quadrangular"—arises from the disturbance or suspension of the "relation between the sign and its reference."[41] In his *Logical Investigations*, Husserl differentiated the field of semantic nonsense—

and the "laws of avoiding" it—along two poles: violations of the "ideal framework," the "pure grammar" of a language, or of the "compatibility" of the constituted meanings to existing entities.[42] Husserl deemed only the first variety to be nonsense "in its literal, strict sense." "A heap of words, like *king but or similar and* is not accessible at all to a unifying understanding; each word has sense in isolation, but the compound is senseless." It violates therefore "the *a priori* laws pertinent to the constitution of the essential forms of meaning." However, these forms "leave quite open whether meanings built on such forms have objects or not, or whether [. . .] they yield possible truth or not." Sentences of the type "this round circle is quadrangular" conform to the laws underlying the formal possibility of sense because they produce a grammatically reasonable sentence. However, they violate the "laws which discourage absurdity" because they lack the "consistency of meanings" or the compatibility to existing entities or both. In the first edition, Husserl relativized his distinction of logical or existential incompatibility from strict semantic nonsense as follows: "This absurdity is also often called [. . .] nonsense, just as after all an egregious violation of empirical truth is called 'nonsense.'"[43]

Following customary usage and Blumenfeld's typology, the field of semantic nonsense in the present study also comprises Husserl's "objective" and "logical preposterousness." The quasi-transcendental "nonsense" of pure "heaps of words," which already transgresses the "primary and fundamental sphere" of the "ideal framework" of possible meanings, does not arise in Romantic nonsense. Even the extreme cases of Victorian nonsense, such as Carroll's *Jabberwocky*,[44] at best only hint at this type of nonsense. Another distinction made by Husserl and beholden to the tradition of logic also has no application in the field of the Romantic poetics of nonsense: the distinction between a purely formal, truth-transcendent sense and a referential or truth-valued meaning. According to Frege, "sense, even considered without meaning, without truth-value, is enough for poetry, but not for science."[45] With this he draws a clear line of demarcation between sense and meaning/reference. However, in the language around 1800 and in the system of hermeneutics, whose concepts were subjected to early Romanticism's playful poetics of nonsense, "meaning" is neither equated with objective referentiality and truth, nor is sense separate from every kind of objectivity. Rather, both are largely used synonymously and moreover for phenomena of linguistic and nonlinguistic nature. The "understanding of a word" means more or less "'the sense, the meaning,' which is inherent in the word in its general usage."[46] Thus, Ludwig Tieck denies not only a continuous sense but also a "meaning" to any narrative or "course of a life" that lacks "unity" and "coherence."

In Blumenfeld's typology, there are four other kinds of nonsense that do not necessarily entail semantic nonsense. *Telic* nonsense or nonsense of purpose occurs when an intentionally guided behavior is incompatible with its purpose. An example is "the Horatian farmer who waits until the river runs dry, so that he can cross it without getting his feet wet."[47] *Logical* nonsense occurs between judgments and their grounds, and therefore does not lie in the statement itself (as in semantic nonsense), but only in its justification.[48] As an example, Blumenfeld recounts the logical schema that Schopenhauer maintained underlies one of Hegel's arguments: "all geese have two legs; you have two legs. Therefore you are a goose." Statements of the type "Severe poverty comes from *pauvreté*" also belong to this form as does the following justification for having returned a borrowed jug in a damaged condition: "Firstly, I didn't borrow the jug, secondly, it was damaged before I received it, and thirdly, I repaired it before returning it."[49] *Motivational* nonsense is present when the relation between a certain behavior and its psychological conditions "does not correspond to our conscious feelings or to what we think we know about them."[50] In *eidetic* or *Gestalt* nonsense, finally, "it is essentially a matter of the *relationship* of the parts to the whole. If we have no dominance, no ruling unity, then sense falls away."[51]

Alfred Liede was the first to apply this classification to literature. He found that in the field of Nonsense Poetry, "semantic and logical nonsense predominate." *Gestalt* nonsense enters "into consideration only in a few cases;" its domain is that of the fine arts.

"Motivational nonsense and telic, or purposive, nonsense are not relevant for us here, since in this relation the poet can wholly do as he pleases."[52] Romantic nonsense presents a completely divergent selection of types of nonsense. Semantic and logical nonsense, the two dominant types of nonsense in Victorian nonsense, hardly play a role in Romantic nonsense. Yet only semantic and logical nonsense can be revealed through an analysis of smaller verbal and phrasal units, such as predominate in almost all studies of Nonsense Poetry. The three other types of nonsense always require the consideration of larger contexts. For Romantic literature, the *Gestalt* and the motivational types of nonsense are of supreme importance. *Gestalt* nonsense in Blumenfeld's use of the term is by no means singularly the domain of the fine arts. Its literary forms, that is, are not at all confined to independently ambulatory knees (Morgenstern) or other grotesque monstrosities that appear as the protagonists and the *contents* of literature. The relationship of the parts to the whole can frustrate the expectations of "dominance," "unity," and "sense" in the *composition* of literary works as well. In Nonsense Poetry this results from its peculiar seriality, the "one and one and one and one and one" of its discrete sequences,[53] the totality of which does not exceed the sum of its parts and which rather dissipates the fragments of meaning instead of organizing them into a *Gestalt*-like surplus. The Romantic poetics of interruption, fragmentation, and above all the appropriation of the grotesque and the arabesque as principles of literary composition launches an analogous attack against a *Gestalt*-based "sense."

Similarly, motivational nonsense in the field of Romantic literature cannot simply be ascribed to an abstract and ahistorical poetic freedom. The Romantic revaluation and redefinition of the novel and the tale correspond to a change in plot motivation: from the motivation derived from the predestined outcome of conventionalized generic plots, characteristic of older prose forms,[54] to the motivation from psychological premises and from the characters of a narrative that typifies bourgeois, modern narrative forms. Where psychological motivation and a coherent causal explanation of both external and internal action—the essential elements of the

Enlightenment poetics of the novel[55]—had only recently been established and incorporated into the bourgeois reader's horizon of expectations, their suspension gains a highly distinctive value. The Romantic recourse to the genre of the fairy tale has a central motive here: with Tieck's fairytale arabesques the indifference of the fairy tale to "meaningful" motivations—an indifference that itself can be seen as a distinctive feature of the fairy tale as compared to myth—is introduced in the form of motivational nonsense into a new system of literature.

Literary Sources of the Romantic Poetics of Nonsense

The theory of the fairy tale that concentrates on the suspension of "sense," "coherence," and "understanding" comes primarily from Ludwig Tieck and Novalis. Contrary to what one might expect, this poetics of nonsense does not find its related phenomena in the famous Romantic "literary fairy tale" such as Tieck's *Der blonde Eckbert* or the Klingsohr fairy tale in Novalis's *Heinrich von Ofterdingen.* For in these works, the poetics of incoherence and nonsense figures more as the means for evoking a *higher* coherence and for creating allegorical, enigmatic ciphers. This Romantic version of the fairy tale, however, is preceded by several arabesque literary works that refer much more playfully to the fairy tale, refraining from any simulation of the "fairy-tale tone" as well as abandoning the suggestion of a "higher" and inexhaustibly "profound" meaning. The most important of these earlier works are Tieck's *Puss-in-boots* [*Der gestiefelte Kater*] and *The Seven Wives of Bluebeard* [*Die sieben Weiber des Blaubart*].

Whereas the fairytale arabesques performed in the medium of other literary genres date from the years 1796 and 1797, most of the Romantic "literary fairy tales," in the narrower sense, were written in 1798 (with the exception of *Der blonde Eckbert*). A poetics of nonsense that is not immediately recodified through a "higher" figural language can be found only in the earliest productions of the German Romantics. Friedrich Schlegel's *Brief über den*

Roman of 1800, in its use of the fairy-tale genre but also in its differentiated treatment of the arabesque, offers insight into this early Romantic poetics of nonsense. At the outset of the *Brief* the arabesque is related only to the "sense for the grotesque" and the comic, and its exemplary pre-Romantic paradigm, Lawrence Sterne's *Tristram Shandy*, can easily be marshaled for a poetics of nonsense. Yet at the conclusion of Schlegel's text the arabesque exhibits features that reflect the process of "restructuring" the Romantic arabesque into a hieroglyph and even into "the dithyrambic."[56] The early Romantic poetics of nonsense has its genuine field only in those "Romantic natural products of our age," as Schlegel says,[57] in which the reception of the fairy tale assumes the shape of an arabesque that playfully flows into the grotesque and the satirical. One of these second- or even third-degree fairy tales is both the key source of inspiration and the literary paradigm of the present study: Tieck's arabesque *The Seven Wives of Bluebeard*. Arno Schmidt called it a "miracle of meaninglessness" and made it the centerpiece of his portrait of Tieck.[58] It is one of the most entertaining and—despite Arno Schmidt's pronounced appreciation—still one of the least known masterpieces of early German Romanticism.

§ 2 Kant on "Nonsense," "Laughing," and "Caprice"

Genius, Spirit, Nonsense

Kant's doctrine of genius transforms the discourse of aesthetic genius into a foundation of hermeneutics. The basis for the production of fine art includes the ability to disclose in its products an interminable, virtually infinite process of understanding. The fundamental hermeneutical theorems of the infinity and interminability of sense are here articulated for the first time and with unsurpassed argumentative force. Among "the faculties of mind that constitute genius," an "enlivening principle" is above all responsible for this "unlimited" expansion of thinking effected by the fine arts, for this "view into a boundless realm" of ideas.[1] As in hermeneutical theory, this enlivening principle is called "spirit."[2] In the *Reflexionen zur Anthropologie* this "word," as far as it is "not used with the article" and can replace the word "*Genie*," figures explicitly as "a new word": "one does not say: the spirit, but rather: spirit, spirit per se [*Geist schlechthin*]."[3] The *Critique of Judgement* defines this "principium of enlivening" ["*principium der Belebung*"][4] as "the faculty for presenting aesthetic ideas." The latter is "a presentation of the imagination which prompts much thought, but to which no determinate thought whatsoever, i.e., no [determinate] *concept*, can be adequate, so that no language can express it completely and allow us to grasp it."[5] Just as in the mathematically sublime, the aesthetic "apprehension" progresses so far into infinity that the faculty of "comprehension" fails,[6] so does genius as spirit render the relations between imagination and understanding asymmetrical and, within the irreducible gap between them, genius institutes the resistance of infinitely rich aesthetic ideas to the boundaries of every determinate concept.

This asymmetricization, however, tends to an extreme at which the foundation of the hermeneutical process inverts into its undoing, or more precisely, at which the conditions of possibility of the fine arts invert into the conditions of their impossibility. Kant laconically termed this extreme "nonsense."[7] The first quality of genius reminds Kant of its affinity to nonsense. A pure aesthetic judgment must not be mediated by purposes and concepts; all art, however, according to Kant implies "a determinate intention to produce something"[8] and a "preceding rule;"[9] therefore, art can only appear beautiful if at least "it looks to us like nature."[10] Kant does not leave this "as if" in the mode of mere illusion. In the doctrine of genius, he gives it an anthropological, indeed an ontological, foundation. This is because genius "is the innate talent of the mind (*ingenium*) *through which* nature gives the rule to art."[11] Hence, the required natural aspect, by virtue of which art is able to dissimulate itself, is at least an objective feature of the power producing it, if not of the artwork's own being.

> One sees from this that genius 1) is a *talent* for producing something for which no determinate rule can be given: not a skillful disposition for what can be learned according to some rule; and consequently that *originality* must be its primary quality.[12]

The subsequent three characterizations do not articulate three further properties of genius but simply mark the area (4) and the effective mode (3) of this primary quality as well as a restriction which it must heed in the field of art (2). Kant, at least in the third *Critique*, limits the "prescriptions" of genius to the "fine arts" and excludes science as a possible domain. At the same time, he emphasizes the unconscious, unplanned, and uncontrollable nature of the productions of genius. However, above all he places the "primary quality" of genius under a restrictive imperative. This imperative is a response to the problem that "there can also be original nonsense." In order to be called "beautiful," however, the "products" of genius "*must*" "at the same time be models, i.e., be *exemplary*; and consequently, though not themselves derived from imitation, (they *must*) serve that purpose for others, i.e., as a standard or rule for judging."[13] Under this perspective, originality—the primary property of genius—conjoins its ability to its failure. It is both advantage and danger, both ground and unground of genius. Between the ability of originality, which includes "nonsense," and the imperative (the "must") demanded of the products of genius a chasm opens up that makes it necessary to restrict the primary essential quality of genius.

It becomes clear in the subsequent paragraphs of the *Critique of Judgement* that the required capability to distinguish itself from nonsense does not devolve upon genius qua genius. Left to its own devices, genius cannot draw the line between nonsense and sense. It requires an intervention by taste and hence by the faculty of judgment, which in this function is in "conflict" with the faculty of genius.[14] Therefore, Kant sees the possibility that "one can often sense genius without taste in one would-be work of art, taste without genius in another."[15] The conflict between these two faculties, to which paragraphs 48 and 50 are devoted, first of all, stages a struggle to determine the role and effect of nonsense:

> If we ask which is more important in matters of fine art, whether they show genius or taste, then this is equivalent to asking whether in fine art imagination is more important than judgment. Now insofar as art shows genius it does indeed deserve to be called *inspired*, but it deserves to be called *fine* art only insofar as it shows taste. Hence what we must look at above all, when we judge art as fine art, is taste, at least as an indispensable condition (*conditio sine qua non*). In order for a work to be beautiful, it is not strictly necessary that it be rich and original in ideas, but it is necessary that the imagination in its freedom be commensurate with the lawfulness of the understanding. For all the richness of the imagination in its lawless freedom produces nothing but nonsense.[16]

Genius had been introduced as the faculty per se for producing fine art; but in the last of the five paragraphs devoted to its discussion, it is thus demoted to being "not so necessary." Taste, which in an earlier paragraph merely figured as the receptive counterpart to the "productive faculty" of genius,[17] assumes the higher authority even in matters of producing fine art. It disciplines genius, "severely clips its wings and makes it civilized, or polished."[18] Kant also speaks of "impairing" or "sacrificing" genius.[19] Because its originality, richness, and freedom on its own "produce nothing but nonsense," they must be curtailed and partly sacrificed in order for them to be able to send us on the infinite and inexhaustible path of sense. Kant's concept of nonsense marks this necessity of a cut, a caesura in the faculty of genius. The productive ground of possibility of fine—and hermeneutically endlessly engaging—art is the tendency toward nonsense and simultaneously the curtailment or circumcision of this tendency. Not the enhancement of genius or its being raised to the highest possible degree but rather its disciplining, conditioning, and curtailing produce the hermeneutical infinitude of aesthetic ideas. In other words: infinite sense is itself an effect of nonsense restrained rather than a multiplication of various determinate meanings.

"Nonsense" was a "favorite word of the Enlightenment."[20] Adelung explains it as an "absence of all understandable and reasonable meaning."[21] Kant's doctrine of genius operates with this difference between nonsense and reasonable meaning. It tries, however, not merely to unmask and exclude nonsense but to tame it by adding a counterweight. It displaces both its enlightenment horizon and its dependence on the earlier critique of Storm and Stress genius through the fact that the finitude of nonsense is no longer opposed to the finitude of an "understandable meaning" but instead to a different and historically new form of incomprehensible sense: infinite meaning. Genius's originality, which in its unrestrained freedom would approach the extreme of nonsense, changes in the mode of tasteful restraint into the productive ground of fine art. Nonsense therefore figures in Kant's aesthetics as an included Excluded.

Nonsense and Madness

The constellation of fine art, genius, and nonsense may to a certain extent be paralleled with another triad: that of the sublime, enthusiasm, and madness. As genius must be restrained by taste in order to produce fine art, so too in the field of the sublime it is necessary "to temper the momentum of an unbounded imagination so as to keep it from rising to the level of enthusiasm."[22] For in its "unbridled" form, "enthusiasm is comparable to *madness*,"[23] just as, on the other hand, genius in its unrestrained freedom and richness tends toward the pathological extreme of nonsense. Yet enthusiasm and madness are not a valid systematic counterpart to genius and nonsense. Whereas genius figures as the faculty for producing fine art, enthusiasm is no faculty at all, but rather merely an "affect of the *vigorous* type."[24] Moreover, it does not play such a universal role in the sublime as genius does in fine art. Enthusiasm is nothing more than a particularly extreme case of the sublime, in virtue of its blindness[25] always in danger of inverting into a merely "stormy movement of the sentiments," which "by no means can claim the distinction of being a *sublime* exhibition."[26] "Sublime in a far superior way" are for Kant such "strainings of our powers through ideas," which—like the (Stoic) "*apatheia, phlegma in significatu bono*"—represent precisely the opposite of enthusiasm.[27]

The *Critique of Judgement* therefore marginalizes enthusiasm in its tendency toward madness far more severely than it does genius in its tendency toward nonsense. However, above all, the two are apportioned different fields of phenomena and also different theoretical values. By virtue of this differentiation, Kant avoids an intersection of these conceptual pairs that would otherwise suggest itself: that of genius and madness. Plato, following common ancient doctrine, had defined the enthused, divinely inspired discourse of the poets as a positive form of μανία.[28] In the 18th century this doctrine of μανία intersected at various points with the unconscious discourse of nature in the modern genius.[29] This suggestive topos of a connection between genius and madness is thwarted by the fine differentiations in the *Critique of Judgement.*

From the *Reflections on Anthropology* of the 1770s to the *Anthropology* of 1798, Kant constantly delimited nonsense and madness against each other: as two diverse, in part even polar forms of "derangement." The disjunction of genius from madness for the benefit of nonsense acquires a polemical accent under this rubric. It acquires such an accent all the more as the *Anthropology* of the 1770s still remains thoroughly committed to the common topos and nowhere produces a connection between genius and nonsense. For instance, on Swedenborg Kant notes: "His originality borders on madness. Thus it is said that genius and insanity lie not far apart."[30] Or similarly: "Judgment and taste define the limits to genius, hence without these [judgment and taste] the genius verges on frenzy."[31] Frenzy in Kant's anthropology is consistently defined as an intensified form of madness: "madness with affect is *frenzy*, which can often be original, yet in being so is subject to involuntary raptures and which then, like the poetic inspiration (*furor poeticus*), borders on *genius*."[32] Kant's painstaking distinctions prevent nonsense and madness from being considered merely synonymous in their relationship to genius. If the extreme value of genius in the early and later anthropology is called "original frenzy,"[33] but in the third *Critique* "original nonsense," then what is at stake is not simply a question of renaming but rather a displacement of the semantic field. If a disturbance is called either "mad or nonsensical,"[34] then nonsensical discourse is no longer a playful form of madness. It is only on the basis of this essential incongruity that the early Romantic poetics of nonsense can again effect linkages to madness.

As the "thing in itself," the pure form and at the same time the innate defiguration of genius, "nonsense" remains peculiarly empty and undefined in Kant's third *Critique*. Only a recourse to Kant's anthropological works can help here.[35] Kant makes several attempts to define conceptual series such as stupid—profound—nonsensical—mad—lunatic or senseless—nonsensical—mad—melancholy—stupid—profound—frenzied.[36] For nonsense there results a clear semantic accent: "nonsensical: he whose thoughts have an unpremeditated mutability and inconstancy."[37] More than twenty years later this reflection finds an echo in the *Anthropology from a Pragmatic Point of View*:

> 1) *Nonsensicality* (amentia) is the inability even to bring one's ideas into that kind of coherence which is necessary for the very possibility of experience [. . .] This first kind of derangement is *tumultuous.*
> 2) *Madness* (dementia) is that disturbance of the faculties wherein everything that the disturbed person says still conforms to the formal laws of thought required for the possibility of experience, but wherein by falsely inventive imagination self-concocted ideas are taken to be perceptions [. . .] This second kind of derangement is *methodical.*[38]

Hence, madness has a method and grounds an experience that despite all its "falsity" nonetheless is coherent in itself. Nonsense, on the contrary, decomposes the very coherence of experience instead of madly creating degrees of high but false coherence. As "unpremeditated [. . .] mutability and inconstancy," without any ordering through motivation or teleology, nonsensicality violates "the coherence necessary for the very possibility of experience." These determinations anticipate the fundamental semantics of Romantic nonsense and no-sense: namely that of being "without any coherence"[39] or motivation. Nonsense does not so much mean the displacement of the "objective" into the "false" but rather the "tumultuous" suspension of the possibility of experience altogether, which indeed for Kant in essence was "the possibility of the unity of experience."[40] To produce this "thoroughly coherent experience" is the chief task and the "subjective principle (maxim) of judgment,"[41] and the pleasure found in the beautiful purposiveness without purpose represents the predestined mode of its fulfillment. Nonsense to this extent questions far more directly and more radically the transcendental principle of judgment than does the coherence still present in madness and enthusiasm. It is only with the displacement of the genius-and-madness topos into the connection between genius and nonsense that the *Critique of Judgement* is able to give the "conflict" between genius and taste a transcendental dimension: genius as the condition for the possibility of fine art tends by its own force toward inverting into a condition for its impossibility, which is the impossibility of a thoroughly coherent experience. Against this background Kant's most succinct differentiation between nonsense and madness attains a powerful significance: "Madness is positive, nonsense negative."[42]

Taste and the Grotesque

According to Kant, in the domain of the aesthetic, "understanding serves the imagination" whereas in the field of theoretical knowledge the reverse applies.[43] The affinity of genius with nonsense prevents Kant from allowing the aesthetic supremacy of imagination to stand without qualification. After all, judgment must violently force the genius's imagination to "conform to the understanding," instead of the latter—as postulated—being "in service" to the former. Yet it is not only the conflict between taste and genius that threatens the central fiction of the *Critique of Judgement*—that of a free and harmoniously tuned interplay of the faculties. Taste itself, the disciplinarian of genius, is in its "reference to the understanding"[44] not as reliable as a non-violent harmony of the two faculties would demand. Left to itself, taste engages "the freedom of imagination rather to the point of approaching the grotesque." Kant gives as an example, and by no means as an admonishment, the "baroque taste in furniture": there "taste can show its greatest perfection in designs made by the imagination."[45] As genius gravitates toward nonsense, so does taste gravitate toward the grotesque: here, too, the third *Critique* anticipates what will be for the Romantics a central concept, one that has less to do with "classical" harmony than with distortion, disproportion, and hyperbolic inappropriateness, and which is less about infinite sense than about finite absurdity. "Grotesque shape," Kant writes laconically in one of the notebooks the third *Critique* draws upon "Caricature. Distortion. Character. Ridiculous. Misshapen."[46] From the first important aesthetic treatise of the 18th century, Jean Pierre de Crousaz's *Traité du Beau* of 1715,[47] up to German Romanticism, the grotesque figures repeatedly as an antidote to an aesthetics dedicated to beauty, unity, harmony, and order. It is not the Romantics but indeed Kant who first transforms the grotesque from an elaborately justified exception into a paradigmatic feature of the aesthetic as such. Several definitions of the grotesque even cross into the field of nonsense and absurdity—so much so that Alfred Liede in his great monograph on "Nonsense Poetry" could assert, "Many of the phenomena treated in my study have until now entered literary history under the rubric of the grotesque."[48] For Kant's third *Critique* there results a vertiginous consequence: because of its tendency toward "nonsense," genius is subordinated to the "disciplining" of taste; but this disciplinarian in turn, because of its inclination to the grotesque, has a penchant for the very same vice.

The "Nothing" of Sense in Music and Laughter

Not only do the affinities of genius and nonsense, of taste and the grotesque not conform to the creation of infinitely meaningful aesthetic ideas; the material media of the various arts as well condemn Kant's generalized definition of beauty as an "*expression* of aesthetic ideas"[49] to partial failure. For only in literature can "the faculty of aesthetic ideas manifest itself to its full extent."[50] Literature's material, language, permits a fortunate suspension between the all too *denotative* medium of painting, which does not reveal sufficient indetermination, and the almost purely *connotative* medium of music, which engages concepts to such a small degree that it "leaves nothing left to reflect upon." Music combines the highest "manifold" and "intensity" of a "transitory" effect upon sensation with a complete deprivation of the power of conceptual thought.[51] In music, "ultimately nothing is thought."[52] Even though music may play associatively with aesthetic ideas as its secondary material, it does not present them in the particular sense that it opens up an inexhaustible "reflection" upon them. Therefore, Kant considered music to be "art without spirit."[53] Because it is unsuitable for arousing[54] the infinite hermeneutical process, because of the vacuity of its transport for thought, music is for Kant "admittedly more a matter of enjoyment than of culture (the play of thought that it arouses incidentally is merely the effect of an association that is mechanical, as it were), and in reason's judgment it has less value than any other of the fine arts."[55]

It would be intriguing to explore the early Romantic reevaluation of music and sound as a positive recodification of this Kantian doctrine that ascribes to music a mechanical idling or interruption of the hermeneutical process. Here, however, music is mentioned only to provide the transition to Kant's aesthetic of laughter. The two intersect precisely in the collapse of the hermeneutical process into a finite nothing: "Both music and something to laugh about are two kinds of play with aesthetic ideas, or for that matter with presentations of the understanding, by which in the end nothing is thought; it is merely the change they involve that still enables them to gratify us in a lively way."[56] "Whatever is to arouse lively, convulsive laughter must contain something absurd"[57] instead of an infinite sense. Grotesque, nonsense, absurdity: three Kantian ways of interrupting the production and reception of infinite sense. It is through laughter that thought is most directly confronted with the "nothing" of its expectations, and precisely this kenotic experience produces a pleasurable affect: "Laughter is an affect that arises out of the sudden transformation of a tense expectation into nothing."[58] This structure, of aroused expectations for sense collapsing into nothingness, corresponds very precisely to more recent definitions of the working of literary nonsense. "The discourse of nonsense," writes Susan Stewart, "refers to 'nothing' [. . .], even though it must manufacture this 'nothing' from a system of differences [. . .] in order to be recognized as 'nothing.'"[59] In a similar vein, Tigges writes that Nonsense Poetry offers and indeed has to offer some meaningful traits in order to be able to disappoint the resultant expectations and have them dissipate into "nothing."[60] Kant strongly emphasizes that this "nothing" is not to be considered as the negation—itself still positive—of a "something," but rather as a, so to speak, free and absolute nothing. Unfortunately, the examples he draws upon to support this intriguing assumption are of only limited use as "evidence" for his definition. Still, they at least make clear what they are *supposed* to show:

> Suppose someone tells the following story: that an Indian at an Englishman's table in Surat saw a bottle of ale opened, and all the beer turned into froth and flowing out, and showed with repeated exclamations his great amazement, and in response to the question of the Englishman, "Well, what's so amazing in that?" he answered: "Oh, I'm not surprised at its getting out, but at how you ever managed to get it all in." At this we laugh, and it gives us hearty pleasure: not because we are possibly smarter than this ignorant man, or because our understanding here brings to our notice anything else which is delightful for us, but rather that our expectation was tense and suddenly disappears into nothing. Or, suppose that the heir of a rich relative wants to arrange for him a very solemn funeral service, but complains that things are not quite working out: For (he says), the more money I give my mourners to look grieved, the more cheerful they look. This evokes ringing laughter, and the reason is that we had an expectation which is suddenly transformed into nothing. We must be careful to observe that the expectation has not been transformed into the positive contrary of an expected object—for that is always something, and may frequently grieve us—but into outright nothing.[61]

Such playing with ideas of understanding, "whereby ultimately nothing is thought," indeed does not provide in itself pleasure to thought, but only through the "influence that the representation has on the body and in the body's reciprocal effect on the mind—and moreover not because the representation is objectively an object of our gratification (for how could an expectation that turned out to be false gratify us?), but solely because it is a mere play of representations which produces in the body an equilibrium of the vital forces."[62] For Kant, a stimulating mechanics that alternately creates and releases tension is responsible for the production of a "healthy motion" in the body when a train of thought evaporates into nothing. In this context, the nothing with which thought is suddenly confronted does not mean the final stasis of the movement triggered by the "material that makes us laugh." The transformation into nothing rather continues to resonate in itself; this resonance, even though it does not disclose any new information or open any new unlimited vistas for "reflection," brings about a "persistent" agitation in the body that "alone, and not what goes on in the mind, is the actual cause of the pleasure at a thought, which in essence represents nothing."[63]

The thought, "which in essence represents nothing," the play, "whereby ultimately nothing is thought": the musical and humorous prescinding of aesthetic ideas, the interruption of their infinite sense are ultimately justified in that Kant accepts their connection to the body and hence their aesthetic impurity. The "*animal*, i.e., bodily sensation" provides an "enjoyment,"[64] in which the claims made by thought that aesthetic ideas provide infinite meaning are not only suspended but are positively disappointed. The pure aesthetic judgment, on the other hand, is neither valid for a "sensation" nor does it provide a "pleasure": its disinterested "delight" is experienced in the mode of a reflective "feeling,"[65] the subject of which is not the body but solely judgment in its close affinity to understanding. The purely beautiful "carries with it directly a feeling of the enhancement of life,"[66] but it affects exclusively the life of the "higher faculties of the soul" (understanding, judgment, reason).[67] The pleasure in laughter on the other hand "seems always to consist in a feeling of the enhancement of the *entire* life of man, including as well bodily well-being, i.e., health."[68] In order to emphasize the purity of the aesthetic and the exclusively "intellectual interest in the beautiful,"[69] Kant previously had repeatedly spoken ironically of the "motions, which we welcome for the sake of our health."[70] In the analysis of laughter, however, he follows a different line of argument. The "impurity" of the aesthetic play and the "nothing" into which the tense expectations of understanding collapse are affirmed precisely because they enhance our *entire* life, including our physical health. Moreover, it is primarily the interference of a bodily agitation that accounts for the more comprehensively beneficiary effects of the aesthetically impure laughter as compared to a pure aesthetic delight. Kant's reflections therefore segue into a virtual plea for the laughing vibration of "nothing." Laughter, wit, and caprice gain supremacy over head-breaking speculation, heartbreaking sentimentality, and neck-breaking flights of genius. This truly Kantian triad of the destructive effects of "profundity" in its turn is broken by three "counterweights":

> Voltaire said that heaven has given us two things to counterbalance the many hardships in life: hope and sleep. He might have added laughter, if only the means for arousing it in reasonable people were as easy to come by, and if the wit or whimsical originality needed for it were not just as rare, as the talent is common for people to write, as mystical ponderers do, things that *break your head,* or to write, as geniuses do, things that *break your neck,* or to write, as sentimental novelists do (also, I suppose, sentimental moralists), things that *break your heart.*[71]

Caprice

Kant's praise of laughter continues to resonate in his evaluation of two related concepts that play a considerable role in the pre-Kantian and pre-Romantic poetics and that shortly thereafter advance to become central ideas of Romantic theory: "wit" and "caprice." Ludwig Tieck begins his *Bluebeard* tale, which boasts everywhere of its incoherence, its nonsense, and its meaninglessness, with an analogous plea for laughter.[72] The conversation that frames the *Phantasus* narratives includes in its "justification" of laughter also ridiculousness and silliness.[73] Tieck calls his *Seven Wives of Bluebeard* "a highly [. . .] capricious book"[74]—just as he explicitly declares "caprice" and "the capricious" to be his element in several of his earlier works. Kant provided the anti-classical rehabilitation of "manner" and caprice with a motto-like definition, which in its pedantic obsession for distinctions is itself already an instance of what it discusses and itself provides what it seeks to legitimate: "material that makes us laugh."

> The *capricious* manner may also be included with whatever is cheerful and closely akin to the enjoyment derived from laughter, and which belongs to originality of spirit [. . .] [which Kant here again strictly distinguishes from the "talent of fine art"—W. M.]. For *caprice,* in its favorable sense, means the talent enabling us to put ourselves at will into a certain disposition of the mind, in which everything is judged in a way quite different from the usual one (even inversely), but yet is judged in conformity with certain principles of reason [present] in such a mental attunement. A person who is subject to such changes

> involuntarily is *moody*; but if someone can adopt them at will and purposively (on behalf of a lively presentation by means of a contrast arousing laughter), he and his performance are called *capricious.*[75]

The pre-Romantic, and even more fully the Romantic, semantics of "Laune" repressed its medieval derivation from the Latin "luna" (moon, lunar orbit, lunar change) and thus the meaning of the "changing wheel of fortune" as well as the meaning of "bad temper" prevalent in the 16th and 17th centuries. Rather, the "merry mood of the spirits" and the relationship to laughter came into the foreground—so much so that "caprice" especially in the domain of literature was often used as an equivalent to the English "humor."[76] Such "caprice in its favorable sense" is not so much passively suffered as rather willfully admitted or artificially evoked. This shift in the evaluation of caprice left intact its basic semantic features of the "arbitrary," "fleeting," and the "unmotivated"[77]—which indeed are also underscored in Kant's definition—but subjected them to a positive reinterpretation. If one further considers that also "the senseless and purposeless [. . . is] a distinctive characteristic of 'caprice,'"[78] then the semantic analysis of this one word produces an entire sequence of central concepts of Romantic poetics. Contingency, arbitrariness, unmotivatedness, senselessness, and groundlessness themselves become in Tieck's poetics the paradoxical "ground" of poetry. What neither has its ground in itself nor can be sufficiently derived from history or from the actual experiences of a subject advances to become the generator of "play." Just as Kant found that in laughter "ultimately nothing is thought" and that the products of "closely related" caprice therefore also disclose no infinite "reflection," so too Wieland once distinguished as polar opposites "the voluntary pouring forth of a fountain of wit and caprice" and "a work of reflection and art."[79]

The license to the "capricious manner" counteracts the strategy of disciplining nonsense even while following it. Caprice for Kant only—and thus he attempts to skirt the impending conflict—"belongs to the originality of spirit, but precisely not to the talent of fine art."[80] Therefore, caprice can be promoted as part of an aesthetics of laughter. However, just a few paragraphs earlier, the same combination of features—"originality" of "spirit" and the failure to produce works of fine art—characterized genius in its affinity to nonsense and led to its "sacrifice" for the sake of the principle of taste as that which is said to be more necessary for producing fine art.[81] Thus, what Kant "curtails" and "clips" under the title of nonsense he reintroduces at the conclusion of the *Analytik* under the title of "caprice." In the *Reflections on Anthropology*, this affinity between caprice and genius is explicitly established: "Genius depends on caprice,"[82] for "caprice has spirit, order doesn't."[83]

Nonsense Displaced: From the Critique of Genius to the Border of the Hermeneutical Field

Nonsense, music, laughter, and "caprice in a good sense"—from the perspective of a caesura in the infinite meaningfulness of the aesthetic and in the hermeneutical expectations of inexhaustible prospects, these categories in the *Critique of Judgement* constitute a coherent sequence. Their coherence need not be "tricked out" as Kant would say, through far-fetched combinations of remote passages. They follow each other, paragraph for paragraph—§50: "nonsense;" §51–53: music, which "leaves nothing left for reflection;" §54: "music and subject matter inducing laughter," "caprice." These five paragraphs do not at all represent a digression in the "Analytic of Aesthetic Judgment," the first large section of the entire work. They constitute its conclusion and therefore occupy an important position. Contrary to what one might expect, though, they do not sum up the preceding arguments; rather, they perform both a confinement and a transgressive opening and thus function as a borderline. The objects of these border paragraphs belong neither to the analytic nor to the "Deduction of Pure Aesthetic Judgments," because by virtue of their reference to the "body," to "pleasure," and to "the pleasing" they go beyond the field of aesthetic "purity." They interrupt the infinity and inexhaustibility of aesthetic ideas with "nonsense" and a "nothing" of thought. However, to the extent that it is the first and essential quality of genius itself that displaces it into the field of nonsense and hence to the border of the Kantian analytic of beauty, the border aspect of the paragraphs in question results from something that is absolutely central for Kant's theory. Such an interaction between border and center is at work throughout the entire third *Critique*: from the very outset the central theses fall under the pressure of a sometimes latent, sometimes manifest marginalization. Conversely, careful reading reveals that apparently marginal elements in fact attain a surprisingly significant import.[84]

The *Critique of Judgement* is a seismograph of discursive displacements. The polemic against the nonsense wrought by an untamed imagination stems from a debate concerning the stormy natural genius, a topic which by the year 1790 had lost most of its relevance. Even the opposition of understanding vs. nonsense—understanding rescuing imagination from its tendency toward nonsense—is little more than an Enlightenment commonplace. Yet at the same time, nonsense enters into a completely different conceptual field. The definition of art as the presentation of infinitely determinable and inexhaustible aesthetic ideas provides nonsense a second and essentially new counterpart: instead of finite understanding, infinite sense. The imperative of infinite sense pursues, like the disciplining of natural genius, not so much a policy of utterly excluding nonsense as rather of overwhelming and incorporating it. However, this incorporation in its turn leads to interruptions of the infinite aesthetic meaning: in the affinity between taste and the grotesque as in the approbation of laughter and caprice or in music that "means nothing." Phenomena, which previously were not significantly related to the distinction between sense and nonsense, (re-)emerge as agents of a new type of nonsense once they operate within the normative horizon of infinite aesthetic meaning. Thus Kant's *Critique of Judgement*, while authoritatively establishing the new hermeneutical paradigm in aesthetics, also differentiates out and even legitimizes a variety of aesthetic forms that do not conform to (and even resist) this paradigm. It does so by drawing on and displacing an older polemic. Similarly, other forms of resistance to the discursive power of infinite "sense" were articulated through recourse to earlier, pre-hermeneutical traditions, which in the conflict with the new paradigm received new valuations.[85] One can suppose with Foucault that the hermeneutical field, like every field of power relations, produced numerous and very heterogeneous kinds of resistance: "resistances [. . .] that are spontaneous, savage, solitary, concerted, rampant, or violent; others that are quick to compromise, interested, or sacrificial."[86] The early Romantic fairytale arabesque articulates its resistance very directly and earnestly in the "theoretical" statements, yet extremely obliquely and with great wit in its literary devices.

§ 3 The Poetics of Nonsense and the Early Romantic Theory of the Fairy Tale

Novalis's "Canon" of the Fairy Tale and Tieck's Poetics of Incoherence

"The form of the fairy tale," one of Friedrich Schlegel's notes reads, "is absolute chaos."[1] Novalis too describes the "world of the fairy tale" as one of a positively conceived "general anarchy" and "chaos,"[2] and not only in terms of the genre's content but most of all because of its narrative form: "In a genuine fairy tale everything must be incoherent."[3] Expressed differently, "Nothing goes more against the spirit of the fairy tale than a regulated coherence."[4] This negatively formulated criterion of a positive absence of coherence allows Novalis to enthrone the fairy tale as the "*Canon* of poetry."[5] Romantic "tales" and "poems" that satisfy this fairy-tale canon must above all be "without coherence,"[6] indeed "without any sense or coherence."[7] Enlightenment's criticism of the fairy tale's "senselessness" is thus being inverted into a positive imperative to disregard or even abandon "sense." Kant's definition of nonsense as a tumultuous displacement of a "coherence" that creates unity no longer characterizes merely a pathological liminal value of genius.

In many ways, Ludwig Tieck's early writings also dwell on the Enlightenment nexus of sense suspension and lack of coherence. Tieck's great early work, *William Lovell* (begun in 1793) remains within the conventional semantics in its explicit use of these concepts. "Incoherence" and "meaninglessness of life" are not yet considered privileged attributes; they merely designate a "vacuum."[8] It is indeed only in this negative sense that the novel speaks of the "incoherent farces" and "senseless arabesques" revealed by a sober description of life.[9] However, in the nearly contemporary *Peter Lebrecht* (1795–96), the lack of coherence already is elevated into a provocative maxim of poetics. For example, the narrator praises himself for the fact that the second part of his autobiography "should no longer cohere with [. . .] the first part."[10] However, at least within the two separate parts, the reader is not troubled by a lack of coherence. It is only with some of the texts published in 1797 under the title *Volksmärchen* that the promise of incoherence and senselessness is radicalized. *Die Geschichte von den Haimonskindern* begins with the following apostrophe to the reader:

> Perhaps you were once ill, dear reader, or perhaps you've found yourself in an unexpected solitude for several hours; abandoned by all diversions, one can at times find pleasure and lose oneself in old marvelous drawings or wood-cuts; one surely attentively contemplates an incoherent and almost incomprehensible image, where in the foreground a council meeting is taking place in the royal palace and in the background one sees the sea with ships and clouds, completely without any perspectival art. O my reader, may you await such a pleasure and no other in the contemporary quaint images that we would now like to present to you.[11]

However, this quaint announcement remained more programmatic intention than anything else. The text, despite its fragmentation into twenty "images," offers a highly coherent story, a completely motivated plot that from beginning to end constitutes a unity. The expected literary analogy to a perspectivally "impossible," confusing spatial composition—for example, characteristic of the grotesque of even the rococo-arabesque—remains an expectation only. The situation is different in the *Bluebeard* arabesque and also in the fairy-tale comedies,[12] especially *Puss-in-boots* [*Der gestiefelte Kater*]. When one of the spectators within the tale appears and finds that "the last scene" is surely "utterly superfluous," unless its purpose is "to introduce some new nonsense,"[13] it's difficult to contradict him: the immanent poetics of the play and its unintentional reversal in the guise of the straight-laced "spectator" could often be stated in the very same words. The interpretation of these fairy-tale comedies has relied on concepts like "farce," "puppet-show," and "satire" and largely avoided the idea of nonsense, mainly because of their numerous interventions in the contemporary literary and political discourse; these satirical allusions offer the reflective mind a thankfully firm support in the whirl of phenomena.

However, these allusions are by no means the "ground" or raison d'être of Tieck's fairy-tale comedies. Rather, Tieck uses the levels of satirical meaning in order "to lure his real spectators/readers into exposing themselves to what the derided [fictive] audience actually fends off, the pleasure in the senseless [. . .] Thus in the field of satire, in the witty joke that the poet together with the real audience indulge in about what is represented, the comedy drives forward the license to and participation in a completely different, truly Dionysian comedy."[14] In this fine analysis of the economy of two forms of comedy and laughter, Bernhard Greiner touches upon a certain pleasure, although he does not pursue its relation to the "senseless." He diagnoses the "fear" of insanity as that pleasure's "dark horizon."[15] "Going crazy" as a pathological displacement, however, in Tieck's comedies is affected, first of all, by the fictional philistine spectators as a defensive gesture. It therefore belongs more to the levels of meaning that are satirically derided than to the sphere that these levels disclose only by means of ironically transcending themselves. By contrast, where it positively distinguishes the Romantic poet and his work, "crazy" signifies an excess of mischievous pranks, of capricious combinations and defigurations, of grotesque and buffoonery—and hence forms of displacement that are less the result of unconscious powers than of intentional acts. To this degree the Tieckian "craziness" distances itself from the Kantian "insanity with affect"[16] and in the same degree approaches the Kantian definition of "caprice," which enables us "to put ourselves *at will* into a certain disposition of the mind, in which everything is judged in a way quite different from the usual one (even inversely)." The term "mischievous insanity,"[17] which Tieck occasionally used in discussing the poetic process, identifies it as *both* a process in which we unconsciously become the victim of a displacement of sense eluding our control (i.e., insanity) *and* a process in which we give free rein to our predilections and bad habits *on our own initiative* and *at our will* (i.e., being mischievous). Just like the ambivalence of the word "crazy," this paradoxical combination refers less to the psychoanalytical concept of paranoia than to the anthropological-poetic concept of caprice; in the meaning of "mood" or "spirits" both *Muth* and *Laune* directly interfere. The borders between the two poles of "craziness," however—insanity (madness) and voluntary caprice—are far from stable.[18]

Tieck's semantics of "caprice"[19] thus essentially includes what Kant only acknowledged as the deepest tendency of the genial (= original spirit) in order to consign it to the "discipline" of taste: the license to mischievous nonsense. Not in any book of early German Romanticism is the rehabilitation of non-sense so programmatic and so refined as in Tieck's 1797 *Seven Wives of Bluebeard.* As a "book without any coherence" it strives to "shake loose" the usual expectations of sense and meaning like a "saddle and bridle;"[20] it provocatively legitimates "contradictory nonsense,"[21] "spectacles about nothing,"[22] and fragmented chains of events that "lead to nothing" and "have nothing to signify."[23] A poetological conclusion is drawn from the diagnosis in *Lovell* that actual existence is nonsensical: since "in the whole of human life there is no purpose or coherence to be found," it is finally time to give up the "foolishness" of "incorporating" "these things" into a poetic "life-story."[24] This resigned acceptance of poetic non-meaning, however, is matched by a euphoric justification that advocates nonsense as the liberation of life and poetry so that they may come into their own in successfully resisting the coercion of meaning: as affirmative craziness, caprice, and excess. The language of love also appears often enough as "the most obvious nonsense."[25]

The boundary lines of nonsense are further complicated by its ambivalent relationship to the contemporary horror novel. Tieck condemns these novels' "poorly cohering adventurisms," on the one hand, as a negative inflation of pseudo-marvelous "nonsense" without "originality" and "convincing nature."[26] (This criticism also playfully inverts the elements of Kant's argumentation: Kant tries to interrupt the connection between originality and nonsense in favor of originality; Tieck, on the contrary, demands such a connection for the benefit of nonsense.) On the other hand, Tieck repeatedly praises precisely these novels for being one of his best sources of inspiration. In fact, his early literary production can almost without exception be classified according to each work's specific nexus of proximity and distance from the horror novel. With its subtitle *A Story Without Adventurisms*, the narrative of *Peter Lebrecht* (1795) announces that its central narrative mode will be its playful departure from the horror novel. The horror novel's elements are present in the form of their negative—or rather polemically avoided—citation. In the "insignificant story" of Peter Lebrecht,

> no phantom or monster appears; I also have not destroyed any castle, have not vanquished any giant [. . .] I am not writing this story from within a prison, less on the eve of my execution, although it perhaps would especially entertain you. I am not melancholic, nor narrow-chested, nor am I infatuated; rather my good young wife is sitting beside me, and we speak constantly with each other without enthusiasm or tender exclamations.[27]

As opposed to this negative inclusion-via-exclusion of the popular novel, the narrative law of *William Lovell* consists in positively incorporating elements of the popular novel.[28] Conspiracies against life and property of the hero and his father, an uncanny stranger, complicated intrigues, and supernatural phenomena—all these standard elements of the popular genre return in the basic plot of *Lovell*, and yet their functionality here lends the work more the character of a psychological-philosophical novel than that of a Gothic novel. The *Bluebeard* arabesque and several of the texts published as *Volksmärchen* occupy an intermediate position in this spectrum. In contrast to *Lebrecht*, they rework the popular novel not in the form of avoiding but rather of ironically quoting it; unlike *Lovell*, then, they never incorporate the entire plot structure but always just certain set-pieces, and they also largely avoid the effects of the Gothic novel. Only in this mixture, whose features largely derive from their conformity to the fairy tale, does Tieck ennoble the "nonsense" of the popular novel into a higher and genuinely Romantic form of incoherence.

"Without Sense," "Nonsense," "Higher" Sense

Tieck's second major novel, his 1798 *Franz Sternbalds Wanderungen*, formulates several times the "ideal" of paintings that "like to renounce plot, passion, composition and everything:" and "delight" solely by their "dazzling colors without coherence." "Meaning in the customary sense" here is suspended as a "condition of art."[29] However, while Tieck's first novel had not yet subscribed to his poetics of nonsense, the second novel already moves beyond it. The "without coherence" functions as a motor for evoking a "higher" and a "marvelous meaningfulness and enigmatic hints."[30] *Color* and *music* are the guiding concepts of this "higher" type of meaningfulness that eludes both concrete and conceptual univocity and that can no longer be modeled on a traditional poetics of plot and composition. The semiotic form of this intensive communication that lets us suspect but "never write down, never successfully guess" "a secret cipher," Tieck calls a "hieroglyph." It implies a genuinely Romantic type of "allegory"[31] (that still has not been sufficiently analyzed), an allegorical writing in colors and sounds. A few years after *Sternbald*—and directly inspired by it—this type of allegory found its visual realization in the arabesque hieroglyphs of Philipp Otto Runge. In Novalis's poetics of the fairy tale a new, "mysteriously"[32] enigmatic and "higher"[33] sense shimmers through the suspension of sense and coherence. Similarly, a higher sense is explicated in musical concepts (the "sounds" and "harmonic series of an Aeolian harp"), cosmological concepts ("*nature itself*," "the whole of nature")[34], and even religious concepts ("similarity of our holy story and *Mährchen*"[35]).

The scholarship on Romanticism therefore has almost never taken seriously and literally the imperatives of chance, incoherence, and non-sense.[36] In general, they were seen to be merely the function and drawback of that "tendency towards a profound, infinite sense," with which Friedrich Schlegel had characterized Romantic irony and the Romantic project *tout court.*[37] In virtue of its mysterious allegorical ciphers, the Romantic literary fairy tale specifically seems to confirm this immediate domestication of the disclosed field of nonsense. However, the provocative formula of narratives "without any sense and coherence" is not equivalent to the function of self-negating literary devices. The present study maps out the tension, the gap between the formula's exact wording and its functional subordination. This study need not only draw on the early Romantic excess in poetology beyond its contemporary literature or on the fact that literalization, and its resultant defamiliarization, is a central stratagem in the fairy tale and the fantastic as literary genres. Nor does it need to produce the intricate, yet by no means impossible evidence that even the profound machinery of meaningfulness in "High Romanticism" itself gives the first and last word to non-meaning by dint of the ironization of all allegorical ciphers and in between takes the greatest pains to deceive both itself and the reader about this.[38] Rather, this study maintains that Tieck's fairy-tale comedies and fairytale arabesques from the years 1796 and 1797 simultaneously exhibit a rewriting of the fairy-tale genre and a poetics of incoherence that had not yet adopted the practice of hieroglyphics that dominates Tieck's work from 1798 onward. Bernhard Greiner has pointed out the unique status of the fairy-tale comedies: if "Romanticization" means the enigmatic enciphering of a sense that can only be guessed at and that infinitely engages the understanding, then these grotesque-farcical fairy tales of the second degree can be described as an "'inversion' of Romanticization."[39] The arabesque narrative of Knight Bluebeard not only does not recuperate the lack of coherence by means of a hieroglyphic poetics; it also offers the most advanced theoretical explanation of that lack. (Forms of nonsense can also be found in Tieck's works after 1798, even occasionally bordering, in the late novellas, on the more conventional type of 19th-century nonsense production. After 1798, however, such nonsense no longer determines the contours of entire works; as well-measured pinches of nonsense, this poetics loses its earlier radicalness and comprehensive, provocative power.)

In view of this material there is theoretical as well as literary-historical significance in the fact that Ludwig Tieck alone has crossed the linguistic border between "without" and "un-." Only Tieck writes of "without sense," "without coherence," and "non-sense;" Novalis, on the contrary, avoids using the word "nonsense" as an affirmative term. Only Ludwig Tieck, therefore, together with Arno Schmidt, can be claimed for a Romantic poetics of nonsense. By no means is the difference between nonsense and without-sense semantically empty, as Alfred Liede asserts.[40] What is without sense need not for that reason be nonsensical in this Tieckian, positive sense. For the prefix *un-* performs an inversion from negation into affirmation that the purely privative "without" does not. A word such as "*Unmenge*" [in English "a vast number, vast amount"] means the indefiniteness of an amount or quantity, not in the sense of a lack or absence of this quantity but rather of its superabundant presence. The same holds for the (philosophical) "*Unding*" [literally "non-thing," meaning both an "absurdity" and a cipher of the absolute]. In an analogous way, the word "nonsense" goes beyond the Romantic affirmative valorization of "without sense." In this word, the mise-en-scène of the difference from the paradigm of sense proceeds from a suspension, a displacement [*Ent-Setzung*] of sense into an affirmative positing [*Setzung*] of its implicated opposition; into a positing in which the suspense—without coming to an end—in its turn is once again suspended and transfixed in a fashion that can tend toward the monstrous. Despite this semantic distinction, in keeping with Immanuel Kant's and Ludwig Tieck's linguistic usage in what follows, there will be no clear line drawn between nonsense and without sense.

The Marvelous, Chance, Incomprehensibility

The category of "the marvelous" receives a new, specifically Romantic definition in the context of "incoherence" and "without sense."[41] It no longer means a subject matter of poetry such as it might result from the imagination's creation of (im)possible (contrary) worlds; rather, it now means a formal mode in which even completely mundane elements might be portrayed. Marvelous are such "elements" or "subjects" of poetry that do not heed any sense of justification or causal explanation but are simply "there, all of a sudden, without any reason or cause."[42] Alternatively, in Ludwig Tieck's words, marvelous is "everything, where we perceive an effect without a cause" and that is "incomprehensible" to the extent that our thought is based on causality.[43] For Novalis, the fairy tale is "an ensemble of marvelous things and occurrences"[44] above all by virtue of these two positive deficiencies: the lack of motivation ("existence [. . .] without reason or cause") and the correlative lack of "coherence." The (Romantic) poet artificially produces this twofold deficiency. His project is that of a "transformation into chance,"[45] indeed he "prays to chance."[46] He thus becomes the agent of a critical experience that makes "ultimately every question—what is that? and why?" become problematic, "a dumb question."[47] Whereas the "classical" form strives to transform all contingency into aesthetic necessity by means of logically coherent construction, the early Romantic theory of the fairy tale proclaims the license and release, indeed, even the conscious production of contingency.[48] The Romantic call for a "new mythology" as the basis for a poetry whose "canon" is the fairy tale, thus combines contrary elements. The new mythology should provide "a new channel and vessel for the old eternal source of poetry;"[49] its project is to lay a foundation, a Fichtean "*Grundlage*." However, the fairy tale transforms the mythological "seeds" immediately once again into products whose logic of "chance" "marvelously" suspends their own ground and lets it become poetry only in the mode of its own unfounding and un-grounding.

Even for Hegel, though with a critical undertone, the form of the fairy tale was defined by such characteristics: "a mere play with [. . .] casual [. . .] connections," pure "superficiality," "staggering juxtapositions."[50] According to Hegel, "the basic trait" of a romantic plot consists precisely in the accidental and "extraordinarily intertwined ramifications" of both characters and collisions.[51] Thus, for Hegel, the philosophico-historical signature of modernity and the genre-specificity of the fairy tale converge in the category of chance. In contrast to the heroic world of the epic, modern life no longer has any essentially concrete contents. Rather, such contents have devolved into contingent inessential characteristics in which a deepening subjectivity can no longer manifest itself. The desymbolizing of all substantive contents that accompanies the process of secularization, the break with the iconographic tradition and society's transformation from a hierarchically to a functionally differentiated organization, enters art in a twofold sense. On the one hand, as Hegel claims, Romantic art allows and even exhibits contingency in plots and objects; on the other hand, it tends to overcome the contingency inscribed within it by the higher "intellectualization" or its subjectivity. In the hieroglyphic arabesques of the Romantic literary fairy tale and in Philipp Otto Runge's paintings, the second tendency dominates: they can be read as attempts to reinvest the desymbolized objects, signs, and images with a meaning through the referential playfulness of arabesque reflection.[52] By contrast, the earliest Romantic arabesque—while likewise taking recourse to the fairy tale—strives to exhibit nonsensical contingency both playfully and critically.

Aleatorics and electronic random number generators share a paradoxical characteristic with Romanticism's slogan for the production of chance: what should evade every rule, every concept, and every intention is itself an intended effect, a negative program. Thus, even when art (voluntarily) submits its productions to chance, it only partially escapes its connection to rule and concept as Kant diagnosed them. Rather, the poetics of chance and contingency radicalizes a Kantian problem: the self-dissimulation that Kant imposes upon all art so that it is beautiful and accessible to a genuinely aesthetic experience. In the sentence "beautiful art must be *seen* as nature," the simulation of nature means nothing other than the bracketing of "intention" and "concept": "it must not seem intentional."[53] In the anthropological reflections, on the basis of which Kant developed the *Critique of Judgement*, the concept of nature and that of chance are thus conjoined: "Chance [. . .] in the conflict or change of presentation: that something is art and yet seems only to be contingency, is nature and yet seems to be art, etc. [in this] actually lies the pleasure."[54] Because the opposition between "nature and art" is explained and replaced by the opposition between "art and chance" and "chance and intention,"[55] the Kantian imperative to simulate nature contains within it the Romantic imperative of contingency. The latter, however, emancipates chance from the framework of a logic of exchange [Tauschen] and deception [Täuschen] in which chance means merely nature's independence from human intentions and concepts. In other words, the Kantian constellation of beautiful art, genius, nonsense, and chance lives on in the earliest Romantic poetics by detaching itself from the systematic problem it was designed to answer in the *Critique of Judgement.*[56]

The imperatives of non-motivation and incoherence also implicitly question the claim to comprehensibility. A contemporary response to the question "What does it mean to understand something?" demands as the goal and condition of understanding the positive presence of what for Novalis (fairy-tale) poetry characteristically lacks: "It means [. . .] to perceive [. . .] the sense and coherence, [. . .] to combine the whole into a unity in consciousness."[57] Schleiermacher explicitly drew the inverse conclusion from this connection between "coherence" and "understanding": whatever "does not follow any law of coherence" is "absolutely incomprehensible."[58] The aggressive formula "without any sense and coherence," the "must" of "incoherence" and "nonsense," thus provokes the cultural praxis of the desire and the injunction to understand that according to Friedrich A. Kittler in the "discourse system 1800" suppressed all other forms of reading and writing.

The theoretical foundation of this hermeneutical praxis, whose central organizing categories are called "sense," "coherence," and "understanding," in part draws on the same authors as does the Romantic poetics of the fairy tale. By virtue of its negative fixation on these categories, the early Romantic poetics of the fairy tale has inscribed within it a resistance to one of the most decisive elements of "Romanticism." The Romantic foundation of hermeneutics[59] undergoes more than a playful restriction when Romantic poetry—at least temporarily and in the literal pronouncements of its theory—is committed to a repudiation of sense, coherence, and comprehensibility. "Truly," Schlegel prognosticates, "it would terrify you if once, as you demand, the whole world actually became completely understandable." For incomprehensibility, if need be an "unbelievably tiny portion" of incomprehensibility, underlies "the dearest things that man has," as well as "the safety and well-being of families and nations."[60] It is the task of the earliest Romantic literary treatments of the fairy tale to present an intensified "portion" of this positive deficiency and to make its critical as well as dietetic functions reflective.

Friedrich Schlegel warns about the abyss of negative certainties into which a "completely" successful act of understanding would topple. The wise moderation of understanding in the interest of the "safety and well-being of families and nations" thus does not lead to a crisis of "sense" but instead avoids it. That moderation rescues and justifies an imaginary "sense" in the modus of its incomplete comprehensibility. Such a suspension of understanding itself continues a central theme of hermeneutics. As the inexhaustibility of "sense" vis-à-vis every finite act of understanding, incomprehensibility itself is part of the project of hermeneutics; admittedly, in this case the incomprehensibility is synonymous with infinite comprehensibility.[61] Literary criticism has repeatedly emphasized in Tieck's and Novalis's fairy tales this "incomprehensibility" that conforms to the strictures of hermeneutics, their resistance to every finite hermeneutical hypothesis by virtue of their abundant sense. Even when in *Sternbald* "incomprehensible hieroglyphs" are praised, which "as it were, stammering or seemingly from a distance, address us,"[62] does by no means challenge the domain of hermeneutical understanding: rather, it is affirmed as infinite. Schlegel's warning of complete comprehensibility undoes this conformity between incomprehensibility and sense. It interrupts the hermeneutical paradigm by the suggestion of a dangerous vacuum instead of an inexhaustible plenum toward which complete understanding would strive. Beyond the incomprehensibility qua inexhaustibility of sense, Tieck's poetics of incoherence in particular raises another, harsher provocation to understanding: the provocation that arises out of the indifference toward "sense" and out of the "nonsensical" withdrawal of "sense."

Goethe's Mährchen

In this respect, Goethe's *Mährchen* of 1795 has a twofold function; it serves both as a manifest antipode and a clandestine ally. The number of interpretations and commentaries that immediately followed its publication—unprecedented for a fairy tale—indicates the text's exoteric side: Goethe had systematically submitted the form of the fairy tale to the hermeneutical paradigm. He had written the first "hermeneutical fairy tale" and to this extent had promoted the tendency that Tieck's Bluebeard arabesque in 1797 would attack. However, at the same time, Goethe also mocked the hermeneutical obsessiveness and, by ultimately withholding the meaning that is suggested and evoked in the tale, he collapsed the intention toward meaning into itself and revealed it to be merely a capricious society game of his age that he ironically "serves up" to the reader. Thus, he also "dialectically" prepares the way for the early Romantic attack against the paradigm of meaning, and his most sensitive readers—A. W. Schlegel, Wilhelm v. Humboldt, and Ludwig Tieck bear witness to such an esoteric reading of the *Mährchen*.[63] (The following summary of readers' reactions consciously avoids direct consideration of Goethe's text; here the sole aim is to present these reactions as a symptom of a cultural system that is both sustained and irritated by the *Mährchen*.)

Perrault's fairy tale and the subsequent *Feenmärchen à la mode* were designed as a means for the aristocracy to pass the time. Reading them (aloud) fulfilled and exhausted their function: one did not go on to subject them to the ardors of interpretation or commentary. The situation was similar for the late-18th-century collections of fairy tales and their increasingly bourgeois audience. Even the most sophisticated, enlightened literary fairy tales such as Wieland's *Prinz Biribinker* require from the reader at most decisions about whether so much fairy-tale nonsense can still be believable, but they do not lead him on an infinite search for enigmatic meanings. Goethe's *Mährchen* therefore represents a distinct *novum.* The "18 figures of this dramatis," Goethe himself says, are "as many puzzles," and they should be "well received by those who love puzzles."[64] Every detail of the fairy tale "invites interpretations"[65]—and, the more complex and resistant the puzzles are constructed, the more interpretations are generated. For quite a while it is not even clear who the tale's "hero" or "heroine" is at all: apparently an intentional violation of the fairy tale's otherwise unwavering focus on its hero. A helping figure may be versed in the following discourse: "Whether I can help I do not know; a single person cannot help, only he who joins with others at the right time."[66] Jack-o'-lanterns offer explanations to their "Mistress Cousin," the serpent, in the vocabulary of idealist aesthetics: "indeed we are relatives only on the side of semblance."[67] A king made completely of gold "pressed the oak wreath on the head of the youth with a father-like gesture of blessing and said: 'Know the highest.'"[68] In view of the uncommonly large role played by dialogue in this *Mährchen,* it is not surprising that the serpent answers the question "What is more refreshing than light?" with "Conversation."[69]

Schiller's first reaction was "Incidentally, with this manner of literary treatment you imposed upon yourself the obligation that everything should be a symbol. One cannot refrain from looking for a meaning in everything."[70] And he prophecies to Cotta: "With this *Mährchen,* the commentators will have something to chew on."[71] Schiller was right. Körner praised the complicated opus with two central concepts borrowed from hermeneutical theory: Goethe's fairy tale ultimately unites the "lightness of the narrative and the wealth of imagination" with "a sense that also does not leave the mind unsatisfied."[72] Likewise, Charlotte von Kalb surmises "much truth and sense" in the tale, and as the good hermeneutical reader that she is, she promises: "I wish to read it again," so as to then convey her "interpretation."[73] Goethe looks forward "to your interpretation of the fairy tale."[74] When her interpretation arrives, he immediately endeavors to establish the unfinalizability of the interpretive efforts: "Send me quickly another explanation that I can send along to her," the author deftly turns to his friend Schiller. "I have quickly noted down several variations on the explanation; if you too can increase their number, then hopefully a confusion without end will arise from these elucidations."[75]

Besides Schiller, who promptly delivers "a small contribution to the interpretation of the fairy tale,"[76] Prince August von Gotha also contributes to the desired confusion. He had "really sunk his teeth into the mystical sense of the fairy tale"[77] and champions the thesis that "the unnamed author of the fairy tale could be no one other than the disciple and evangelist John, who must still be alive."[78] To this Goethe responds: "Regarding the discovery that your reading has made, that the disciple Quaestionis must still be alive, I am all the more amazed as the closer familiarity with the text itself has completely convinced me of your hypothesis, which initially seemed all too bold."[79] Despite his being completely persuaded, in the same letter Goethe promises his own "interpretation [. . .], but which I do not think to make known before I see my 99 predecessors." Further promises "to produce [. . .] something elegant [. . .] about the interpretation"[80] are proffered only to be subsequently retracted: he would prefer, as he says in the following letter, "to glide over the interpretation [of the fairy tale]."[81] However, ten days later Goethe "hopes" for his own interpretation: "My thanks for the contribution toward the interpretation of the fairy tale; we"—that is, Goethe—"would like to wait and see a bit. But I hope for a fortunate turn in the Conversations, where I can have my own self-indulgent fun with it."[82] In the *Xenien* this self-indulgent fun takes the form of a hexameter and pentameter:

> More than twenty persons are involved in the fairy tale.
> "Well, what are they all up to?" "The fairy tale, my friend."[83]

No wonder that in view of such (non-) elucidations the *Journal of Luxury and Fashion* in the 1796 March issue diagnosed an abiding "desperation among the interpreters and exegetes" of the *Mährchen.*[84] Instead of contributing his own interpretations Goethe preferred, for the sake of the unfinalizability of the hermeneutical exercise, to collect those of others and even "tried to preserve [them in the form of a] chart" (that unfortunately is lost).[85] Over the course of more than 30 years, there are diary entries like the following: "The evening at Madame Schopenhauer. After dinner the fairy tale"[86] or "At Frau von Eybenberg. The fairy tale and to what degree it has a meaning."[87] It is always "women" who are read to and who "willingly" take up the invitation to interpret. "The feminine eye suspects there is meaning in it," Carlyle reports in May 1830 from Craigenputtock about his "housewife" having read the *Mährchen,* and says he is "more often asked for explanations than I can provide."[88] Yet neither Mrs. Carlyle nor Marianne Willemer receive the requested "golden key"[89] to the *Mährchen*—that magical object from the Bluebeard tale that also represents a central hermeneutical fiction. The discursive practices that Friedrich Kittler has analyzed as the "discourse network 1800" enjoy perhaps their first distinctive paradigm in Goethe's flagrant hermeneuticization of the pre-hermeneutic form of the fairy tale.

However, at the same time, the *Mährchen* of 1795 inaugurates a decisive subversion of these emergent practices, with which the tale plays so masterfully. This counter movement is completely overlooked in Kittler's portrayal of Goethe and the German Romantics. If there exists an initial sustained meaning of this memorable "product of the imagination"[90] (as Goethe characterizes his tale), then it is that of suggesting meanings everywhere and inviting interpretations. If there is a second meaning, then it is that of reneging on precisely this suggestion and of compromising this hermeneutical seduction by unmasking it as "self-indulgent fun." However, whenever this counter tendency in the *Mährchen* was detected by Goethe's contemporary readers, it was seldom relished as "fun" with their reading practices but instead registered with disorientation as the suspension of those practices' presuppositions. "People complain," Wilhelm von Humboldt reports to Schiller, "that the fairy tale says nothing, has no meaning."[91] In the journal *Deutschland*, it is lambasted as "a vapid little ghost story," that "diverts German readers [. . .] from [. . .] the genuine great interest of humanity."[92] Karl Grün finds the best conceptual expression for this experience of emptiness and the withdrawal of meaning: the *Mährchen* is "the naked desperation of sense and understanding and the pathological enjoyment in this desperation [. . .] We are not used to this from Goethe, we won't stand for it even from him [. . .] we protest."[93]

Even if they could articulate this experience only as a perversion, Karl Grün and his predecessors perceived something in Goethe's *Mährchen* that mainly escaped the praise of its hermeneutical readers because it questioned hermeneutics' very responsibility and competence. This is because the criticized deficiency "in sense and understanding," expressed positively, represents the common denominator for the esoteric reception of the *Mährchen* and even an explicit slogan from Tieck's Bluebeard arabesque. Wilhelm von Humboldt praises Goethe's *Mährchen* for this suspension of the constraint of significance: "Your fairy tale," he writes to Goethe on February 9, 1796, "seems to me to be the first example of this genre in our literature. Most readers, whose judgments have reached me here, have tortured themselves to the extreme in order to read out of it, or at least read into it, a philosophical sense, and since several have turned to me, as though I must possess revelations about it, I have in my responses divided the readers into two classes. For those whom I immediately despaired of convincing, I composed an explanation extemporaneously; to the others I endeavored to demonstrate that none is needed."[94] Four weeks before Humboldt's great letter to Goethe, culminating in "a proper theory of the fairy tale," A. W. Schlegel's review appeared in the *Allgemeine Literatur-Zeitung*. It too masterfully avoids performing hermeneutical contortions upon Goethe's *Mährchen*. Instead of "interpretation" and "meaning" the review speaks of "arrangement and expression," of "language" and "elegant manner,"[95] that is, categories from rhetoric and stylistics. A hermeneuticization of these categories is explicitly avoided. "The search for a secure thread of meaning" Schlegel leaves for such readers who "cannot amuse themselves with an uninhibited mind."[96] He "contents" himself with the non-interpretive "delight" in the "charming delicacy of the depiction," and how "the entire fairy tale hovers," how it "exhausts what it should represent, and [. . .] yet lightly glides over it, like nymphs over the grass."[97] The praise and enjoyment of the lightness is thus directly contrasted with the gravity of reading for "meaning." Ludwig Tieck's discourse on Goethe's *Mährchen* in the introduction to *Phantasus* (1811) likewise operates on the distinction between a conventional hermeneutical reader and a non-hermeneut who understands more about art. The first reader grants the *Mährchen* the title of "masterpiece" only insofar as we "can be satisfied with a poem that has no content."[98] The non-hermeneutical reader on the contrary wants to separate the enjoyment of the "presentation" from such a qualification. A "poem" according to him could also be "perfect" if it "lacks a mid-point and genuine coherence." Reading here no longer remains shackled to the hermeneutical chain of "coherence"—"sense"—"understanding." If a "poem" in spite of deficient meaningful coherence is nonetheless executed "perfectly" in its "separate parts," then—affirms Tieck's non-conformist reader—"the soul [can . . .] forget that demand for an inner coherence."[99] The "gentle wisdom of an amusing sense"[100] permits the compulsive search for sense and meaning to be suspended.

These remarks apropos of Goethe's *Mährchen* also represent an echo of the much more sophisticated critique of hermeneutics that Tieck had made in 1797 in the form of a "folktale"—the *Seven Wives of Bluebeard.* The correspondences in terminology and argument show that Tieck was one of Goethe's "esoteric" readers and therefore could see his *Bluebeard* as a radical development of—instead of an adversary to—Goethe's "hermeneutical" fairy tale, just as Novalis's demands for fairytale-like incoherence were a direct and positive reaction to Goethe's complicated "product." Goethe pursues his "self-indulgent fun" with the new hermeneutical practice of reading by making more gambits of intelligibility than any other author and yet in the end confronting the hermeneutical effort with a void rather than infinite meaning. Gervinus sensed this at least as a disturbing politics of "teasing the reader," which he interpolates from the "problematic compositions": Goethe would like, Gervinus guesses, "to laugh quietly into his hand as Schiller and the others torture themselves on the knots [. . .] in his fairy tales."[101]

"Vainly devising an interpretation for the whole,"[102] as Johann Friedrich Reichardt wrote in the journal *Deutschland* he edited, Goethe's readers face the choice between criticizing either the Olympian or their own reading habits and hence a contemporary discursive praxis. Ludwig Tieck chooses the second alternative. Goethe's sublime hermeneutical-critical twist in the medium of a hermeneuticization of the fairy tale pursued to the point of exhaustion gives way to an open provocation of the hermeneutical discourse. This move does not only devolve upon the fairy tale by virtue of the need to invest it with an actualizing function; it also possesses a solid *fundamentum in re* in the original fairy tale. Therefore, this provocation has also produced distinct effects in the most important theories of the fairy tale in the twentieth century. Such effects form the subject of the concluding chapter of this study; yet in anticipation they already enter the presentation and discussion of Perrault's *Barbe-Bleue* and its arabesque overgrowth in Tieck's *Seven Wives of Bluebeard.*

§ 4 Between the Addition and Subtraction of Sense—Charles Perrault's *La Barbe-Bleue*

The full title of Charles Perrault's small collection of fairy tales is not often cited. In the standard edition of 1697 the title is *Histoires ou Contes du temps passé. Avec des Moralités.* For eighty years, up until the sixth edition of 1777, this complex title of the type "'A ou A.' Avec des B" was maintained as an integral whole. Since that time, however, Perrault's fairy tales usually bear another title: *Contes de fées, Contes du temps passé,* or simply *Contes.*[1] The original addition *Avec des Moralités* vanished from these titles, and with it a difference important for genre theory. In the latter case, the title *Conte* comprises the texts in their entirety, including the *moralités,* just as the concept of "fable" includes the *moralité* which summarizes it. In the former case, on the contrary, the *moralité* is excluded from the *conte* and explicitly marked as a supplement exterior to it. What the original title conveys is precisely this: not everything included in the book corresponds to the concept of the fairy tale or the *conte du temps passé*; rather, something is appended to the fairy tale that is itself not a fairy tale. Only in this conjunction with a difference from its own concept does Perrault introduce the genre of the fairy tale into literature. In other words, Perrault's fairy tales are also reflexive considerations of their own genre. They are not simply narrated as fairy tales but are in every single case caught in a textual movement that urges the reader to draw a distinction between the fairy tale proper and its external supplement.

It is widely upheld that Perrault's *Contes de ma mère Loye* or *Histoires ou Contes du temps passé* derive from orally transmitted fairy tales.[2] However, numerous variants collected by ethnologists and the common stylistic features of fairy tales identified by genre theory support a supposition that at least apparently enjoys more validity than its contrary: that Perrault did not simply record an extant corpus of orally transmitted fairy tales. Rather, their written form exhibits a recognizably literary-political strategy and devices of literary modification that have been less explored than the thematic preoccupations of Perrault's small selection. Viewed formally, Perrault's transcription only occasionally follows the rhetorical operations of omission [*detractio*], direct transformation [*transmutatio*] or exchange [*immutatio*]. It favors the form of—sometimes marginal—additions (*adiecto*), quite in line with the title whose "avec" points to the figure of *adiectio*. The structure of an "avec" is by no means restricted to the *moralités* (alien to the genre of fairy tale and borrowed from the fable) that Perrault adds to the narrative conclusion of the fairy tales as emblematic signatures. Rather, this structure wholly characterizes his narrative technique. His fairy tales are complete and largely and seemingly "authentic" fairy tales *plus* something else.[3] These additions do not simply transcend the fairy tale. Rather, they respond to problems in the genre's definition and execution: they make the form's boundaries and laws reflexive by breaking them. These addenda constitute the focus of the following readings.

"There was once a man who owned grand houses in the town and country, gold and silver dinnerware, tapestries and gilded carriages."[4] This opening immediately identifies Bluebeard's first distinctive feature: his wealth. Regarding his second characteristic feature—his blue beard—Perrault does not limit himself to simply mentioning the fact without commentary. Rather, he adds a motivation that is as inconspicuous as it is momentous. Instead of "but this man had a blue beard," Perrault writes, "but unfortunately this man had a blue beard" ["*mais par malheur cet homme avait la barbe bleue*"]. If this motivation is taken literally, it has the effect of removing motivation altogether: if the blue beard is a natural and fateful misfortune—as the ugly disfigurements of Riquet à la houppe (or of Perrault himself)—then no symbolic significance can be ascribed to it. Then the blue beard may well serve as a striking signal, as a conspicuous (colored) spot in the plot surface of the fairy tale (and performs narrative functions that need to be defined), but it does not permit any hermeneutic that aims at some deeper, inner character of the person wearing it.

Encyclopedias and reference works offer an abundance of highly contradictory meanings of "blue" and "beard." According to tradition, blue is the color of divine purity and of infinite longing (the "blue flower" of German Romanticism) as well as of the plague (the black death as "blaue Flamme," "blue flame"), of alchemy or of vanity and futility ("ins blaue reden" [in English "talk 'til one's blue in the face"], "blauer Dunst" [sheer invention, hand-waving], *Contes bleues, faire des coups bleus, ne voir que du bleu*). Furthermore, blue figures as the color of loyalty and constancy, evil and deceit, catastrophe and grief. The beards of ancient Egyptian gods, the skin of the Indic Krishna, the coat of Wotan, the vestments of the Holy Father, and the veil of Mary in Christian iconography are all blue; even Satan too is sometimes portrayed as a figure in blue. On the one hand, blue has the connotations of profundity, purity, truth, divinity, royalty, infinity, immateriality, and on the other hand, of vacuity, futility, and coldness—including the coldness of death itself. The beard may be viewed as a sign of virility and (animal) strength as well as of wisdom and dignity. Gods and demi-gods or saints are regularly bearded; no magician worth the name can get by without a beard. However, the moment grooming starts to lapse, the beard abruptly turns into a sign of insanity. One swears by the beard of the prophet; *fair la barbe à qn.* can mean bringing terrible shame on someone, and there are other examples. Moreover, the attribute of "beard" can also suggest having the key—keys have a "beard" in German ["bit" in English]—or even the age of the plot—a story that "has a beard," as one says in German.

If one collates these multiple (potential) meanings of the words "blue" and "beard" and relates the resulting number of semantic overlappings to the prevalent feature of (fear-inducing) deviance produced by the pair's unusual syntagmatic combination, then several varieties of metaphorical significance emerge. The most common interpretation operates with only a few of the negative connotations and arrives at the unambiguous conclusion that the blue beard refers to the coldness and malice of its wearer. Other readings try to rescue some of the polyvalence by seeing the connotation of knowledge and of the magician also actualized—for instance, noting Bluebeard's possession of a magic key. All of these moves interpret the blue beard as an instance of metaphorical signification and hence postulate an expressive relation of similarity between the beard and the character attributes of its wearer. Since the blue beard symbolizes coldness, the beard's wearer is also cold; since magicians have beards, so Bluebeard too is a magician. In place of this motivated relation, Perrault introduces the contingency of a "malheur" and thereby interrupts the continuum between ethics and aesthetics that traditionally interprets ugliness as evil. With this move, Perrault, precisely by adding a (de)motivating formula, stands closer to the fairy tale than do the metaphorizing transferences of "beard" and "blue" onto the nature of their owner.

In fairy tales, beautiful young women are also as a rule morally good. This aesthetic-ethical parallelism is, however, subject to a decisive requirement and an often overlooked restriction. It is effective only if these women are—at least temporarily—poor, abandoned, enchanted, or in some way lacking something. If there is no external deficiency, an ethical defect assumes its role: comfortably situated beautiful princesses are then prideful, cruel, and lazy. In numerous fairy tales, therefore, beauty figures more as a license for morally questionable actions than as a guarantee of impeccability. The syllogism from aesthetic appearance to ethical character, the continuum between beauty and goodness in fairy tales thus either relies on preconditions or is immediately broken. The same is true for the complementary relation between ugliness and evil. Only rarely does ugliness simply accompany and reinforce the moral baseness of character, as for instance in the case of the witch who cooks children. More often ugliness is diagnosed as a mere veil that unfavorably and, in many cases, only temporarily conceals either an enchanted beautiful person (for instance, the frog prince) or a morally "good person" (for instance, Perrault's Riquet à la houppe or King Drosselbart in Grimm's tales). The "ugly dwarf" Perrault noticeably favored this last variant of the non-identity between appearance and essence. Even in "Barbe-Bleue," he interrupts the equation between ugly and evil that generally defines this figure: Bluebeard is not ugly because he is evil but solely "par malheur."[5] The fact that to women he seems "so ugly and frightening" no longer allows a deeper interpretation of the blue beard as a metaphor of his demonic essence. What remains is the color blue, a favorite color in fairy tales, hair as an often mentioned feature of a human being's look, and above all their disturbing syntagmatic conjunction, which because of its aspect of deviance seems repulsive and evokes presentiments of evil-doing. For the purposes of advancing the plot, this wholly suffices. Only as a vague signal of subsequent action—and later as a metonymy of its actual performance—does the conspicuous attribute have a clear narrative function.

To be sure, even the "original" fairy tale at times raises questions about the "why" of deviant appearances, but it usually offers only pragmatic and not psychological-hermeneutic answers. Just as the misshapen figures of enchanted princes and princesses do not signify anything per se about their essence (the frog-prince "actually" has nothing frog-like about him) but rather refer to a past intrigue and elicit future action, so too the blue beard circulates solely on the plot surface of the fairy tale. Unlike the disfigurements wrought by enchantment, however, the beard is not the very subject of the evolving plot but instead only an accompanying sign—a replaceable and even wholly superfluous sign, as several variants of the tale indicate. The metaphorical charging of the beard is itself due to a double metonymic relation: the relation to its owner and the relation to the murder. As the point of intersection between these two metonymies, the blue beard is prone to a metaphorical short circuit. The fairy tale, however, removes every further motivation from this short circuit, since it suggests no reason at all for Bluebeard's behavior and exclusively executes the pure facticity of the plot. Thus, while the "original" fairy tale offers the metaphorization of a (double) metonymy only to the extent that it immediately disregards it and lets it come to naught, Perrault by his addition "per malheur" explicitly prevents any psychological motivation at the very outset.

Perrault's reservation against any metaphorical interpretations of ugly deformations thus, as a supplemental addition, does not break the laws of the genre "fairy tale" but rather merely parallels Bluebeard with other ugly misshapen figures, among whom King Drosselbart ["King Choking-Beard"] comes to mind, simply by virtue of his name. Probably in order to forestall the equation of the physical scandal with an evil nature and to introduce the possibility of an (indifferent) difference, Perrault delays Bluebeard's marriage and the discovery of the secret chamber by introducing an intermezzo during which the aesthetic-ethical identification is expressly dislocated. As each of the three daughters rejects the uncanny groom and prefers that one of her sisters marry him, and as the mother also makes no decision, Bluebeard resorts to courtship and marriage in a thoroughly progressive-liberal way:

> In order to get to know them, Bluebeard invited the girls with their mother, three or four of their best friends, and a few young people from the area, to one of his houses in the country, where they stayed for eight whole days. All they did was hold picnics and parties. They hunted and fished, danced and ate, and no one slept a wink; they were too busy playing the fool. In fact, all went so well that the younger sister started to believe that the lord of the manor did no longer have so blue a beard and that he was a very fine man after all. As soon as they got back to the town, she married him.

Bluebeard figures of the oral tradition do not care at all about the will or the sympathy of their brides. They rely entirely on the distress of the parents, their own wealth, or other means of enchantment. Perrault's addition of a formally consummate courtship once again fulfills the double function of making the tale contemporary and providing (demotivating) motivation. The otherwise rather barbaric Bluebeard acquires an aristocratic, upper-class culture of conviviality: he hosts country outings, proves himself a "maître de plaisir," and knows how to win people over. Thus, the marriage acquires the dignity of an informal mutual recognition instead of being merely a function of power and wealth. At the same time, this informal motivation of sociality demotivates and empties out the initial "sign" of the fairy tale. In the face of the winning personality of its owner, the blue beard loses every offensive aspect. It is no longer read as the sign of an ominous deviance; indeed, with its scandalous semantic character, it seems to vanish entirely out of the world (of perception): "the younger sister started to believe that the lord of the manor did no longer have so blue a beard and that he was a very fine man after all."

Does the post-marriage discovery of the murders disavow the desymbolization of the blue beard as a mere effect of masterful disguise? In the light of the evil deeds, does the difference between aesthetic appearance and ethical essence itself become an illusion? Is thus the metaphorical identity, while rejected in the first place, reaffirmed in a second reading? Such a double turnaround of the relationships between aesthetics and ethics and between appearance and essence would contradict at least one fundamental characteristic of the Bluebeard figure, if not of the conventions of fairy tales in general:[6] brutal honesty and a seamless identity between word and deed. Bluebeard does not conceal his offensive facial feature;[7] he openly threatens to kill anyone who is disobedient, and he just as openly condemns his wife to death and performs the ritual of execution—at least in Perrault—even while others are present. He lacks the virtues or vices of social rhetoric and disguise rather than possessing them in abundance—the latter being typically, both in Perrault and later in Rousseau, a reproach to the female sex only. In accordance with that, Bluebeard has never been faulted for his powers of rhetorical disguise.

In Perrault's version, when Bluebeard prepares for his journey, he once again proves to be a cultivated and generous "honnête homme." Instead of expecting his wife to wait on the threshold until he returns, he asks her "to amuse herself during his absence. If she liked, she could invite all her friends and take them to the country; anything that would keep her happy." This request, itself an addition to the "original" fairy tale, introduces another supplemental motif: the wife's friends who keep her company. Viewed functionally, this supplement once again not only violates the laws of the fairy tale, but makes them reflexive. First of all, this motif doubles the opposition between the protagonists: Bluebeard is "ugly," whereas his wife is "perfectly beautiful;" Bluebeard has neither family nor friends, whereas his wife has both. The presence of these secondary figures grouped around the wife figures as a medium into which Perrault immerses the time of the courtship as well as the absence of Bluebeard, the discovery of the corpses as well as the scene of the near execution. The second appearance of the friends and neighbors clearly signals that this motif is not about realistically motivated conviviality, for "the neighbors and friends didn't wait to be asked to visit the young bride." No sooner has Bluebeard suggested to his wife that she invite some of her friends than they are hurrying to the spot, like remote-controlled puppets, without waiting for any kind of invitation whatsoever. This magical short circuit of suggestion or word and action has the effect that the intentionality of the wife arises too late and robs her of every possibility to cause the event. Through its very improbability, this bewildering phenomenon lays bare a general law of the fairy tale, namely "that the feelings and intentions of the dramatis personae do not have an effect on the course of action in any instances at all."[8]

The disruption of a comprehensible link between the intentionality of the female protagonist and the visit of her friends becomes fully manifest when Bluebeard's wife leaves her "guests" in order to open the forbidden door. Surprisingly, she does not communicate the grisly discovery to the group of friends luckily present at the time—which might have increased her chances of being rescued. Instead, she withdraws to her chamber, and the neighbors and friends are never even mentioned again. Without having performed any recognizable plot function, they vanish from the house and from the text just as magically as they were first conjured up. Because it remains so "void of coherence" and "functionless," Perrault's ghostly supplement to the fairy tale functions in a way that is characteristic of the fairy tale: as an "obtuse" or even "blind motif."[9] Furthermore, the way the group of friends is suddenly treated as non-existent reveals another "a priori" of the fairy tale: the imperative isolation of the hero in the initial phase of his development.[10] The guests whom Perrault has tossed into the tale serve to demonstrate a social isolation on the part of the protagonists that is characteristic of the genre and wholly indifferent to psychological motivations: in certain sequences of its plot, the fairy tale itself simply cannot use company even when such company could be of use to the protagonists.

The unsummoned appearance of the neighbors and "good friends," while on the one hand pointing to a constitutive lack of psychological probability and function, is on the other hand recuperated through introducing into the text the motif of "impatience." The friends are not just impatient to finally see Bluebeard's treasure; they are obsessed with "impatience" and are almost staged as allegorical prosopopeia of this vice. This anticipates the behavior of Bluebeard's wife, to whom the "being-possessed"[11] by "impatience" and "curiosity" is then metonymically transferred. The wife is "so consumed with curiosity" that she simply abandons her guests and rushes down the tiny secret stairway with such speed "that two or three times she thought she was going to break her neck." With this emphasis on curiosity Perrault once again fills a motivational vacuum. The ideal-typical fairy tale does not require any motivation through curiosity in order for a prohibition to be broken. For this purpose, the mere existence of the prohibition suffices, since in a typical fairy tale a prohibition is precisely pronounced in order to be invariably violated[12]—if not by the hero then by some contrastive figure. What is put to the test is at most obedience. Whether curiosity or some other reason induces disobedience is generally of no interest to the fairy tale. Not *why*, but *that* there is a lapse of obedience is of primary import. The plot schema itself requires the prohibited act regardless of the "feelings and intentions of the persons undertaking the action."

Perrault's move to provide a supplementary, psychological reason for a course of action required by the very genre of the fairy tale appears again to amount to rationalization. Furthermore, this supplement conforms well to the contemporaneous Christian ideology: under the sign of accursed curiosity, the story of Bluebeard and his wife becomes a variation of the sinful Fall. Yet upon closer scrutiny, the Christian adaptation as well as the rationalization do not hold up. Bluebeard may indeed be a satanic tempter, but he does not induce a prohibited act; rather, he first issues the prohibition and thus rather plays the divine role. When we turn to Eve's role in the Fall, the parallel fails completely. For far from causing her eternal misfortune, the heroine's curiosity in the fairy tale ultimately brings her a large fortune and thereby the chance of happiness both for her and her family. Eve-like curiosity, which as a feminine vice may motivate the prohibited act, cannot likewise account for that act's fortunate consequences. Once again the rationalizing supplement becomes entangled in self-critical contradictions, and the addendum of motivation, with which Perrault is often reproached for having simplified, even banalized the fairy tale, turns out in fact to be the withdrawal of motivation.

"At first she couldn't see anything" reads the text after the forbidden door has been opened, and the reason given for this seeing "nothing" is darkness, where only "after a few moments" can one begin to make anything out. There are, however, other readings of this "nothing." The first one would claim a pathological imagination: Bluebeard's wife in fact sees "nothing," but her fear—she had turned the key "trembling"—produces in the darkness visions of horror, which reflect her uncertainty about the fates of the previous wives. This interpolation, though, is both at odds with the fairy tale genre and does not agree with Bluebeard's own statements. Another more viable and more valuable way of reading the "nothing" literally could point to the fact that the series of Bluebeard's wives must not only conclude with a final instance—which is the heroine of the fairy tale—but that it must also begin with an initial one. What, now, did this first wife see in the forbidden chamber? It follows logically that she did not see any predecessor, any corpse, or any blood—she saw precisely "nothing." One could object that this argument is too logical to be true. Psychologically, the Bluebeard plot requires a thinking which sees him always already as a serial killer. His action implies from the very beginning the figure of seriality and repetition or, in other words, his action implies the paradoxical figure of an originary repetition. Such a withdrawal of a "pure" first time, the logic of a -1, of an emptying out of the position of origin, certainly offers an interesting perspective for a post-Freudian reading sympathetic with a deconstructive reformulation of traditional metapsychological assumptions. However, there is yet another reading of the "nothing," one that is more congenial to both the genre and the plot.

Bluebeard's prohibition in several respects recalls the archaic form of taboo. It does so primarily through its lack of motivation: "taboo prohibitions," according to Freud, "have no grounds" and are "unintelligible to *us*." Regardless of this lack of motivation, "they seem self-evident" to those "who live under their domination."[13] Apparently, Bluebeard's wife is not one of them. For her the unfounded prohibition is anything but self-evident and sacrosanct. This is in line with the general tendency of the fairy tale to incorporate traces of archaic rites and customs without their social and religious underpinnings and thus to transmit them as estranged, incomprehensible relics. In the field of taboo "this and that is forbidden, (primitive peoples) do not know why, and it doesn't occur to them to ask why."[14] Bluebeard's prohibition as well is a matter only of "this and that is forbidden," not of the knowledge, pleasures, or material profit that might result from its transgression. Bluebeard's wife is punished for opening the door, not for what she discovers behind it. This mystery *behind* the door is "nothing" in terms of the logic of taboo. The mystery can be completely empty, less a mystery of nothing than a nothing of mystery; for the sanction elicited by the transgression of the taboo all this changes—nothing. The nothing that Bluebeard's first wife sees and the nothing that his last wife sees thus do not destroy the *skandalon* but rather in their literalness indicate what according to the logic of taboo is the "proper place" of the *skandalon*: the door and the turning of the key, the threshold itself rather than what lies beyond it.

In his reading of Perrault's *Barbe-Bleue*, Ludwig Tieck strongly emphasized and literalized this "nothing" of the mystery. Where the corpses of Bluebeard's wives end up does not interest him; indeed, it goes unmentioned. In any case, they are not gathered in the forbidden room. Not only did the first woman to enter see "nothing out of the ordinary in the room."[15] The next one also "was surprised when she entered and found an empty chamber [. . .] It was all empty."[16] And another one found much "ado about nothing! There is nothing in the room but the bare walls."[17] "Elle ne vit rien"—this sentence of Perrault's leads deeper into the opaque structure of taboo the more it withdraws (psychological) motivation from it. By rupturing the connection between the prohibition and the corpses, this sentence destroys a central link in the traditional hermeneutics of the plot.

After the magic key reveals that the prohibition has been transgressed, the sanction is immediately announced: "'Madam, you must die,' he told her. 'you must die right now.'" In this impersonal linguistic form, Perrault's modernized *conte* signals that Bluebeard's personal cruelty is as little at issue here as is his ugly beard a sign of his evil nature or the forbidden chamber evoked for the sake of its secret. Perrault both forces and revokes the de-archaizing and de-ritualizing of the fairy tale, in the wake of which curiosity becomes the motive for transgressing the taboo and evil, cruelty, and sexual desire become the motive for excessive "punishment." The form of taboo and the style of the fairy tale do not at all require such rationalizations in order to "motivate" the scandalous phenomena. Taboos include the notion "that any violation of them will be automatically met by the direst punishment,"[18] in most cases a fatal one. Similarly, "the death sentence is virtually the only punishment in the fairy tale and the severity of such judgments often has no relation to the crime committed [. . .] The very different levels of guilt often find no corresponding gradation in the punishment."[19]

Max Lüthi recognized this to be a consequence of the abstract style of the fairy tale that is unfavorable to making subtle distinctions: "Extreme crimes, fratricide, infanticide, vicious slander are the order of the day in the fairy tale, as are cruel forms of punishment. The many *prohibitions* and harsh *stipulations* contribute substantially to shaping the precise style."[20] "The extreme and starkly graphic punishments are in accord with the sharp contours and disdain for nuance characteristic of the fairy tale's style."[21]

If the genre itself operates with harsh stipulations and almost always requires the death penalty, Bluebeard cannot simply be made "personally" responsible for it. In repeatedly pronouncing "You must die," he acts rather like the representative of an anonymous law than as an individual subject driven by the lust to kill. Moreover, other figures from fairy tales significantly outdo his cruelty in choice of punishment. Therefore, Bluebeard's possible motives play no role in the folk variants of the tale—not because the motives are self-evident but because they are superfluous or insignificant to the unfolding of the plot. In particular, these folk variants "reveal nothing of the piquant charm of a sexual crime." They are more focused "on the fates of the heroine," whereas in drama, opera, and film, Bluebeard becomes the "actual hero."[22] It is only in this modernist shift of focus that the psychologization of Bluebeard's deeds first emerges and is then *post festum* read back into the fairy tale. Perrault's *Barbe-Bleue* both yields to the demands of "modernization" while at the same time continuing to resist it.

The fairy tale grants a reprieve between the verdict's pronouncement and its execution. In some oral versions, Bluebeard commands the heroine to retire to her room "pour revêtir ses habits de noces ou ses plus beaux habits, plus rarement pour les poser;"[23] the corresponding scenes of ritual disrobing and donning ceremonial attire especially point to the "archaic" character of the action. Perrault, the advocate of the "modernes," spared his contemporaries the provocation of this ritual, which had already become opaque to the fairy tale itself. In his version the heroine herself requests the reprieve "to say my prayers"; yet in fact she doesn't pray but asks her sister three times whether she can see her brothers coming to save her. The Christian coding of the event is thus proffered only in order to be immediately withdrawn again as a mere pretense.

Regardless of their specific motivations, set deadlines in fairy tales always have two distinctive characteristics. The first concerns their duration: deadlines are either met in the very last moment, or the time granted is even slightly exceeded.[24] This is in keeping with the abstract style of fairy tales, which functions favorably through extremes. The heroine in *Barbe-Bleue* experiences the suspense of slightly exceeding the time granted: her brothers arrive seconds too late, the deadline of "a quarter of an hour" is already elapsed, and Bluebeard already raises his sword. She survives her *dead*line, is a *survivante* in the intriguing sense that her life extends past the limit set upon it—which lends her virtually the characteristics of a *revenante.*[25] The second distinctive characteristic of deadlines in fairy tales concerns their plot function: they enable a difficult task to be achieved or a catastrophe to be averted because they represent the time needed for helping figures or helping objects to arrive or, in the case of the time exceeded, to at least come close. The original fairy tale does not care for any explanation whence these figures come, why they come, and how their magical capabilities are to be accounted for. The only thing that counts is *that* they come at just the right moment, and that they possess precisely the capabilities that the hero lacks, in short: that they supplement his shortcoming exactly and perfectly. For example, some oral variants of the Bluebeard tale suddenly provide the heroine in her moment of need with a talking bird or a clever dog, who then fetches the brothers,[26] while in others she flees and, just as she is about to be caught, uses magical helping tools to repulse or confuse her persecutor.[27] The function of the wondrous events is not at least to stylistically establish this abstract symmetry between problem or danger on the one hand and solution or rescue on the other. Perrault, however, avoids every hint of the marvelous and magical in his helping figures and tries to be "realistic." Yet the metamorphosed helping figures can only fulfill their fairy-tale function by in turn destroying their increased verisimilitude and negatively presenting the abstract law of the fairy tale in the failure of its undoing.

"When she was alone," Perrault says of his heroine, "she called her sister Anne and said: 'My sister Anne (for that was her name), I beg you, go to the top of the tower and see if our brothers are coming. They promised me they would come to see me today, and if you see them, signal them to hurry.'" In other contexts, under other conditions, the call to her sister may seem more natural than the miraculous appearance of supernatural helpers. In Perrault's *Barbe-Bleue*, however, it assumes the character of a magical citation, for nothing earlier in the tale suggested the presence of the sister in Bluebeard's house. She was not part of the group of "neighbors" and "good friends" that appeared immediately and unsummoned at Bluebeard's departure. Just as these people shortly thereafter vanished into nothingness without a mention, so too "sister Anne" materializes out of nothingness just at the moment she is needed: a classical characteristic of helpers in fairy tales. Though the sister does not possess any supernatural capacities and does not perform magical acts, nonetheless, there is something extraordinary about her. Perrault has underlined this with two addenda that are alien to the very genre of the fairy tale. The first is the proper name Anne. In a linguistic universe largely composed of abstract functional concepts like Father, Mother, Sister, Husband, Wife, King, Prince, Magician, or significant names such as Red Riding Hood, Cinderella, and Bluebeard, this name seems a stranger. The second supplement strengthens this effect by making the bestowal of the name self-reflexive: "My sister Anne (for that was her name)." When a sister addresses her sister as "sister Anne," it is usually self-evident that this is the sister's name. The additional commentary "(for that was her name)," which is not included in the first version of 1695, represents an intervention, highly unusual in fairy tales, of the narrator into the midst of a speech in direct quotation; moreover, its grammatical form—that of parentheses—occurs extremely rarely in the genre of the fairy tale. Above all, however, the additional commentary is superfluous; it says nothing that was not already said in the address "my sister Anne." It is a supplement that adds nothing to the "sense" but that—in the excess and emptiness of the additional message it conveys—highlights the supplementarity itself. Encompassed in parentheses and thus neither wholly inside nor wholly outside the narrative progression, it refers to what is already a supplement to the fairy tale: the proper name Anne. What was to "naturalize" the helping function of the fairy tale is itself attenuated into the supplement of a supplement, and occupies *in* the tale an excessive, superfluous position *outside* the tale, a position that is more exorbitant and less probable than all the threats to verisimilitude it was designed to avoid. The addition that promises motivation ("for . . . ") becomes a tautological self-disclosure of unmotivated contingency: Anne is called "Anne" because that is what her name is, or, in Novalis's words, "Because things are that way, that is the way they are" ["Weil es so ist, so ist es so"].[28]

The question of how the rescuing brothers could be summoned in the first place, if neither the heroine nor her sister has magical powers or animal emissaries at their disposal, leads to a similar structure of self-negation in the rationalization of the tale. Perrault's answer is consistent: the required call for help is impossible. Therefore, it must be replaced by its being made superfluous. The solution: the brothers do not need to be summoned, since they had already promised "they would come to see me today." However, there was just as little mention earlier in the text of the brothers and their promise as there was of the presence of the equally helpful sisters. In keeping with the entire narrative logic of the helping figures, the ad hoc improvised promise to pay a visit on precisely the fateful day and the brother's appearance at precisely the fateful moment eliminate the magical elements and increase the tale's "realism" only at the expense of a high degree of improbability. Magical help disregards motivation and realism of the helping figure's powers; that is precisely what makes magical help in fairy tales probable, indeed "natural." On the contrary, the unmagical help in *Barbe-Bleue* tends toward motivation and excludes supernatural powers; precisely for those reasons, however, the help is improbable. Only because it cannot obtain its excess of rationalization without paying a complementary tribute to the fairy tale, does it not simply negate the genre's characteristic features, but presents their chiastic reflection. In helping figures, who by their "realistic" capacities are not as suitable for this effect as magical helping figures would be, the abstract symmetry between danger and rescue, running out of time and redemption is chiastically enacted.

Bluebeard is slain by the brothers, his riches distributed to his wife's family, the heroine happily married, and the sisters cared for, as the fairy tale swiftly reaches its conclusion. Not so Perrault: he continues it beyond its conclusion, similar to how the heroine survives beyond her own appointed downfall. His fairy tale is a complete fairy tale plus a postscript, an encore, "with Morals." All supplements to the fairy tale, the internal as well as external ones, interrupt the narrative *intentione recta* for the purpose of oblique acts of reading what is narrated. The narrator's parenthetical interventions such as "(for that was her name)" comment on particular aspects of the *récit*; those supplements that are integrated into the narration of the (ideal-typical) fairy tale present readings of earlier versions as well as reflections upon provocative properties of the genre; and the *moralités* submit the entire fairy tale to a belated reading. The change from prose to verse marks the fact that the *moralités* no longer disrupt the level of *récit* but rather have abandoned it completely. The *moralités* continue both forms of *récit*-internal addenda: the sequence of narrator's parenthetical interventions, because the *moralités* too assume the authority of commenting and interpreting; and the narrative supplements, because the *moralités* partake of their potential to reflect on the genre. In purely formal terms, *moralités* and *récit* share complex relationships: by their mere existence, *moralités* disrupt the narrative closure of the *récit*; they indicate its need for hermeneutical supplementation while at the same time offering themselves as the means to fill this gap. Moreover, the doubling of the *moralités* entails a further division within the *récit* through the very act of a reversed reading, which is designed to establish the meaning of the *récit*. Even on the level of their "contents," the twins "Moral" and "Another Moral" prove to be mischievous supplements.

The first moral repeats the supplementary motive that was already introduced in the narrative to explain and condemn the violation of the prohibition: the motive of curiosity. It thus adds what already had been added to the fairy tale and therefore reduces itself to the empty repetition of an addendum that adds nothing (more). On the other hand, this external repetition revalorizes the *récit*-internal supplement, for it now is elevated into the didactic kernel of the whole fairy tale instead of being simply one of its elements. Curiosity, as the first moral addresses itself to women, is a dangerous and evanescent pleasure:

> As soon as you've got it, it ceases to be,
> And it always costs too much.

Thus, the fairy tale appears as an edifying exemplum of a traditional rhetorical topos: the critique of curiosity leveled at Eve's daughters under the sign of the Christian narrative of the Fall. Yet in several respects the text stands in an ironic relation to the extraction of a "lesson" by means of the selective presentation of a single element. The privileged element is not even an integral part of the plot but only an optional additional motivation: something that is so inessential as to be entirely missing in some folk variants is charged with the role of that which is so essential that its absence would rob the fairy tale of its fabula docet-like right to exist. Furthermore, this "something"—while formally promoted to represent the lesson of the whole narrative—is itself being taught a lesson about its own arbitrary partiality. For the fairy tale portrays by no means only the dangers and negative costs but also the unheard-of productive force of curiosity: it is curiosity that leads to the discovery of the crimes, the just punishment, and the windfall inheritance. Moreover, the conventional topos contains a provocative inversion of the burden of guilt in the fairy tale: instead of masculine violence it is feminine curiosity that is castigated; thus, it is woman's own sinfulness that is made responsible for her downfall.

After the *moralité* has first halved the achievements of the (supplementary) curiosity in this way and thereby inversely displaced the emphases of the whole plot, this entire effort invested in rhetorical deflection rather than in the hermeneutical attainment of sense is devalued as useless. The second moral praises contemporary men for not, like Bluebeard, demanding "the impossible" from their wives. Yet if the stipulation of taming curiosity is fruitless from the very outset, because tantamount to demanding the impossible from the supposedly Eve-like nature of every woman, the lessons of the first moral lose every practical use value. They fail to grasp the events whose sense they are supposed to provide, and on top of that are fully useless. They relate ironically to their own role of being an emblematic-allegorical subtitle below the events, although they avoid any ironic tone and although Perrault's marked tendency toward misogynist ideologemes raises doubts about any ironical intentionality.

The second moral shifts perspective from the role of women to that of men. By analogy, one would expect a critique of male power and cruelty toward women here. Not a sign of it. The crucial element and mystery of the Bluebeard tale, symbolized in the forbidden chamber, eludes the supplementary determination of its "lesson." It even explicitly loses every claim to be able to provide any practically relevant sense. For the only "lesson" that Perrault derives from Bluebeard's behavior is the conclusion that such men have long since ceased to exist:

> Even the less sensitive spirit
> Who knows little of the world's spells
> Will see very soon that this story
> Is a tale of times past;
> There's no more husband as terrible,
> Nor one who demands the impossible
> [. . .]

As a historicizing commentary, the *moralité* ceases being a *moralité* of the *récit* itself: it no longer claims to apprehend the sense of the events; rather, from its transcendental standpoint it claims only its anachronism, its complete obsolescence. Along with the function of providing meaning, so too the function of a practical lesson dissolves: maxims are no longer needed for a problem that no longer exists. The *moralité* becomes a *moralité* about the superfluity of a *récit*, which no longer provides any useful lesson. The moral lesson empties out the text whose sense it is supposed to establish. The (here fully ironical) supplement of the fairy tale supplements not the lack of a meaningful coherence, but rather contributes to its withdrawal and fragmentation. In the "(passage) du déchiffrement linguistique [. . .] au décryptage herméneutique,"[29] the fairy tale's resistance against hermeneutic becomes virulent and reflexive. Perrault's additions to the tale are therefore not satisfactorily described—as is usually done—with shorthand such as actualization, motivation, rationalization, de-ritualization, and de-archaization. These additions also draw on their excessive exorbitance to reflect upon the specific properties of the genre at the critical moment of its transformation into literature. Perrault's tales not only represent the first written fairy tales of "modern" European literature, but also a highly sophisticated form of their reflexive investigation.

§ 5 "A Book Without any Coherence"—Ludwig Tieck's *The Seven Wives of Bluebeard*

Charles Perrault's fairy tale of *Barbe-Bleue*, which comprised only a few pages, was developed by Ludwig Tieck in short succession into two completely different works of book length. In 1796 he wrote the drama *Knight Bluebeard. A Nursery Tale in Four Acts*; it appeared in 1797 both as a separate publication and as the first volume of the *Folktales*, edited by his fictional character "Peter Leberecht." In the same year there followed the narrative *The Seven Wives of Bluebeard*, edited by "Gottlieb Färber." The bibliographical mystification here was extended to the place and time of publication: "Istanbul by Heraklius Murusi, Court Bookseller of High Gate; in the Year of the Hedschrah 1212." Twenty years later Tieck even planned a third version of Bluebeard, as a "reworking" of this "juvenile book."[1] However, it came to nothing more than a sketch—just as the fourth volume of *Phantasus*, for which this new version was intended, remained an unfinished project.

The Bluebeard drama and the Bluebeard narrative encountered a very unequal and "unjust" reception. Not only was the drama reviewed by A. W. Schlegel in highly flattering terms (in the first issue of the *Athenäum* in 1798)[2] and declared by Solger to be the epitome of "purest irony;"[3] it also had the good fortune to be included, in a slightly revised version, in one of the completed volumes of Tieck's *Phantasus* (1812). Later editions of Tieck's selected works primarily drew on these *Phantasus* volumes as well as on the major novels. Philology has also paid its respects to the Bluebeard drama: not only did it become widely acknowledged, following Solger's canonization, as one of the preeminent embodiments of Romantic irony; it also served as the basis of historical and genre-theoretical comparisons of Tieck's fairy-tale dramas with the marvelous and the fairytale-like in Shakespeare's plays or with Carlo Gozzi's *Fiabe*.[4] By contrast, the Bluebeard tale suffered a completely different fate: no prominent mention among the contemporaries, no later publication and no inclusion in one of the editions of Tieck's selected works, no philological monographs, and only cursory attention in the more comprehensive studies on the author.[5] Buried in the ninth volume of the 28-volume edition of his *Schriften* of 1828, the Bluebeard prose text, as Arno Schmidt lamented, remained "unfortunately absolutely unknown."[6] Tieck himself appears to have shared Arno Schmidt's high estimation of this "juvenile book": despite considerable irritation due to the censor's interventions, for him it belonged "at least not to the worst of my works."[7]

The following reading largely has the character of a running commentary, even if it treats the middle third of the text more summarily than the beginning and the conclusion. The reading does not simply single out textual reflections that challenge the constraint of meaning and expectations of significance and unity, but rather seeks to weave them into the twist and turns of the narrative development. Following the composition of the text, the explicit poetics of non-sense therefore first appears at the conclusion of the reading. That is because to appreciate the subtlety and nuances of the licenses that permit non-sense, it is critical first to consider which character utters them at which point and to whom.

Arabesque

The pseudo-Turkish title of the Bluebeard story,[8] on the one hand, alludes to the (pseudo) orientalizing vogue for *Märchen* in the 18th century. On the heels of the "breakthrough" by Perrault, the fairy tales à la Madame d'Aulnoye and the first translation of the *Tales of 1001 Nights* by Antoine Galland (1704) came to identify the fairytale-like with the Oriental and vice versa. This conjunction made it possible later for the disquietingly violent aspects of fairy tales—such as the serial murder of women—to be blamed on its oriental pedigree. The Bluebeard tale in particular, however, also shares completely unideological connections to the tales of Sheherezade: it is widely accepted that the motif of the forbidden chamber is borrowed from the tale of the second mendicant monk. On the other hand, Tieck's peculiar title contains a concealed reference of a purely formal kind. In the second printing of 1828, this reference is exposed through a metonymic displacement in the elements of the paratext: while the oriental place of publication is removed, a genre category is added that again points to the Arab world: the four narratives of the ninth volume of Tieck's *Writings* are called *Arabesques.*

"Arabesques: floral lineaments are all and sundry sorts of composed leaf- and floral-work, such as the Arabs are wont to do for decoration, since otherwise they are forbidden to make any images of animals or people." Such is the definition given in a *Lexicum Architectonicum* of 1744.[9] At about the same time, a new treatment of ornamental leaf forms and shell forms becomes the catalyst for the formation of an absolute aesthetic object. In the rocaille ornament, shell work and leaf work is extended from the frame onto what is enframed until it largely comes to substitute for the image itself. From this a hybrid emerges that is neither simply image nor ornament.[10] In becoming an image-object whose representation provides the impression of a spatial depth, the ornament gradually emancipates itself from the flatness of the surface to which it is applied and thus from its traditional definition as a "pattern against a ground" (Riegl).[11] On the other hand, sufficient ornamental traits remain in order to prevent an outright mode of imagery from developing. Oscillating between the modes of ornament and imagery, the new treatment of ornamental framings brings forth a "world of its own"[12] that consists of ideal (quasi-) objects. This puzzling play—exhibiting elements of beauty, eroticism, mortality, and also chthonian threat—has been designated by the art historian Hermann Bauer as a "stage of transition to Romanticism"[13]—an insight that has received all too little attention in literary scholarship. Like Romantic literature, the rocaille ornament combines a movement of "idealization" and of the absorption of representation with an ironic moment that puts art at a distance from itself.[14]

The Rationalist polemic against the Rococo ornament[15] seizes primarily upon the characteristics of semantic emptiness, non-representation, and the apparent ungroundedness of such play. Thus, it anticipates not only the Enlightenment critique of the arabesque but also the invectives against Romantic irony at the beginning of the 19th century. To a great extent, the Rationalist critique is shared by Classicism. However, Classicism strives to appropriate the language and forms of rocaille by modifying it.[16] Winckelmann in his critique of the Rococo arabesque had in 1755 already set a criterion for the eventual rehabilitation of the arabesque. Only "by a more thorough study of allegory," according to Winckelmann, could the "meaningless paintings in our chambers [. . .] be purified and attain truth and understanding." Otherwise, "the flourish and the much beloved shell work" are only "there to fill their space, and to cover the spaces that cannot be filled with goldplate [. . .] The aversion to empty space thus fills the walls; and paintings empty of thought are to replace the void."[17]

The Romantic arabesque from 1798 onward[18]—in particular, the paintings of Philipp Otto Runge—can be described as *one* way of fulfilling Winckelmann's requirement. It ennobles the arabesque by giving it a new allegorical weight—even though the Romantic type of an enigmatic scripture or "*Hieroglyphe*" surely goes beyond Winckelmann's concept of allegory. Werner Busch has depicted the Romantic hieroglyphic as the "natural mystical" or "natural historical" phase of the arabesque in the early 19th century. In its subsequent "historico-critical" phase, the arabesque is used to present internal positions and conflicts within painting, the academies, and the art world, and also serves to illustrate texts and book covers.[19] In the middle of the 19th century, the modern arabesque is appropriated by capitalist aesthetics; it adorns stock certificates, bank notes, and the designs of industrial parks. These three, well-researched "major phases" and forms in which the arabesque "vacuum" is allegorically "filled" are preceded, however, by attempts to liberate the arabesque from Winckelmann's imperatives of "meaning" and "truth."

The Enlightenment critique considered the project of saving the arabesque by allegorizing it to be impossible, indeed wrongheaded. Rather, this critique tended to declare the arabesque unredeemable and hence to entirely condemn it. In a polemical text of 1788 that continues the older critique of the rocaille ornament, A. Riem calls arabesques "meaningless scribbling" and "veritable monsters of the most unbridled imagination." Viewing them as "senseless" and "most capricious serial patterns without purpose or intention,"[20] he places them on the index of aesthetic criminality.[21] In contrast, the classicist, the Kantian, and the earliest Romantic poetics attempt to legitimate the arabesque without relegating it to a mode requiring the infusion of an allegorical "sense." Instead of overcoming the vacuum—the lack of an object and therefore of meaning—the characteristics in question are rather submitted to a new theoretical elaboration. It was precisely the ornament's lack of purpose and significance that suggested itself as a paradigm of aesthetic autonomy, and the difference between central and marginal, between frame and enframed, underwent several theoretical revaluations. Karl Philipp Moritz's classicist aesthetics of the ornament constitutes a compromise between the critique, which is still clearly perceptible, and an affirmative appreciation of the arabesque as both an autonomous play and a liminal art. Moritz shared in the condemnation of the useless "games of chance"[22] and demanded that the "ornament" "contain nothing *foreign*, which could draw our attention away from the subject matter itself."[23] At the same time, he legitimated the ornament by functionalizing it as an art of demarcation: "The ornament becomes the border guard of aesthetic autonomy internally and externally. It must redirect the surplus emanating outward from the artwork inwardly and it must outwardly protect the artwork against the tasteless and the uncultured."[24] Moreover, Moritz let the ornament itself partially partake of aesthetic autonomy rather than restraining it to a mere function in service of that autonomy. The chapter "Arabesques," in his treatise *Vorbegriffe zu einer Theorie der Ornamente* (1793), concludes with the proposition that "It is the very essence of ornament that it is bound by no law, because it has no purpose other than to give pleasure."[25] This license of lawlessness, however, does not challenge the fundamental subordination of the ornament to what it adorns. For in no case were the purposeless forms of ornament allowed to militate against their service to the "subject matter itself;" on the contrary, they continued to be required to "in every way suggest, and indicate, the essence of the subject, to which it is attached."[26] Otherwise, the contemplation of the ornament would run the danger "of giving way to a completely rambling imagination."[27] Even Goethe defended the "cheerfulness, carelessness and pleasure" of arabesques only as a "subordinate art,"[28] consequently as an art that should be aware of its limits and its inferiority to an art that is *not* arabesque.

In the field of the "playful varieties of taste," under which he comprised the arabesque, Moritz diagnosed a puzzling inversion of the classicist postulate of the unity of the manifold: "In the playful varieties of taste the manifold dominates over unity, whereas with genuine taste the manifold is subordinated to unity."[29] This delimiting of the manifold, this de-regulation of the difference in "play" tends to obey less and less the functional limitation of the classicist ornamental aesthetic. It "tempts" us rather, as Moritz says, through the free "flight of imagination [. . .] with a kind of pleasure into labyrinths."[30] In Tieck, the labyrinth loses every negative connotation: in the preface to the first edition of *Ritter Blaubart*, Tieck calls his "meaningless *fairytales*" delightful "labyrinths of rock and tree," whose "multifarious characters without coherence" compromise the concept of unity.[31] The de-limiting of the arabesque, against which Moritz warned, becomes a programmatic part of the early Romantic project.

As an art of the border and a borderline art, the arabesque frame is designed to confirm and to reinforce the identity of the artwork and thus to demarcate the field of aesthetic autonomy.[32] As such, it is a reaction to a new problem in aesthetics, for it is only with the emergence of the modern autonomous system of art that a precise demarcation between inside and outside becomes an urgent desideratum. The Kantian attempt to ground an absolutely "pure" and solely aesthetic judgment of beauty rigorously responds to this desideratum. The arabesque frame now provides the sought-for border demarcation: as a crossing between inside and outside at the outermost edge of the artwork, it expressly represents the difference between an inner and outer realm. Without directly using the concept, Kant's *Critique of Judgement* (1790) formulates an elaborate philosophy of the arabesque that then serves as a major touchstone for the reevaluation of the arabesque in early Romanticism:

> There are two kinds of beauty: free beauty (*pulchritudo vaga*) and merely adherent beauty (*pulchritudo adhaerens*). Free beauty does not presuppose a concept of what the object is [meant] to be [. . .] Thus designs *à la grecque*, the foliage for frameworks or on wall-paper, etc., do not mean anything on their own; they represent nothing, no object under a determinate concept, and are free beauties. What we call fantasias in music (namely, music without a topic [*Thema*]), indeed all music not set to words may also be included in the same class.[33]

§ 4 had already struck a similar note: "Flowers, free designs, lineaments aimlessly intertwined—technically termed foliage,—have no significance [. . .] and yet please."[34] Kant's flowers and foliage directly correspond to the definition given above of arabesque ornamental decoration, and the "free designs *à la grecque*" present an analogy in contemporary fashion, where *à la grecque* indicated "the straight ornamental ribbon in Greek art which is called 'meander,' which in the 18th century was once again applied particularly to knitting and other decorations, above all to the hems of clothing."[35] Even Jean Paul drew this parallel between arabesque and *à la grecque*: "Our conversations today are full of arabesques and *à la grecque*," he writes in *Hesperus*.[36] Kant's strict distinction between a free beauty (*pulchritudo vaga*) and a merely adherent or "fixed beauty" of purposeful "objects" amounts to the aesthetic privileging of the unnamed arabesque; at the same time, it excludes the traditional "ideal of beauty," the human body, because of its purposiveness from the region "of an entirely pure judgment of taste."[37] This has already been noted with as much concision as concern by Schiller: "Kant [. . .] claims, rather strangely, that every beauty which stands under the concept of a purpose is no pure beauty: that is, that an arabesque and similar things, considered as beauty, are purer than the most perfect beauty of man."[38]

Perhaps provocatively taking up Winckelmann's and Riem's earlier critique of arabesques as "meaning nothing" and also anticipating a central theme of Tieck's *Bluebeard* arabesque, Kant especially emphasized two aspects when he equated the arabesque with insignificance. The a-significance and non-representationality of the arabesque, its break with the rationalist paradigm of aesthetic representation, rests for him solely on the fact that the arabesque lacks concept and intentionality; however, it is not due to the strict lack of an object in the oriental sense.[39] Arabesques *can* lack an object, but they are not required to do so. Indeed, even foliage and flowers still evoke objects, and certainly Raffael's arabesques do not lack an object. What for Kant is essential here is not that the arabesque represents "no object," but that it represents "no object under a specific concept," that it "presupposes no concept of that which the object should be." For the object-representation without a specific concept, *in the strict sense*, represents "nothing" for Kant; as a representation of nothing it is also a non-representation. Only in virtue of this lack of concept and purpose does the arabesque permit a disinterested delight in the pure form, a delight "in the mere exhibition or faculty of exhibition."[40] A few years before, Karl Philipp Moritz had already drawn the conclusion from the non-signification of the arabesque ornament that one must "surely be on one's guard" against the desire "to interpret everything" here. To the extent that the arabesque "is merely a work of caprice"—here Moritz anticipates under the proviso of "merely" the Kantian and Romantic definition of "caprice"—"absolutely no interpretation is possible anymore."[41]

Kant's theory of a "free" beauty without concept and signification furthermore emphasizes the difference between minor and major work, between frame and enframed—the fact that an ornament in essence is an accessory, an addition, a marginal decoration. Kant emphatically incorporates this quality of the ornament into his analysis of the "pure" aesthetic judgments. With a remarkable and even puzzling consequence, an entire series of examples elaborates on the concept of a parergonal beauty:

> In painting, sculpture, indeed in all the visual arts, in architecture and horticulture insofar as they are fine arts, *design* is what is essential; in design the basis for any involvement of taste is not what gratifies us in sensation but merely what we like because of its form [. . .] What we call *ornaments* (*parerga*), i.e. what does not belong to the complete representation of the object as an intrinsic constituent, but [is] only an extrinsic adjunct, does indeed increase our taste's liking, and yet it does so only by its form, as in the case of picture frames or the garments on statues, or the colonnades around magnificent buildings.[42]

Certainly not every decorative adjunct or parergon named by Kant is an arabesque in the traditional sense, but the arabesques that in the form of ornamental "additions" establish a frame, clearly represent the most relevant paradigm of parergonality itself. The *à la grecque* ornamentation in the narrower sense, on clothing hems or on designs, obviously corresponds to this paradigm. In Kant's meaning, however, the *à la grecque* fashion of the neo-classicist tunics stands in a parergonal relationship to the beauty of the human body and, mockingly called "statue-suit,"[43] they can be directly subsumed under the "garments on statues." Pursuing this interest in arabesques as parerga, Kant unhesitatingly equates the garments adorning statues with the frames of paintings; thus, he conceives them not as integral parts of the statues but rather as an addition or ornamentation. As the parallel example of the colonnades around a magnificent building shows, Kant's interpretation of the statues' garments does not so much aim to take a stand vis-à-vis the question of whether such garments were in some cases posteriori additions to the sculpture proper. Rather, Kant is solely concerned with establishing a synchronic difference between ergon and parergon and with grounding the very definition of a "pure" beauty of art in this difference. The same holds for Kant's perspective on "ladies' attire": in its function as "ornaments [. . .] at a luxurious party," he "includes" this attire under the arabesque decorations of "rooms"[44] and thus equates it with the ornamental wallpapers. Even the "free beauties of nature"—"wild flowers"[45] and animals like "the parrot, the humming-bird, the bird of paradise"[46]—are viewed as colorful dots added like ornaments to a nature that otherwise, and as a whole, is not supposed to be devoid of purpose. In a classically anthropocentric gesture, Kant holds that the human being is the only entity of nature that is a purpose in itself (*Selbstzweck*),[47] and that most other animals (like the horse) are subordinate to human purposes. For this reason he excludes all these natural beings—just like the artworks and man—from the ambit of purely aesthetic judgments.[48] The exoticism of many of the animals given as examples therefore serves the bewildering yet consistent construction of parergonal margins of nature, which Kant did not yet view as subjected to the central ergon of creation, namely European man. Even in Kant's time this task obviously required extended travels (of imagination).

In a different way, "shells" or "crustaceans of the sea,"[49] which Kant evokes several times throughout the entire third *Critique*, are also marginal to human beings' realm of dominion. Kant thinks of them apparently not in terms of fishing and eating—rather, he imagines them as free creatures that occasionally lend themselves to man's aesthetic contemplation at the liminal margin between land and sea. Furthermore, shells enter into this contemplation as empty enclosures, as "coverings" without "contents" or as a frame without a center, and these empty frames in turn are used for decorative frameworks—a doubled arabesque structure. Even the "shell-work" decried by Winckelmann thus undergoes a legitimization as a free beauty. But why Kant's amazing obsession with "foliage for framework" and other arabesque parerga?

For Kant, "art always has a determinate intention to produce something."[50] Since in this way "art always presupposes a purpose in the cause (and its causality), a concept of what the thing is intended to be must first of all be laid at its basis;"[51] otherwise, "its product cannot be ascribed to any art at all."[52] Pure aesthetic judgments, however, are applicable only to what pleases without purpose, intention, concept, and interest. In drawing on examples taken from nature, Kant avoids this dilemma, but vis-à-vis problematical art he confronts it by a double strategy. On the one hand, "fine art," in order to be beautiful, must produce the illusion that it is no art at all but rather "nature." Its unavoidable purposiveness must "appear unintentional, although it is intentional."[53] At least in the mode of illusion, of an "as if"—that is, "as if it were not art"—fine art can be rescued for a pure aesthetic judgment. To be sure, Kant only follows this route toward the final paragraphs of the "Analytic of Aesthetic Judgment." At the same time, with the emphasis of a "must," an imperative of illusion, he runs the danger of falling into contradiction with himself, namely, with his likewise categorical assertion that poetic composition should not "deceive by means of a beautiful illusion" as rhetoric does, but rather that in it "everything proceeds with honesty and sincerity."[54]

In the first paragraphs of the "Analytic of Aesthetic Judgment," on the other hand, Kant looks for a beauty of art that corresponds to the requirements of a pure aesthetic judgment *without* deception and illusion.[55] Since artworks in the genuine sense are disqualified here, Kant resorts to the accessory or "adjunct works," the decorative "parerga." These are beneficiaries of a negative-parasitic economy: they draw their freedom not positively from the "genuine" works but from the fact that the latter by their very definition include the moment of purpose and intention and thus remove the aesthetically "impure" component of art from their ornamental supplements. The artwork incorporates and, as it were, "handles" the problematical element, so that in the difference between the work and the arabesque addendum, a possibility of a "pure" and "free beauty" opens up that otherwise would remain unattainable for art.[56] Consequently, parerga are para-sitic in a double sense: first, they are spatially situated next to an ergon; second, they profit functionally from this para-situatedness in that they draw from it their power and the particular surplus of their being. Only as a parergon, as an addition to itself, is it possible for art to be "purely" beautiful without having to deceive. The free play of all faculties becomes possible to the extent that beauty—its Kantian correlate—is banished from the work to its frame. The arabesque "foliage for frameworks" and its analogs are thus not only prime examples; they even represent the condition of possibility of purely aesthetic a significance and of conceptless non-representationality. An echo of this revalorization of the "parerga" can also be heard in Kant's theory of "supplementary representations" ["Nebenvorstellungen"] or aesthetic attributes:

> If forms do not constitute the exhibition of a given concept itself, but are only supplementary [*Neben-*] representations of the imagination, expressing the concept's implications and its kinship with other concepts, then they are called (aesthetic) attributes of an object [. . . They present] something that prompts the imagination to spread over a multitude of kindred presentations that arouse more thought than can be expressed in a specific concept determined by words.[57]

Although itself a part of the aesthetic work, this para-representation produces a similar side step, a spreading and straying along the borders similar to what the parergon of beautiful frames does. Both evade the center because both evade the concept for the sake of the aesthetic.

To put it formally, the purely aesthetic beauty of art thus resides in establishing and processing the difference between ergon and parergon. Both of these types of beauty in art—that of the ergon and that of the parergon—are equally dependent on the positive absence of a determinate concept. Yet in each respective case this conceptual indeterminateness generates a different and even opposing effect: in the case of the "authentic" artistic productions of genius, it reveals precisely the infinite meaningfulness of the aesthetic idea; in the case of the parerga, however, Kant explicitly speaks of their "meaning nothing." Hence, there results a series of several correlative oppositions: parergon vs. ergon, aesthetically pure vs. aesthetically impure, free vs. adherent beauty, "meaning nothing" vs. infinitely meaningful. To be sure, the *Critique of Judgement* does not develop these correlative oppositions simultaneously. Rather, its focus shifts successively from one side to the other: from the pure beauty of ornamental parerga at the beginning to the theory of infinitely meaningful erga, which, however, do not allow for an "entirely pure" judgment of taste, at the conclusion of the Analytic.

By virtue of his emphasis on the parerga, Kant radically reevaluates the margins, frames, and digressions as compared to the "actual" artworks. He locates the inner and "pure" field of the beauty of art in precisely those parergonal figures of framing that constitute the crossing of inside and outside, or more precisely—that articulate the inside/outside difference at the outermost margin of the work. Kant is no longer concerned here with the frame's effects on what is enframed—regardless of whether it playfully defigures the enframed image, as in the Rococo-arabesque, or whether it confirms and enhances it, as in Classicism. On the other hand, he also does not transform the ornament into a self-sufficient abstract artwork, as would occur later on in modern art. That is because Kant insists that the arabesque has its genuine place on or beside a work and thus indeed is a parergon. However, this "para" is little more than a transcendental metonymy. It signifies nothing but parergonality itself as the condition of the possibility of a pure aesthetic judgment and does not imply any specific interaction between the particular content levels of ergon and parergon. The assumptions traditionally underlying the ornament—"that the ornament emphasizes the value of the object it decorates and must itself be appropriate to it, that it simultaneously 'interprets' what it decorates"[58]—are suspended in this now entirely abstract relationship. By virtue of this naked and transcendental metonymy, the ornament ends up in the rigorously sought-after position of aesthetic autonomy because it is the "only genre of art that cannot exist autonomously."[59] Even so, the ornament is not required to surrender its para-sitical dependence on some other ergon.

Kant's insight into the autonomy of the aesthetic is thus essentially an insight into the para-heteronomy of this central phantom of modern aesthetics. A consequence of this insight is, however, that Kant suspends the requirement of aesthetic purity for all nonparergonal and hence for almost all of art, just as for the "ideal of the beautiful;" in fact, he superimposes on the tendency toward aesthetic purity a contrary tendency toward enhancing the aesthetic by contaminating it with practical and theoretical dimensions. It is only with regard to this shift toward legitimating aesthetic impurity that one can account for the fact that when Kant finally addresses the beauty of artworks near the end of the "Analytic," he no longer mentions the parerga at all—though at the beginning they had served as a pivotal paradigm for the exposition of the very concept of beauty and of "entirely pure" judgments of taste. This displacement in the diachrony of the Kantian text reflects a fundamental tension about how to determine the autonomy of the aesthetic in terms of its pure self-reference. On the one hand, the third *Critique* strives for a completely autochthonic principle of aesthetic judgment and excludes from it every theoretical concept as well as every purpose and every practical interest. On the other, the field of the aesthetic is construed as a reconciliation between theory and praxis and hence as a function of a systemic architecture that is presupposed in its basic elements. The concept, as an "indefinite" one, is allowed to return in this field as well, indeed Kant demands—despite the polemically accentuated disinterestedness—that both artist and recipient take an "intellectual interest" in the beautiful as a veritable seal of quality in aesthetic appreciation. The theory of the parergon thus marks the puristic self-referential pole of a fundamental ambivalence perceptible throughout the third *Critique*, while the theory of the ergon marks the integrating function of art. Only when seen together,[60] these conflicting elements point to a cardinal desideratum of the Kantian as well as of the subsequent Idealist aesthetics: how can art follow only its own "rules" and at the same time, in virtue of its formal structure, generate effects that bear on ethical and theoretical problems? Under two conditions this intervention does not compromise the autonomy of the aesthetic: first, its effects must be unattainable by anything other than the aesthetic; second, they must relate to problems not solvable at the levels proper to theoretical and practical philosophy (namely, to the problem of their unity). Moreover, rather than solving these problems of theoretical and practical philosophy, the aesthetic only sets them in motion, "agitating" what cannot be solved at all in any coherent theoretical sense.

Kant's intervention in the discourse on the arabesque has been largely, often completely, ignored by literary historical research on the theory of arabesque (for example, Karl Konrad Polheim's comprehensive treatment *Die Arabeske*[61]); the absence of the word[62] evidently occluded the argument as well. In research on Kant, the situation is widely similar.[63] To be sure, in a brilliant study Jacques Derrida analyzed Kant's orientation toward the parergon, but he related the overdetermination of the frame above all to a theoretical problem of the *Third Critique* itself: namely its taking its own frame from the *Logic* without any further justification and, moreover, taking it tacitly from an implicit anthropology.[64] Following Derrida, the logic of the parergon has then been generalized into a universal subversion of occidental reason and its principle of identity.[65] This standpoint, however, overlooks the contemporary aesthetic locus of the *Third Critique*'s apparently eccentric series of examples. The entire argument of the text begins to speak differently, and far more specifically, only when the frame circumscribing the frame obsession, namely, the theory of arabesque, is itself brought into view.

For Friedrich Schlegel the arabesque was "the original form of painting [*Pictur*]"[66] and also "the genuine mother, the embryo of all of modern painting"[67]—a determination that is most persuasive with reference to the Rocaille forms and their predecessors in traditional ornament. But Schlegel went further than this. He declared the arabesque to be indeed "the oldest and original form of human fantasy."[68] Consequently, it is the return of the "arabesque" that, according to Schlegel, accounts for "the entire advantage of the so-called novel of the age."[69] Schlegel reappropriates the prime features of the Kantian arabesque and enriches it with further characteristics. The arabesque's non-signification as emphasized by Kant is modified into a fantasy *about* nothing, even into the idea of "poems composed of nothing."[70] Schlegel's own novel *Lucinde* is called both a "*Naturarabeske*" and a "poem composed of nothing."[71] Schlegel consequently ranks "novellas out of nothing" among "the arabesques as exempla of irony."[72] At the same time, the Kantian parergonality breaks through from the margins of the work into its center; indeed, it becomes the very essence of the work itself as an unending ironical reflection. Schlegel's "Letter on the Novel" (1799) compares the "delight in Sterne's humor" with the delight "which we often feel when contemplating the whimsical playful paintings called 'arabesques.'"[73] As a second example of a literary arabesque full of playful wit, he mentions "Diderot's *Fataliste.*" In both works the narrative core and the continuity of narration are permanently interrupted by digressions such that these digressions produce an ironical as well as completely arabesque structure of the whole text. *Tristram Shandy* furnishes the pre-Romantic point of convergence for both the arabesque and the poetics of nonsense. Schlegel himself did not set out to demarcate a genuinely romantic type of arabesque as distinct from Sterne's; however, some basic differences can be easily marked out. First, the romantic arabesque no longer operates only or predominantly through staging differences between textual levels of narration and para-narrative enframings. Rather, arabesque patterns are already employed on the level of the "actual" narration itself. Thus, the basic plot of the *Seven Wives of Bluebeard* does not necessarily require the additional parergonal "leafwork" of the narrator's reflection in order to be thoroughly arabesque. The romantic arabesque furthermore blends with elements of both the fairy tale and the fantastic, and as a rule it is more in line with the tradition of the grotesque than with that of *humor.* Finally, in Sterne, nonsense elements do not yet operate against the horizon of infinite aesthetic meaning. Rather, they still inhabit a field that is more rhetorical than hermeneutical. To this extent, they are not yet a polemical component and margin of the discursive network of 1800.

Friedrich Schlegel transposes Kant's arabesque parergonality into the ergon's own principle of form.[74] The adjunct work ceases to be a mere addition and is elevated into the condition of possibility of the work itself. The ornamental addendum is transformed into an ironic-reflexive supplement. To this extent, the difference between ergon and parergon is re-introduced into the ergon itself, and possibilities for endless re-entries of the Kantian difference in the interplay of different textual levels are being opened up. The arabesque no longer merely demarcates, in the mode of an ornament, the inner field of art against its exterior; inversely, it also no longer merely displaces the purity of the aesthetic onto the external borderline of inside and outside. Rather, it turns the entire distinction toward the inside. This entropic movement does not sublate the central distinction of frame and enframed but rather permits it to propagate itself all the more obstinately and diversely in the mode of delirium. In the media of painting and architecture, the Rococo arabesque had powerfully anticipated these textual deliria of inside and outside, or of enframed and frame. The Romantic arabesque intellectualizes and de-aestheticizes such techniques. Whereas rocaille is essentially a "beautiful" art, and an art of beautiful idealization,[75] the Romantic art of ironic interruption interrupts that very appearance of the beautiful.[76] Furthermore, whereas in rocaille, ornamental framing motifs engulf the image and destroy the laws of representation and referentiality, in the Romantic implosion of the frame—particularly in its smashing of symbolic orders—a phantom of the real returns. This phantom is essentially linked to the Romantic cipher of "chaos." Schlegel speaks of an "artificially regulated confusion"[77] that is continually being produced by the parergonal disruption of a work from its own tendencies. Another name for this effect is the romantic cipher of "chaos."[78] Hence, Schlegel parallels "chaotic form—arabesque, fairy tale."[79] This connection between chaos and arabesque is also reflected in the "Discourse on Mythology"[80] and in the sequence "Romantic Chaos," "*Naturarabeske*," and "Poem composed of nothing" in the self-advertisement of *Lucinde*.[81]

Embellishments of rooms, preeminently those done by Raphael in the Vatican, were for Moritz still the paradigm of the aesthetic of the arabesque—just as they were earlier in Heinse's *Ardinghello* (1787) and in Goethe's article "Von Arabesken" (1789). This discourse, which primarily pertained to the fine arts until 1790, was then widely appropriated by philosophy, poetics, and literature.

The intersection of all these disciplines in the term "arabesque" marks the origin of a new thinking about art in general. Kant, in his search for a pure and free beauty, discovered parergonal structures in numerous natural and social phenomena. Between 1797 and 1801 Friedrich Schlegel applied the concept in an original and persuasive way to literature. He had precursors in some remarks by Herder[82] and especially in the context of the poetics of the fairy tale [Feenmärchen]. In 1790 Friedrich Justin Bertuch compared Count Anton Hamilton's fairy tales with the "famous arabesques in the loges of the Vatican," and he named precisely the same characteristics of the pre-Romantic traditions that were then developed in the earliest Romantic poetics: "the maddest and most hilarious imagination, playfulness, caprice [, . . .] the most colorful and most hilarious texture." Bertuch's introduction to the *Blue Library of all Nations* contains similar wording: "The Blue Library of all Nations will be a universal and ongoing collection of all wondrous tales, legends and adventure stories and novels, of all peoples, so to speak, the arabesques and grotesques of all known literatures."[83]

The affinity between arabesque ornament and fairy tales is based above all on two characteristics. Like the ornament, the fairy tale suspends the practical ends and theoretical concepts of everyday understanding and establishes its own proper arena of "mischievous imagination." Herder in his *Adrastea* (1801) still calls fairy tales "flower[s] of arabesque," precisely because they are "stories without understanding and purpose;" he requires, however, that the "caprices and whims" of this "extinct world" be given a new, "most unexpected turn."[84] The second common characteristic is the structure of interlacing in ornamental patterning and wondrous fairy tales. Meanders, snake-like lines, and even the snake itself are preferred forms in arabesque decorations in architecture; narrative interlacings—and likewise often the snake as an old fairy-tale motif—characterize the fairy tale and its Romantic rewriting as linguistic *figurae serpentinatae*, as analogs of the famous line of beauty.[85] The "free," never entirely predictable, curved line at the same time accounts for the interrelation of fairy tale and the Romantic idea of chance; one of Schlegel's literary notes laconically explicates the "fairytale-like, arabesque" as "the infinitely capricious and contingent."[86] What Moritz had called the "play of chance" in his incrimination of the arabesque now becomes the central concept of a Romantic theory of the "chance" and "non-coherence" of the fairy tale.

Romantic poetics certainly goes far beyond this close connection between a literary concept of arabesque and the fairy tale. It enthrones the arabesque—above all by emphasizing the "frame effects," the relations ergon-parergon, frame-enframed—as the central concept of poetics per se. In Schlegel's *Letter on the Novel* (1799), the fairy tale is not mentioned at all as a paradigm for a poetics of the arabesque; in its place appear Diderot's *Jacques le fataliste* and Sterne's *Tristram Shandy*. The definition of the fairy tale as an "arabesque composition for fantasy's pleasure"[87] nonetheless unmistakably continues the pre-Romantic conception of the fairy tale. Schlegel certainly never explicitly applied this definition to *Feenmärchen* but exclusively to their radical Romantic modification. One of his earliest comments on the theory of fairy tales refers to the "poetic arabesques," "which [Tieck] formed out of several old fairy tales."[88] One of these, the *Bluebeard* tale, is much more than simply one of the many works upon which Schlegel practiced the permutations of his conceptual alchemy: this tale's theoretical reflections directly anticipate many of Schlegel's thoughts and also exhibit elements that go beyond his ruminations.

In Tieck, the disputed "meaninglessness" of the arabesque is no longer justified by the constraints of a philosophical system that requires art to be without concept and intention, but instead by a critique of the constraints and ideological violence inherent in the imperative to be meaningful. It is also not, as in Schlegel, dialecticized into a prerequisite for infinite meaning. On the contrary, "meaninglessness" is functionalized into resisting the new hermeneutical paradigm. A poetic figure's life story, conceived as a narrative that exhibits unity and meaning and precisely to that extent "is to be read and understood" (190),[89] is denounced by none other than the Bluebeard-figure himself as a perfidious plot by "readers of unlordly rank" (189–90) and "bad writers" (106). The sober realization, that "in the whole of human life there is no goal and no coherence to be found," and that life quite literally "means nothing" (193), should finally produce consequences in literature: on the one hand, as an anti-idealistic "realism," and on the other hand, as the emancipation of life from the expectation that it should be poetically meaningful. As an arabesque pattern, literature should "shake" the hermeneutical postulates of meaning "loose like a saddle and bridle" (220). Instead of infinite meaning, literature should rather produce "miracles of meaninglessness," as Arno Schmidt has already characterized the major achievement of Tieck's Bluebeard arabesque. Whereas Kant and later Schlegel too harness the meaninglessness of arabesque to the new hermeneutic paradigm of indefinite and infinite aesthetic meaning, Tieck's earliest arabesque expressly articulates a source of resistance to this central paradigm of the contemporary "discourse network" (Friedrich A. Kittler). Tieck thereby polemically exploits a possibility that the arabesque accrued only against the background of the new paradigm of sense. As a beauty, free in the Kantian sense, that is, without concept, purpose, and interest, the arabesque principally transcends the difference between sense and nonsense: it is without sense, without, however, being nonsensical. Yet the arabesque can also become the producer of nonsense effects, where its indifference toward sense is itself placed and exploited within the field of sense.

Kant's arabesque parergonality finds a more literal counterpart in Tieck's text than in Schlegel's theory. The entire narrative presents one single parergon to the plot of the fairy tale itself: it describes only its margins and avoids the center. Bluebeard tales preeminently, and often exclusively, narrate the story of the final wife who brings the murderous career of the fiend to an end. It is precisely this narrative core that Tieck leaves out. It becomes merely the subject of an allusion to Tieck's recently published *Bluebeard* drama: "I am therefore not obligated to add anything here, because I assume that each of my readers has read the Bluebeard, and therefore it is very easy for me to write this last chapter, in which I do not need to present anything" (241). The allure of the blue beard and the title in the style of Perrault (*La Barbe-Bleue*) easily mislead the reader into believing the serial murderer to be the protagonist of the fairy tale. However, a purely negative hero is unknown in genre theories of the fairy tale. In the sense of Propp's morphology, Bluebeard figures solely as the evil counterpart of the positive heroine who brings the serial murders to an end. Because this main protagonist of the Bluebeard tale disappears from the circle of Tieck's arabesque "presentation," the fairy tale's distinctive focus on the hero is inverted into figurations of the hero's literal exclusion: into the involutions and branchings of a plot that finally consists only of secondary figures and antagonists. The repeat offender and serial killer Bluebeard thus becomes the ideal subject of a form that is essentially defined through serial proliferation and through repetitions of a recurrent pattern.

Although the removal of the heroine, on the one hand, reinforces the narrative role of the male villain, on the other hand, the title *The Seven Wives of Bluebeard* rather de-emphasizes the male figure. The promise of the title is broken upon reaching the decisive number seven, so popular in the fairy tale. Only the first six wives are "presented"—whereas in the original fairy tale these serial victims are at most merely summarily mentioned but never appear as characters themselves. What otherwise is merely an aspect of the concept, of the very paradigm of the Bluebeard figure, is transferred by Tieck into a syntagmatic sequence, which is wholly "an addition" that "isn't really part of the subject at all."[90] In the portrayal of the women, the original fairy tale and Tieck's arabesque supplement each other in a twofold fashion: the heroine of the fairy tale is mentioned merely as a quotation (and moreover as a quotation to Tieck's own previously published drama), but her deeds are not depicted; the other women, who in the fairy tale are only mentioned abstractly as earlier victims, are individually portrayed. In virtue of the omission of the center and the supplementary distension of the periphery, the title's invocation of ornamental arabesque quite literally becomes the law of the narrative. What Tieck in the *Letters on Shakespeare* (1800) had praised in his favorite author—"those arabesques with their flourishes and embellishments that have come alive"[91]—he himself has inscribed in the margins of a fairy-tale plot in the *Seven Wives of Bluebeard.*

After the "conclusion" of the "story," in which Tieck, while alluding to his Bluebeard drama, simply announces that he will forego depicting the said conclusion, there follows a further, explicitly entitled "final chapter." What comes on the heels of the "*Beschluß*" (the subtitle of the 32nd chapter) of the thereby concluded "story" as a "thirty-third, or final chapter" [p. 241]—as supplementary note, appendix, or paralipomenon—can easily be called a parergon in the strict sense. By nonetheless integrating this parergon—this "final chapter" *after* the final chapter—into the ergon, Tieck once again lays bare the work's pervasive and literal pargonality, which like an arabesque snakes about the margins of a narrative center that is both omitted and yet presupposed. "The parergon [*Nebenwerk*]," as Tieck elsewhere had put it, "is made into the main subject."[92]

Morality

In the supplementary *moralités*—and hence from a standpoint exterior to the fairy tale itself—Perrault's *Barbe-Bleue* is subjected to a double reading that promises to establish the tale's (missing) sense. However, because these *moralités* contradict the foregoing text, and even each other, they ironically undermine any plausible meaning and thus become treacherous supplements that, in the very form of adding it, withdraw the missing sense all the more completely. To the extent that they fail in their task—to extract the meaning of the narrative—Perrault's *moralités* already approximate a free parergonal reflexive arabesque in the Romantic sense. Ludwig Tieck begins his *Blaubart* narrative by citing Perrault's concluding gesture and elaborating upon it. "*Moralité*" and "*Autre moralité*" are the titles Perrault gave his additions to the fairy tale; "*Moralität*" is the heading Tieck chose for the first chapter of his book. The integration of "morality" into the running series of chapters—rather than its extrusion in the form of an introduction or epilogue exterior to the "proper" story—already indicates a different understanding of the relations between *texte* and *hors-texte* and thus also of the arabesque parergonality. Rather than offering a *moralité* and then immediately refracting it as Perrault did, Tieck ironicizes and satirizes the idea of giving a moral. Indeed, he even ironicizes the very word and concept of "morality":

> First Chapter
> Morality
> Whenever I reflected upon this word, I have always sensed that thinking about it is bound up with many difficulties. A man, who is much experienced in a thousand things, wanted to assure me that in reflecting much [about this word] one even easily runs the danger of becoming confused with all this brooding and suddenly, without knowing how it happened, of acting immorally. Yes, he added, there are such wonderful sides to this science, such strange aspects, that a refined mind can consider to be highly moral what the typical dilettante would call a disgrace to morality; and just as with all the other arts, so here too one becomes an expert only by losing one's one-sided enthusiasm. The man, whom I will not name here because his modesty would blush, swore to me that the whole world calls him the most wretched egoist merely because he is actually too unselfish, and at times he's even hit upon the idea of relaxing his strict virtue a bit, so that people would better understand him. (89)

Whereas typical fairy tales beginning with "Once upon a time . . . " evoke a past (ir)reality that is irrevocably prior to the narration, Tieck's fairytale arabesque begins with the reflection on a "word" that the author himself has just placed as the chapter heading. The "once upon a time" is countered by an "often" and "always." The traditional fairy tale, after identifying its protagonists by generic names (the youngest son, the stepmother, and so forth), would quickly establish an initial lack on the part of the hero and proceed to the subsequent plot moves. By contrast, Tieck's "fairy-tale" gets caught up in its first word—just as the hiatus between "*so*" and "*oft*" immediately brings the first sentence close to a stylistic stumbling. Does Tieck's reflection on semantics ironicize only the subjective-intentional confounding of morality and amorality in hypocrisy and mendacity? Or should his statements also be taken literally as indicating an "objective" aporia in the definition of the quoted word in question? In any case, right from the moment it first appears, the problem of understanding is set in a radically disturbing light. The "man with much experience in a thousand things" conjoins successful understanding with a serious distortion of that which is understood. The negation of what is understood is made into the condition of possibility, into the transcendental a priori of understanding.

Following analogous reflections upon the tendency of radiance to "blind" its observer and small vices to undermine "great virtues," Tieck first indicates that "I will break off here":

> The reader cannot possibly demand that I should carry on this discourse at too great length here, since none other than he would have to compensate for it with boredom: for I consider myself forced to have the honor of reassuring him that I don't much care what I write, as indeed must be the case for every honest writer. (90)

Yet following the nonsensical formula of being "forced to have the honor," the text does not live up to the "break off" it announces and pretends to justify ("for . . . "). Instead, unconcerned about this patent contradiction, the subsequent paragraph continues the reflection about the title and hence about the conclusion of Perrault's *Barbe-Bleue.* Morality is denounced as an awkward economic and societal form of communication that is no longer needed in the "enlightened world": it only disturbs mobility and makes "all commerce impossible" (91). In a society that has evolved into differentiated functional spheres, this "iron money" has its place only in the museum, where it will no longer disrupt "sciences and arts, trade and factories and philosophy." This allegorical critique of the obsolete clumsiness of morality as a communicative medium abruptly turns into ironic and nostalgic expressions of regret at morality's disappearance from the "doings and dealings" of enlightened modernity. At this point, poetry comes into play. This "do-nothing, slight, nimble vagrant" becomes the target for modernity in its attempt "to find a home somewhere" for the now functionless morality, a place "where one can get hold of morality right away and without ado"—in contrast with a visit to the antiquities collection—"if one feels an urge for it during one's idle hours." In the form of a fable, Tieck explains the liaison between poetry and morality that flourished in the 18th century—the other side of their functional differentiation—as one moment in a process of societal evolution:

> Poetry struggled and wanted to leap away at one moment, to fly away at another, but the sprightly arms of the businessmen were too strong for her, she had to surrender and was brought before the council. First she was rebuked harshly for her idleness, but since she had no other use anyway, she was told to at least gather up in her flower basket all the morality lying about and not dare to offer even a single rose without also breaking off a little piece of morality to go along with it. Poetry shook her head, but the judges paid her little concern, for the verdict had been spoken and they were glad to be completely rid of morality; only now and then one of them hurries on over to Poetry to see if she is obeying the command. Poetry doesn't dance anymore, now she has to bear a heavy burden. (92)

This fable goes far beyond a purely aesthetic critique of art's moral obligations. It diagnoses this obligation as an effect of the redistribution of societal functions in a time when "businessmen" and "factories" become the dominant power. The functional conjunction of poetry and morality amounts to the further debilitation of each rather than to a mutual rejuvenation. Under the "heavy burden" of iron morality, poetry ceases to dance and to offer "visual splendor and sweet fragrance." Inversely, the aesthetization of morality ratifies its "actual" downfall: for the apparent salvation via aesthetization only anaesthetizes the awareness of morality's functional obsolescence and so finally allows modernity "to be completely rid of morality."

Thus, the fable of the do-nothing vagrant Poetry and the vigorous arms of businessmen has a clear *fabula docet*: it rejects the very principle of *fabula docet* and thus paradoxically ironizes its own argumentation. The critique of *moralité*—which includes not only outright moral maxims but also general "propositions of prudence"—is itself presented in the guise of a fable and hence that literary form that *per definitionem* contains a "moral." For precisely this reason, Tieck wanted to exclude the fable as a "strange apparition" from the "new poetry;" indeed, he did not even acknowledge it in its "old form [. . .] seriously as a genre."[93] In its own literary properties, Tieck's narrative mimetically assimilates that "odd [. . .] strain of literary art," from which his predecessor had derived his supplements to the fairy tale. In the guise of a fable, it denounces that "connection" between poetry and morality whose prototypical form is the fable itself—and hence the very genre that Perrault, in however refracted a manner, had superimposed on the fairy tale.

Perrault's *moralités* are at odds with each other and with the text whose moral sense they purport to provide; Tieck's morality, by contrast, appears in the form of a fable that altogether and quasi-transcendentally destroys the very principle of the fable and hence also the principle of the "moral of the story." The apparently smooth transitions between fairy tale and fable in Perrault give way to a strict demarcation of genres according to whether they provide or subvert a totalizing meaning. Wilhelm von Humboldt similarly defined the fairy tale by its contrast to the fable: "the fairy tale should not be the metaphorical or poetic expression of a preconceived proposition, that is, not a fable or allegory." Hence, according to Humboldt, the fairy tale is related less closely to traditional minor forms of literature than to the (modern) field of "narrative in the widest sense (novel, novella, etc.)."[94]

After the ironical critique of the very form of a "moral," Tieck's fairytale arabesque issues correspondingly rhetorical praise that ironicizes its content. The praise concludes by postulating the reducibility of all poetry, by means of an image that both resonates with the "iron money" and foreshadows another of the narrative's major motifs, that of the "leaden head," the secret of the forbidden chamber:

> If one wants to smelt down all poetry, then from every artwork a moral proposition must be left over like a caput mortuum, and the arts of separation that art critics apply to every book demonstrate how quickly the airy invention and its watery trappings can be evap-

orated, leaving behind the dry earth, the moral, the basic element of art. (93)

Caput mortuum used to be the name for the glowing residue (red iron oxide) of the smelting process; yet literally it also means "dead head." The derivation of a "moral proposition," according to this simile, can be achieved only at the price of the life and body of poetry: the moral is a lifeless residue of a violent meltdown. Referring to his previously published play *Knight Bluebeard,* Tieck accuses himself—or rather his pseudonym, "the otherwise excellent *Peter Lebrecht*"—of having undermined all chances to distil such a caput mortuum: "for neither poetic justice nor morality hold sway adequately in it [. . .] if one were to reduce his fairy tale in a crucible, nothing intuitable would be left over" (94). Elsewhere Tieck explicitly prescribes—in keeping with Kant's third *Critique*[95]—precisely what he blames his *Bluebeard* play for: "each and every work of art" should *not* be "dissolvable into concepts."[96] Accordingly, poetry would by definition resist the "arts of separation" employed by the "art critics" and frustrate every procedure for "smelting down" its "clothing." Its relics would represent "precisely nothing at all"—at least nothing that would mount up to a concise "proposition" and hence to a "caput mortuum." With the allegorical-literal figure of the "leaden head," then, Tieck stages a prosopopeia of this caput mortuum. He entangles it within in a story in which it goes to ruin, indeed, which in many senses "buries" it. Poetry becomes the gravedigger of the very caput mortuum that was supposed to be the indestructible element of poetry left over after the distillation process of critical reading.

The (self) criticism of the *Bluebeard* drama for being too free-flowing a "fantasy" is followed by the reassurance that the present narrative will avoid this flaw and without fail provide "sufficient moral lessons":

So now I move on to the story at hand. The reader may very well note that in it many perish, and I am already now, ahead of time, more sorry for the persons than the reader is. But there is nothing to be done about this, for the story is nothing else than a great sacrificial

> celebration set in motion in order to improve the reader [. . .] The reader should therefore not worry about not receiving sufficient moral lessons, for wherever the least opportunity presents itself, I will not refrain from making him aware of his vices. (94)

This edifying pronouncement is unmistakably ironical. Nevertheless, Tieck fulfills it quite literally: namely, as a critique of the reader. If one reads carefully, he promises no "lessons" that could be drawn from his narrative as its caput mortuum. Rather, while unfolding the narrative, Tieck looks for "opportunities to make the reader aware of his vices." This will turn out to mean: wherever the story lacks "unity," "coherence," and "meaning," the opportunity will be seized to denounce the need for these features as an ideological vice of the reader and to call for a different sort of reading. Just as the fable of the vagrant Poetry and the businessmen "transports" the critique of *moralité* as the fable's own *moralité*, so too the "book without any coherence" (220) and meaning does indeed provide a lesson: the lesson, namely, as to why there is no lesson. This lesson, despite all criticism of understanding, is well intended to be understood by the reader. So complications are in store. "O understanding!"[97]

The question of a totalizing meaning of fairy tales is accompanied by the question of whether and how their individual elements are motivated. Although these two questions are closely related, neither one is reducible to the other: a fairy tale could very plausibly come down to a lesson, even though many of its elements might remain opaque, inaccessible to a "motivation from the beginning" (Lugowski). Thus, along with the problem of extracting an overall meaning from the fairy tale, Tieck also addresses this often flagrant lack of motivation in its textual details. If one accepts his later report, then the occasion for the *Seven Wives* was in fact his publisher Nicolai's wish that Tieck should "try his powers in presentation, development, and motivation"[98] with the *Bluebeard* material. This demand implies a displeasure at Tieck's *Bluebeard* drama, which was published shortly before. The younger Nicolai, who believed he had "inherited a sense of criticism from his father,"[99] evidently—and quite correctly—had not found in the drama any inclination toward "development and motivation." Similarly, Gottlieb Färber, the pseudonymous "editor" of the *Seven Wives*, blames Peter Lebrecht for "leaving too much obscure" in his *Bluebeard* drama: "one doesn't know why the main protagonist has a blue beard, just as one doesn't know why he hates his wives." By contrast, "Gottlieb Färber" praises himself for filling these gaps: "I flatter myself that I have placed all these circumstances in the best light" (242).

The reverence for Nicolai's suggestion implied in these phrases, however, tumbles into barely concealed mockery, when one considers more closely the vaunted motivations: Bluebeard's beard is blue because he was so un-gallant as to remind his fairy protector of her advanced age; and he hates women because, given his own choice of misfortunes, he chooses women. Such motivations are their own parody, a "self-parody of what is presented"[100] rather than what Nicolai wanted. Accordingly, Tieck tersely declared: the publisher's "demand, even if I had been able to fulfill it, could have no interest for me, for similar books, which exist in all languages, had always left merely an embarrassing impression upon me, precisely because they contain the requested sort of willful psychological depictions. And yet I took on this work, because I was struck right away—and without looking for it—by the opportunity, that instead of a philosophical novel an utterly fantastical, strange and capricious book could be fashioned upon this subject matter."[101] At the conclusion of the introductory chapter, Tieck already offers a logically nonsensical formula for his capricious (de)motivations: "By the way, I call this story a true story because it really is true, just as true as anything else that one can read" (95).

The Beginning of the Story and the Education of the Hero

The relationship of the second chapter to its title is just as arabesque and parergonal as that between the first chapter and its title. The second chapter's title promises the "beginning of the story," but the chapter itself is comprised entirely of reflections on how one can begin a story, how the reader can frustrate the author's tricks by immediately turning to the last page of the story, and so on. The "beginning of the story" is not the beginning of the story, at least not the story of Bluebeard and his wives. It certainly is, however, the beginning of another story, one whose intermingling with the Bluebeard plot constitutes one of the narrative's fundamental characteristics: the "heroes" of this other story are the author and above all the reader.[102] Their interaction is not limited to the author's ironical addresses to the reader, as in the first chapter. Rather, both author and reader become active protagonists in the narrative: Bluebeard's mentor figure sees himself as the author of the life of his protégé and worries about the reviews of this "work" in the literary journals; in the end, Bluebeard himself rejects the poetics of his master along with the corresponding politics of reading that demands unity, meaning, and understandable coherence in the life story of a literary figure. In Tieck's sketch for yet another version of the Bluebeard narrative in 1817, the theme of the reader entirely displaces the central plot of uxoricide and becomes the main plot itself rather than being a reflexive, arabesque appendage. Thus, under the heading "On Academies," a first part of the sketch lists chapters on "book fairs" and "perhaps on book manufacturing." A second part promises letters "about the lack of a [coherent] narrative," about "the difference between modern and ancient authors," and about "Gozzi and fairy tales." The actual plot replaces the story of the "seven wives" with seven different reading situations: it is divided according to "seven places where reading occurs."[103] In the Bluebeard version of 1797 that we are considering here, the narrative not only reflects discursively but stages and narrates the process of reading it.

> "The unleashed storm raced through the forest with its full force, and dark clouds hung heavy from the skies; in a remote castle burned a solitary light, and a traveler wandered through the night upon the great thoroughfare." (97)

Thus begins the plot, in its more circumscribed sense, in the chapter that follows the "beginning of the story." It begins as a citation, a foreign body of speech whose source is alien to the text itself: the opening sentences of the "actual" plot are framed in quotation marks. This graphic marking is made all the more striking by the fact that Tieck nowhere in the rest of the text makes use of quotation marks for direct speech or for citation. Their use is reserved solely for the first contact between parergon and ergon, between the arabesque ornament and the central narrative. The quotation marks thereby signal the inversion of their hierarchy: in a context where framings are made absolute, the "actual" story appears as a foreign body and a citation of itself; the ergon appears paradoxically as a supplement to the parergon. Only when after a long digression Tieck once again takes up the story of the hero's education (99), does he forego citing it as another's speech; henceforward, the "story"—and its "deficiency" (220)—threads itself without typographic distinctions into the fabric of its supplementary arabesques.

The opening sentences of the plot may also be read as a quotation in the more familiar sense, in that they provide a pastiche, if not a genuine quotation, of the setting of a typical gothic novel.[104] However, as the narrative's countless other allusions to gothic stories indicate, this kind of quotation alone would not have sufficed to legitimate the use of quotation marks. Tieck's presentation of Bluebeard and indeed his approach to the fairy tale in general weave through the contemporaneous genre of the gothic novel, which shares many forms and motifs with the fairy tale:[105] the forest solitudes, helping figures, talking birds, and the figure of the creepy old woman. As the mentor figure for Tieck's Bluebeard, Bernard unmistakably belongs—like the stranger in *Wilhelm Meister's Apprenticeship*—to that series of fate-arranging figures in gothic novels who pull all the strings behind the scenes; at the same time, Bernard alludes to the supernatural helping figures of the fairy tale. Mechthild, Peter Berner's (= Bluebeard's) housekeeper, exhibits traits of a "gothic" old woman as well as those of the evil witch of fairy tales. To be sure, the proximity to fairy-tale motifs does not figure as a condition or license for including elements of the gothic story genre into Tieck's Bluebeard narrative. This is proven for instance by the gothic scenarios at the beginning of the story and during the descent into the fairy kingdom, or by the intrigues of Bluebeard's relatives concerning his genealogical identity—all motifs that have no direct counterparts in the genre of the fairy tale. However, in the context of the fairytale arabesque, these gothic story elements undergo a revaluation that shows many indications of a direct counter-determination.

The gothic scene that opens the story on a fairly serious tone is immediately and expressly mocked for its "ridiculously exaggerated manner," and the popularity of this manner is recast into a critique of the readers who, for all their thirst for excitement and all their sentimental excitability, "hardly know how to laugh" (97). The "monopoly on laughing enjoyed hitherto" by human beings, Tieck prophecies, will probably "be left to the innocent enjoyment" of animals (99); comedy, as a consequence, will henceforth be hardly esteemed (98). By scolding the reader in this way Tieck calls attention to the opposing tendency in his treatment of the Bluebeard tale: wherever possible to wrestle comical aspects from the gruesome plot and to uncover the hilarity that is the inverse side of the horrible. Effects pointing to the uncanny and the demonic in Bluebeard's actions are rigorously avoided, even though—or precisely because—nothing would be more natural than to portray them in such gothic terms. In this regard, Tieck's fairytale arabesque stands just as opposed to the popular novel of his time as does the original fairy tale, of which Freud has written: "I know of no genuine fairy tale in which anything uncanny occurs."[106] For according to Freud, the "emotional effect" of the fairy tale, by virtue of its genre a prioris and its style, is entirely "independent" of its "subject matter" and thus has the power to suspend—as is the case with *Bluebeard*—even strongly uncanny plot elements.[107]

On the dark and stormy night of the story's opening, the "wayfarer" notices "a solitary light burning [. . .] in a remote castle." As a horror-novel figure, he would have unerringly sought out this conventional gothic locus. But in Tieck's story the castle serves merely as an ornament, a signpost, and is never again mentioned. Its light does not guide the wayfarer to the castle itself, but instead to a "small house." This small house too combines elements of both the fairy tale and the gothic novel: it is remote, inhabited by an "old woman," and has a talking bird on its roof. Yet here once again these props are devoid of any mysteriousness, any uncanny plot function. The house turns out to be a little boarding school where, without any use of witchcraft, two pupils from noble families are being raised: Peter Berner—later Bluebeard—and Adelheid, his childhood friend. The wayfaring visitor reveals himself to be Berner's genius and "guide;" following the death of his last protégé he now wishes to make Berner's "career" his "work" (105).

Although living under the same roof, Adelheid and Peter are subjected to two strictly opposed pedagogical "discourses." In Adelheid's case, a bird serves "as a kind of tutor, who incessantly sings to the child the most trivial songs;" her "young foolish caretaker [. . .] lets her sleep when she wants, wake up when she wants, and plays childish, almost silly games with her. Thus, one does not hear a single sensible word pass between the two" (104). Peter's old tutor, in contrast, is an "utterly philosophical mother or nurse" who constantly berates him with profound "moralistic hymns" in which "joy and suffering" or "pain and life" appear allegorically in all their inconstancy and vicissitude (100, 102). With these satirically overdrawn pedagogical styles, Tieck initiates a sequence of parallel oppositions that extends through the whole text. The imperative of meaning that reigns over both the old woman's songs and the "career" poetics of Berner's genius comes under duress from the very outset. It is being opposed by a critique whose first representative is a pedagogy of lassitude, a license for silly nonsense and unregimented children's games. But while having melancholy songs continually sung to him, in conjunction with too much sleep, may indeed be annoying for little Peter, it by no means accounts for why he later murders his wives. The psychological-pedagogical portrayal of the "hero's education" fails grotesquely to meet the expectation that, as opposed to the portrayal of characters in fairy tales, it would seem to suggest: to provide an explanation of how Bluebeard became what he is. The schema of the psychological novel is only cited and parodistically executed in order to compromise the idea of a psychological "development and motivation" from the outset. What the fairy tale lacks naturally and implicitly is now refused, explicitly and provocatively, in its ironical simulation in Tieck's fairytale arabesque.

Instead of providing a motivation for the hero's deeds, the chapter recounting the "hero's education" introduces a fundamental opposition that extends well beyond its first representatives to other textual positions, thereby assuming a structural function. Seen in terms of genre theory, the correlate to this opposition is that of gothic novel versus idyll: Bernard and the old fairy fall under the heading of gothic novel, the beautiful antagonist Almida under idyll. While working within the medium of the fairy tale plot, Tieck simultaneously stages a battle between the gothic novel and the idyll as genres. Right from the beginning the protagonist Bluebeard belongs to the horror-novel pole of this opposition. Yet again and again he declines, and at the conclusion categorically refuses, to follow the laws of the gothic novel; on the other hand, he also fails in his attempt to move into the space of the idyll and "Romantic love." Suspended in this way between the polar impossibilities of the gothic novel and the idyll, the fairy tale finds a genuine early Romantic literarization.

Horror Novel Without Horror; Critique of the Sublime

The old governess and tutor can "say nothing more" about the history and provenance of the boy "than that he was entrusted to me by an unknown knight" (103). When this old knight, "a distant relative," later comes to claim the grown-up charge from his caretaker, the author explains in plain terms the boy's lineage and the reason for his concealed upbringing:

> The castle and the property of young Peter were seized by greedy relatives after the sudden death of his father; an old knight had rescued the boy Peter Berner from their persecutions and sent him to be raised in this remote dwelling. Now the boy was grown up, and the knight had collected more knights and a number of servants in order to help him regain what is rightfully his. (108–109)

From this material a horror novel would have made an extensive "puzzle plot" with numerous complications, since legitimacy and illegitimacy of pedigrees (unknown to the hero himself) and intrigues against the sole rightful heir are the basic components of the popular gothic novel.[108] But with a few sentences Tieck lays the gothic plot to rest. As a "very brave warrior" Peter is able quickly to convince his relatives of his rightfulness:

> The other relatives who had assumed control of the castle had declared him to be a fake, a foisted child from the moment he first appeared. For and against this genealogical opinion there ensued violent arguments from both sides, and the inquiry was pursued so heatedly that many a knight and servant lay dead in the disputation even before it was finished. At first those in the castle would not yield at all in their claim, but in the end they were constrained to make peace. Through this peace agreement Peter became a genuine and true son. (109–110)

With the sentence "Peter was now the lord of his castle" the preliminary tale of Peter Berner comes to an end, along with his career as a happy hero in a horror novel extract without uncanny intrigues. His career as "unhappy" husband and Bluebeard can begin. In horror novels, the restoration of family relations and acceptance into the inheritance is typically crowned with a happy marriage—one that had earlier seemed hopeless or was blocked by malevolent rivals. A typical candidate for this is also offered in Tieck's arabesque: Adelheid, to whom Peter was bound by "youthful love" during the years of their shared upbringing (107). However, the later attempt spurred by Bernard to develop that into the happiness of "romantic" love turns out to be a failure, and Adelheid is indeed the only woman whom Peter courts unsuccessfully. Thus, Tieck strictly divides martial from marital good fortune and precisely out of this division constructs the second career of Peter Berner.

Elements of the horror novel still intrude into the details of the Bluebeard plot; yet they definitely do not serve to produce effects of horror. The gap between quoting a genre-based set piece and suppressing its corresponding effect is strikingly showcased when Peter is led by his mentor into the subterranean kingdom of the fairy, who enjoys power over both of them. Tieck evokes a "classical" horror-novel landscape: jagged mountain peaks, a bottomless rocky gorge, terrifyingly steep ridges and cliffs. Yet to the consternation of his companion, Berner shows no signs of feeling any dizziness or fear (115–116).[109] Even the plot's most obvious horror effects are rigorously avoided: Bluebeard's castle apparently is not outfitted with the obligatory stairwells, twisting corridors, and underground vaults; furthermore, the forbidden chamber is explicitly moved from the dark cellar into a bright pavilion on the roof (145); the murders are not actually depicted, and there is no collection of corpses in the forbidden chamber.

> In this way the reader has it very good and comfortable, since I always take the gravest things upon myself, hushing up the best part of what is emotionally dramatic [*das Pathetische*]: this is done merely out of love for the reader, so that even persons of a weak and nervous constitution may read and understand this story without any detriment to their health. (187)

Giving up the "emotionally dramatic" and the terrifying while citing their conventional causes accords with a basic differentiation between the horror novel and the Romantic fairytale arabesque, whose elements have passed through the horror novel. The horror novel inherits and plunders the aesthetics of the sublime—especially the sublime in Burke's sense—while the fairy tale and Tieck's Romantic arabesque, on the other hand, avoid or refract those sublime "sensations." The popular folktale contains so little of the sublime that it even appears as its determinate negation. The protagonists are predominantly of the "lower" estate: the miller's son, the farmer's daughter, and poor children mostly with only one parent. Even where princes and princesses figure as heroes and heroines, the kind and the course of the conflicts do not aspire to the sublime at all. It is typical for the fairy-tale conflicts—no matter how severe and seemingly impossible to overcome they are—that the protagonists succeed in the decisive things effortlessly: whether by means of their own stupidity, which inverts into cunning; or by means of intervention through those helping figures and magic objects that reliably solve insoluble problems. In contrast, the aesthetics of the sublime would bring into convergence what the fairy tale happily disjoins: the magnitude of conflicts and tasks on the one hand and the degree of subjective exertion in solving them on the other. Moreover, the sublime would favor a tragic or sad end, whereas the fairy tale subscribes to happiness and, by means of its stylistic devices that reduce affect to a minimum, distances even the plot's opening misfortune from any emotionally dramatic-sublime shading. The "objects" of fairy-tale happiness—the bride, the chest full of gold—are beautiful and "trivial," never sublime. Often enough they are explicitly called "beautiful," just as beauty in general represents one of the highest values in fairy tales.[110] However, "the sublime"—and with this comment once again Wilhelm von Humboldt proves an invaluable authority on the advanced theory of the fairy tale at the end of the 18th century—"was probably not made for this genre."[111]

By contrast, and although several of its figures and props are related to those in the fairy tale, the horror novel instrumentalizes all the registers of the sublime. Bluebeard's fateful guide Bernard intends for his protégé "extraordinarily great things": he wants to see "combined" in Peter Berner "[e]verything that made Alexander, Caesar and Hannibal and the others great" (188). The first thing he criticizes therefore is Berner's typically fairytale-like lack of dizziness and fear when confronted with the canonically sublime cliffs and crags into which his mentor leads him: "You will be brave, but never sublime" (116). Almida's anti-sublime position, on the other hand, which demands nothing meaningful from her protégé and dispenses with any plan, is from the outset tied to the complementary praise of beautiful triviality. The old fairy's subterranean and flowerless kingdom is associated with the sublime concepts "night" and "future," whereas the flowery island of beautiful Almida is all spring, sun, and love.[112] Silly games, laughing communication without one "sensible word" (104), life without a plan, indeed even happy successes that cannot be interpreted as destiny or given a higher sense[113]—all these phenomena are praised for lacking the pretense of meaning and thus serve to make reflexive the Romantic poetics of freedom from the constraint of meaning, of the "senseless" fairy tale and the "meaningless" arabesque.

The Figure of the Genius; Fate, and Fairy Tale

The most striking relic of the popular novel in Bluebeard's tale of murder is the guide figure Bernard. Only from a distance can he be mistaken for a helping figure typical of the fairy tale. His more specific attributes prove him a descendant of the contemporary society novel [*Bundesroman*].[114] This genre's genius figures are almost always old men, "decrepit, intellectually strong rationalists. Hence the frequent denomination: the elderly man, the old man [*der Greis, der Alte*],"[115] the latter of which Tieck also uses. "He comes and goes mysteriously. Suddenly he's standing there, as if sprung from the earth, on the highway, at the edge of the forest,"[116] even this characteristic introduction of the "fateful figure" fits Bernard. However, the corresponding effects—the mysterious, the demonic, the terrible—are once again absent. Instead, Peter Berner increasingly treats the old man more like an annoying burden, duping his intentions to guide his fate and finally sending him packing. The fact that Bernard's power is not his own but only lent to him from a higher authority is something he shares with his literary-generic relatives. The genius of the popular novel is the messenger of a secret league, a society operating behind the scenes. (This feature survived its "trivial" earlier models to become the "tower society" in Goethe's *Wilhelm Meister.*) In the case of Bernard, this league is replaced by a figure more befitting the fairy tale genre: a fairy who rules a subterranean kingdom.

Tieck's fairytale arabesque reflects yet another characteristic of these fateful figures: their omniscience. As a rule, Bernard knows everything about Berner's activities, just as genius figures "appear to be omniscient once they establish a close personal contact [to their protégés—W. M.]."[117] However, not only is this magical omniscience marked by a striking exception—of all things, Berner's acquisition of the blue beard escapes Bernard's attention, forcing him, "amazed," to ask a question that normally ill-befits the concept of a genius figure: "What's that?" (146). At the same time, as knowledge about itself, omniscience also turns into an unhappy consciousness. For he who knows everything, Bernard remarks, is "without curiosity" (104–105) and hence unhappy because listless and desperately hungry for something new. To be alive means nothing other than to be curious and not to know everything. Analogously, Bluebeard's wives turn unhappy and become literally lifeless as soon as they "know everything"—in this respect Tieck, too, like Perrault warns against wanting to know all secrets. At the same time, however, from the very beginning Tieck undermines Perrault's criticism of (female) curiosity, with which he then later ironically agrees: lack of curiosity would indeed be a transcendental misfortune; for instead of saving one from a fatal threat, omniscience would bring decrepitude and lifelessness as its recompense.

Of all the characteristics of genius figures, Tieck especially emphasizes the one strangest to the world of the fairy tale: the "relation to the idea of fate."[118] This enables him, in turn, to stage in literary terms a "theoretical" conflict of genres. In the popular novel, the secret society's entirely rational "play of intrigue" is transformed for extended periods "into a web of fate" for hero and reader—not least in order to perpetuate this genre's otherwise impossible terror effects. As emissary of the league, the genius is a key instrument for this transformation: he appears as an "intermediary creator," even as a "magician" of fate.[119] It is as such a figure that Bernard presents himself. He intimates foreknowledge of Berner's fate, particularly regarding the figure who will ultimately kill him (114), and he offers his assistance in salvaging at least an interesting "career" (105) from such an unfavorable fate and even, with "much skill," rendering some of its "unfavorable influence harmless" (111). Neither the author nor the mere harbinger and companion of fate, Bernard is rather its demonic intermediary, a literary adapter who seeks to assist in rendering the inevitable into readable and summarizable forms of eventuality. For this he uses three key philosophical-poetic concepts: unity, coherence, and meaning.

Ultimately, Bernard must confess the complete failure of his "writerly sins" when applied to a real "life story;" consequently, his pretensions to being a shaper of fate are foiled. Nevertheless, his protégé's reasoning—not without some comic distortion, of course—remains suffused with the idea of fate. Despite having been given the free choice of a specific form both of "happiness" and of "unhappiness"—that is, the opposite of a "destiny" dispensed by the gods—Bluebeard still speaks of "his future fate, that he himself had chosen" (116). After the education based on philosophical-melancholy songs, this fatefulness of his own choosing is the second motivation offered to explain Bluebeard's uxoricides. Its logical deficiency is again striking: a self-chosen unhappiness with women does not necessarily entail the methodical rigor with which Bluebeard in turn condemns them to misery and even kills them. Once again, instead of providing a motive for Bluebeard's actions, Tieck's parodistic citation of the model of fate provides a genre-theoretical insight: the idea of fate must pay for its admittance into a fairytale arabesque with its comic-reflexive distantiation, if not its determinate negation. Otherwise, the idea of fate would have to destroy or disfigure an a priori of the fairytale genre.

Indeed, fairy tale and fate are mutually exclusive: the space of the fairy tale knows no fate; its heroes have escaped fate.[120] Their happiness is neither merit nor fate. It is enough that the hero finds his way to good fortune and it need not further be comprehensible why he follows every command and breaks every taboo, or why at this point an opponent descends upon him and at that point a helping figure suddenly stands at his side. Admittedly, there exist rudiments of a doctrine of virtue that in many ways motivates the "fairytale like" road to happiness: a simple but good heart, pity, courage, endurance, diligence, willingness to sacrifice, and obedience; by contrast only very rarely particular intelligence and almost never martial qualities.[121] However, often enough fairytale fortune also favors swindlers, con men, lazybones, and gamblers. Even the supposedly positive heroes are as a rule shockingly cruel, vengeful, wholly implacable toward their enemies, and ungrateful toward their benefactors. Likewise, in their behavior toward secondary figures they allow themselves, in interest of their "success," every possible type of lie, deceit, and falsity—behavior which, on the part of their antagonists, is unfailingly punished severely. Such traits testify to the priority of the path to fortune itself above all merit or any motivation.[122] This is precisely what is fairytale-like about fairy-tale fortune: that it can never be understood *sufficiently* as the result of work or by merit of virtues (which are at most its *necessary* conditions). Rather, it always maintains the character of a free gift, something that cannot be derived from the qualities of the hero or the conflict he overcomes but that is bestowed solely by the form of the fairy tale itself. This moment of essential contingency, seen from the viewpoint of the hero and the plot, means that fortune ultimately always eludes understanding and must simply be accepted like a gift from a donor. Ludwig Tieck's phrase "man never *deserves* happiness"[123] is especially appropriate for the hero of the fairy tale.

According to Walter Benjamin, the concept of fate is completely irrelevant in the field of happiness—and even unhappiness; it makes sense only in the field of guilt.[124] To be sure, the fairy tale frequently evokes the appearance of a merit on the part of the hero, but it avoids completely the pretense of a fateful course of action: Cinderella's happiness is not her fate and also not—*pace* André Jolles's definition[125]—her merit or just reward. Theologically, it would have to be described as grace,[126] its duration ("and they lived happily ever after") as blessedness. The fairy tale's relationship to redemption—and this is not restricted to the "redemption fairy tale" in the narrower sense[127]—is directly opposed to the idea of fate. For redemption, after all, is not at least redemption *from* fate. Just as grace interrupts fate and the law—which is why Kant also understands the "right to grant clemency" to be a paradoxical self-negation of law and to amount to a right of "doing injustice"[128]—so too the fairy tale's happiness negates all mythic fate, instead of itself being one. This moment of redemption inscribed in the form of the fairy tale applies not only to the hero's ultimate happiness as the content of the fairy tale,[129] but also to the form in which it is realized. This is why fairy-tale happiness can be woven into the entire fairy-tale world from the very outset and communicate its peculiar "lightness of being" before any "redemption" of the hero and despite the severity of its conflicts. This formal redemption effect is connected not least of all with the form-specific "redemption" from mythical motivation and accordingly with the suspension of collectively binding justifications and ascriptions of meaning.

By overtly distancing from the constraint of meaning and parodistically distancing from the constraint of fate, Tieck brings both these constraints into parallel opposition to the fairy tale. Thus, he indicates a secret affinity which is openly stated in Benjamin's theory of myth. Myths provide explanations, elucidating the origin and significance of a ritual or a singular event; by contrast, fairy tales forego etiology and ascriptions of significance, immunizing their "world of events that is blissfully self-sufficient"[130] against successful hermeneutical reduction. The fateful nexus of ancient tragedies is grounded in myths, whereas fairy tales know no fate (and hence also no tragic sacrifice, which would break the fate while fulfilling it).[131] In the context of this opposition, the peculiar resistance of the fairy tale to clear meaning and functional explanations (which distinguishes the fairy tale from other "simple forms") would cease being merely a negative, unresolved problem in the scholarship on fairy tales and could become a positive characteristic of the form. The emancipation from the constraint of meaning would then in itself be, as a semantic correlate to the fairy tale's redemption [*Er-Lösung*], the very meaning and function of the fairy tale's form.

The early Romantic definition of the fairy tale as an antidote to the discourse of "sense," "coherence," and "understanding" anticipates such an insight. Tieck's Bluebeard arabesque lends that definition a highly complex articulation. Passing through the contemporary gothic novel, this "folktale" is (parodistically) haunted precisely by what it rejects: the law of a "deeper" meaning and concealed motivation. In the gothic novel everything is significant and everything is motivated, even if (often enough) only virtually so and in the form of a "suspenseful" mystification. The reading process is aimed essentially at discovering the temporarily obscured—and therefore all the more charged—meanings of its enigmatic entanglements. The horror novel is thus completely dominated by the imperative that Tieck's fairytale arabesque refuses to heed. However, since this refusal is itself entirely motivated, and since the critique of the constraint to meaning and the desire to understand is in turn quite "meaningful" and understandable, it remains haunted by the very specters against which it writes. The fairy tale's implicit achievement, to which this refusal appeals, is thus turned into reflexive knowledge only at the expense of being simultaneously inverted and destroyed—a paradox that accords with the Romantic insight into the nature of reflection. The critique of meaning and understanding succeeds only by transgressing against itself, by exempting itself from its own argument and thereby directly contradicting itself. Together with what it criticizes, the "ideal" of arabesque meaninglessness loses its own integrity and itself becomes a phantom of motivated nonmotivation. With this, however, the critique and the parody no longer can avail themselves of a secure standpoint distinct from the object of its critique and parody. For this reason, critique and parody too are no longer provided with a secure standpoint distinct from the object of criticism. They become, in Tieck's own words, entangled in a "willful frenzy, which often destroys the very laws it invented."[132] Entrusted with the task of a "critical" passage through the horror novel, the arabesque reflection on the margins of the fairy tale succeeds only in the mode of compromising its "intentions" in the very process of their articulation: the promise of emancipation and redemption—"purity" from sense and purpose, "freedom" from motivation—is unavoidably contaminated already in its own wording.

Fortune and Misfortune

Fairy-tale plots take place "in the olden days, when wishing still helped."[133] This famous phrase from *The "Frog Prince"* is even more true for the form of the fairy tale than for its protagonists.

Sometimes good fortune befalls them without their having wished for it, and is thus by no means merely a correlate of their own magically enhanced intentions. The freely and explicitly chosen wish whose fulfillment is guaranteed by helping figures represents less the norm than a special border phenomenon. Within the fairy tale itself, the magic wish becomes reflexive primarily through its failure: as soon as characters in fairy tales can and should make their wishes freely, wishing no longer helps. In fairy tales like Perrault's *Souhaits ridicules*, for example, the final remaining wish at best suffices to undo the adverse effects of previous wishes and to restore the modest contentment of the status quo. By contrast, fairy-tale happiness is regularly botched through such wishing. The beginning of Berner's "career" and Bernard's "work" on it[134] is highlighted by an analogous moment of fairy-tale fortune becoming reflexive in a freely chosen wish.

> Well good, continued Bernard, this is an important moment for you. Your whole life now stands still, and all the stars come to a halt, for soon they will begin a new epoch. A man can never unite all the happiness on earth in one career, and he is already to be called blessed who, like you, is given a choice. So then, in what way do you wish to be happy? Do you want wealth, honor, luck against every enemy, love? Just name what you want and it is granted to you—but you better collect your thoughts first. Peter looked doubtfully at his friend, who was offering him more happiness here than the lottery could ever bring him, even more than the heaven on earth that Mr S. promises for 1 and 8 pence. He wondered whether this stranger maybe took him for a fool.
>
> Choose! shouted Bernard, before the propitious moment passes.
>
> Well, since it must be, said Peter, just give me luck against my enemies, and to the devil with all the rest.
>
> It is granted unto you, said Bernard solemnly, but you must know that now the rest of happiness will shrink to make room for this one. (112–113)

Not only does the explicit intentionality of Peter's wish for happiness push that critical limit where the rashness of subjective desire endangers the fairy tale's otherwise generic guarantee of happiness.

In the wish's contents and even more so in its implications, the reflection of the fairy tale is driven to the point where its promise turns into its exact opposite. Indeed, the explicit promise of happiness for an entire sphere of life itself belongs more to an astrological or popular-psychological discourse than to the fairy tale. The fairy tale's hero usually encounters exactly that fortunate assistance that he requires in order to solve a difficult task, pass a test, or escape from a dire situation. What he is given by the helping figure or helping object is context-bound rather than a general lifelong prognosis, even if the hero's happiness in the end is awarded the promise to be a lasting one. Similarly, the wishes made by characters in fairy tales almost always refer to very concrete and singular "objects" rather than to abstract qualities operative across one's whole life: this one princess rather than "happiness with women," the chest of gold rather than wealth in general, the triumph over the evil stepmother rather than "luck against every enemy."[135]

The extension of a wish to "structural" objects is repaid with a radical contraction of its power to bring luck and happiness. As a consequence of its own excess, fairy-tale fortune thus turns into the freely chosen wish for a "misfortune." This "dialectical" transition, by means of which Bluebeard's wives come into play, is based on a premise unknown to the fairy tale, a premise whereby each increase in "fortune" is bound to a complementary increase of misfortune. Such a logic of retribution, of like for like, perpetuates the very logic of fate that fairy-tale happiness transcends:

> You must know that now the rest of happiness will shrink to make room for this one [luck against one's enemies, the form of happiness Peter had chosen—W. M.] and to let your misfortune through. Here too you have to choose. Therefore tell me without pausing to consider: which sort of misfortune do you fancy?
>
> Peter thought about it for quite some while, as it seemed a bit too impudent and unabashed that he himself should select his misfortune out of the immense dark mass. He couldn't make a choice, or a decision, despite all the old man's efforts to help him along.
>
> I won't even mention the worst misery, Bernard finally shouted im-

> patiently, but if I can give you some friendly advice, then choose one of these three evils: disgrace, bad luck with your wives, or to be childish in old age.
>
> Stop! said Peter, I'll take the bad luck with women, for more than one reason. For first of all these words contain a prophecy that I'll have several wives, which I don't mind; and secondly with these weak creatures you can always come out on top. So, that will be it. (113)

With that, Peter has fallen completely out of the fairy-tale world where promises of happiness come true and plunges into its grotesque parody: he *must* select *his* misfortune ("You have to choose"). If the fairy tale's "you *may* choose" was itself already undermined by the implicit negation of all the unchosen possibilities for happiness, now, in the imperative wish for a misfortune (you *have to* choose), it passes over into its direct antithesis. To this is added yet another refraction: the wish for "fortune against one's enemies" that Peter chose, and which was granted with such ceremonial solemnity, does *not* come true. Rather, Peter loses two battles, indeed, two quite important ones: against the witch-housekeeper Mechthilde, whose magic is superior to the power of his sword; and against the fiancé of his adolescent beloved, who wounds Peter severely during his futile attempt to abduct her before the wedding.

Alongside the distorted continuation of both the magical wishing power and the fairy-tale happiness also comes their direct negation. The forms this negation assumes are the refusal to fulfill wishes, the discourse about the impossibility of happiness, and the veritable anti-fairy tale. In the case of Peter Berner's two wishes, whose fulfillment is guaranteed, he lets his genius insinuate two or three possible objects from which he then chooses, without ever questioning this radical preselection. These wishes are just as little *his* wishes as those open chances to "make a wish" are for some other fairy-tale figures, who waste them on thoughtless phrases or even slips of the tongue. By contrast, when Peter later does find a wish of his own, wishing doesn't help anymore. This wish, born of melancholy night thoughts on death and a "cold dread" at contemplating his own "body," reveals Bluebeard to be surprisingly sensitive to the awareness of temporality: "make me forget my mortality so that I can live as though today would always remain today, as though no tomorrow were to follow, and another tomorrow after that and so one day shakes hands with the next and in the end delivers me like a prisoner to the last ghastly day" (193–94). Psychological interpretation could see in this fear of death a reason for Bluebeard's murders—namely, as a substitute sacrifice to mortality—as well as for his sealing death up in a separate room.

From the perspective of genre theory, on the other hand, all Peter wishes for is what the heroes of fairy tales have always already been granted. The radical dynamism of the fairy tale in which today's pig farmer is tomorrow's king presents a heightened experience of temporality, a sense of the positive instability and mutability of existence. At the same time, the fairy tale refuses to accept death as a final and irreversible event. Rather, it allows the dead to be resurrected just as easily as it foresees the possibility of an indeterminately long life: "and if they haven't died, they're still alive today," is the formulaic conclusion of German fairy tales, the equivalent of the English "and they lived happily ever after." The feeling of being-unto-death is just as alien to fairy-tale characters as is dread regarding the abstract mortality of their bodies; indeed, they generally lack any awareness of their bodies at all (as long as those bodies are not targets of spells or such). Hence, Bluebeard's wish is really to be brought out of the arabesque-reflexive framework of the fairy tale and back into its center.[136] What this wish rejects is not so much a hybrid impossibility as rather an experience of temporality that the characters in fairy-tale chronotypes—when wishing still helped—do not need to wish for because they are always already living in it.[137]

The inverted reflection of wishing and fairy-tale happiness in the arabesque achieves greatest clarity in a character who, as entirely Tieck's own invention, has no equivalent in the original Bluebeard tale: the housekeeper Mechthilde. In her case, Tieck indeed provides what is alien to characterization in fairy tales and what in the case of Peter Berner is offered only in an ironical self-demontage: a narrative of how she became what she is. She narrates her life like an abbreviated summary of a psychological novel, an *éducation sentimentale* of bitter disappointments. Her adolescent wishes and her love go to ruin as they would in a novel of utter disillusion; thus, they trace a strictly anti-fairy-tale career. Explicit reflection upon the fairy tale a priori—"which in our coarse, awkward language we call *happiness*"—here takes the form of a critique of illusions: that it is "incomprehensible to expect this happiness in this prison [= real life—W. M.]" (154). For "old, indifferent mother Time" is "unmoved by lamentation" and "goes along her way without looking after the whining children of man" (155). Wishes, dreams, and the idea of happiness exist for us not for the sake of their (fairytale-like) fulfillment but only so that we might tolerate our non-fairytale-like lives, for without those dreams and wishes, we would simply sacrifice our lives to the "wish for death." Anticipating Freud's theory of the death drive, the fairy-tale impulses of life are integral parts of an economy in which they are merely the detours by which death finds itself:

> What we call life is nothing but the wish for death, towards which we inwardly strive and for which we secretly yearn; but outwardly, in turn, wretched man is terrified by the horrible image that reaches towards him out of the darkness. Hence we have to soothe ourselves about everything; our wishes are there in us only to keep us involved in a lively activity, but they never come true. (154–155)

This astonishing sketch of a metapsychological economy of life and death drives is far more than a rejection of the "illusions" of fairy tales. It integrates that very element (wishing) whose fulfillability it denies into its own anti-fairy-tale functionality and thereby does not simply demand the renunciation of unfulfillable desires.

However, as was the case with the introduction of the concept of fate into the realm of the fairy tale, so too here: neither the parodistic continuation of fairy-tale wishing and fairy-tale happiness, nor its critique in the face of an implacable mortality, nor finally its refunctioning into an economy of non-fulfillment are sufficient to explain Bluebeard's motives for murdering women. Rather, the satirical and theoretical levels of Tieck's arabesque stage a play of reflection; a play that conforms to the Romantic theory of the novel as the genre that reflectively mixes all other genres. The specific literary forms combined in Tieck's arabesque—especially fairy tale, psychological and horror novel, but also satire, idyll, and the fantastic—*as* forms draw and redraw their own boundaries, and within this play they also, indeed most importantly, articulate a theory of genres. In this way *The Seven Wives of Bluebeard* anticipates, more than any other work other work preceding the *Athenaeum*, Friedrich Schlegel's Romantic idea that a philosophy of genres must itself be expressed in the very medium of these genres.[138]

The Leaden Head

Upon entering the forbidden room, Perrault's heroine at first saw nothing. The same holds for Agnes in Tieck's Bluebeard drama: "when I opened the door I saw nothing but an empty chamber."[139] However, Agnes's seeing nothing is no longer just an inability to see because of darkness; instead, positively, it is her seeing an "empty chamber." Her murdered predecessors are shielded from view through "a green curtain" in the "background." Then Agnes too makes the terrible discovery. Tieck's Bluebeard narrative, by contrast, interrupts this transition from seeing nothing to gruesome certainty. It eliminates the corpse from the forbidden room. The impression that "everything was empty" (166) therefore ceases to be merely a first, temporary phase of heightened suspense as she enters the room. In fact, none of the wives discovers that inconspicuous secret that Tieck substitutes for the spectacular image of the rows of corpses: the leaden head. Only the housekeeper Mechthilde by chance awakens its capacity to speak. It is precisely this incidental discovery that makes her immune to Bluebeard's wish to punish her, since she understands how to use the powers of his secret against him. Thus, what she finds in the forbidden chamber turns out to be a highly effective helping object—a course of events for which one also finds examples in other fairy tales drawing on the motive of the forbidden chamber. To Bluebeard's wives, on the other hand, the head is nothing and signifies nothing. It merely "fills" marginally an empty space without eliminating the emptiness: Winckelmann's definition of the arabesque "flourish." Hence, that bloody central phantom of the Bluebeard plot, the shocking presence of the corpses, yields its place to a more than discrete arabesque. Not only its spatial positioning but its metamorphic ability as well reveal the leaden head to be a derivative of those controversial room decorations. When Bluebeard smashes the head, a small serpent shoots out of it: that (fairy-tale) creature that appears as both represented object and as the formal principle of interlacing and the "serpentine line" in Raphael's Vatican arabesques.

A "blue spark" leaps out of the leaden head when the old fairy pours his "spirit" into it in the form of a droplet (140). This alludes to the blue flames of the occult tradition of alchemy, which in popular novels before Tieck and Hoffmann were frequently evoked as a demonic appearance of light.[140] A wondrous object in the idiom of contemporary novels, the leaden head also bears an abundance of metaphorical relations both to the dead women whom it so surprisingly replaces and to the Bluebeard fairy tale in general. The women seek and find knowledge in the forbidden chamber; the leaden head is an allegory of knowledge itself. The correlation between lead [*Blei*] and knowledge has a literal referent in the use of "*Bleisatz*," hot lead used in print setting that fueled the explosion of "knowledge production" in book form in the 18th century. The knowledge the women gain despite the prohibition not only bears on the subject of (their predecessors') death but is also itself bought at the price of death. By the end of its career as advisor, the leaden head meets the same fate as these women: it is "killed" by Bluebeard. Nevertheless, throughout its life, the head is a sealed-off, dead knowledge, that cannot regenerate itself and thus lacks the very power of life. Furthermore, ever since Perrault, the females' curiosity about the forbidden chamber has been given Biblical connotations referring to the story of the Fall and the serpent's seducing Eve into tasting of the Tree of Knowledge. Tieck's combination of a leaden head of knowledge and a serpent here has a second horizon of allusion. In both cases, knowledge is related to unhappy consciousness. The bitter consequence of attaining (forbidden) knowledge, as in the banishment from paradise, is at least implicitly present in the leaden head through the associative chain: leaden head—heavy head (headache)—melancholy. In a tradition stretching back to Aristotle, the capacity for prophecy is associated with a melancholic disposition.[141] Bernard, Bluebeard's genius figure, also evokes this correlation between knowledge and melancholy.

All these positive parallelisms are combined with negative ones. The sealed-off leaden head does not so much represent knowledge that the women lack, i.e., "revelations" about Bluebeard, but rather a knowledge that Bluebeard himself lacks. The head is the reified supplement of Bluebeard's stupidity—a stupidity to which his own "helpers" formally attest (114, 120). Also in its relation to time, the head's knowledge reverses the order of the original fairy tale: whereas the forbidden chamber usually provides knowledge of Bluebeard's past and only in the form of this past indicates the women's own implicit future, the leaden head as counselor and prophet exclusively and directly subscribes to the future. In both cases, the living present is lost in the chamber. The chamber functions like a time machine in which every present tense is swallowed up by a past or future tense. The correlation between lead, future, and prophecy may also allude here to the popular New Year's custom of telling fortunes by dropping hot lead into cold water and observing the shape it takes. Moreover, "*bl*eiern" ["lead"] alliterates with the "*bl*auer" ["blue"] spark to which the head ultimately owes its wisdom and with the "*bl*auer" beard—just as lead also has a bluish hue.

Bluebeard consults his leaden counselor exclusively in regard to the two fields (war and women) where his fortune and misfortune are already defined, and it is in those two fields alone that his counselor lives up to expectations. In this way the leaden head—by virtue of its prophetic gift and its resolution to bestow even unwelcome advice—poses a contrasting image to the advisor of the Bluebeard drama, who only echoes his master foolishly. However, whenever this "leaden Minister of State" (121) exceeds the two domains of war and wives—which in any case tend toward tautology because they are already ordained by "fate"—his advice is definitely harmful. The head's first recommendation—"get yourself a housekeeper" (123)—brings Peter under the sway of a witch-like hag who promptly ruins his leaden counselor in the course of extracting so much secret knowledge from the head that she henceforth dominates Berner. Bluebeard therefore rightly damns the "whole family" of his helpers—fairy, genius, counselor—as "not worthy of the hangman" whom they claim to serve: "Your counselor—him too I'd like just to melt right down and make soup spoons out of him, so that our mouths could finally taste something healthy from him" (147). The leaden head's wealth of metaphorical references only serves to lay bare all the more grotesquely the "capricious mischief" inherent in the act of substitution to which the head owes its place in the story. The wished-for transformation from advice giver to soup server does not so much destroy the head as exhibit the logic of the arabesque non-sense that institutes it.

Stupidity and a Blue Beard

In place of blood and dead bodies, in Tieck's tale a bodiless and bloodless being appears that consists only of a head. Despite this inversion and also despite the unmistakable masculine nature of the head—a "leaden State minister" (121), a "great man" (240)—what remains sealed within the forbidden room is a feminine "principle." In Tieck's arabesque all knowledge and all understanding originate with women: the beautiful Almida embodies the highest wisdom, the old subterranean fairy has command of at least the "wisdom and understanding" of the leaden head, and the latter is useful ultimately only to another woman, namely, the housekeeper Mechthilde, who for a short period of time also was Bluebeard's mistress. In this space of feminine knowledge, Bluebeard is above all one thing: an idiot. "You are brave and courageous, but you lack wisdom and understanding [. . .] You are now young, and it can be foreseen that with increasing years you will become dumber" (120). Thus says the old fairy, and to cover this deficiency she gives her protégé the leaden head, "which will think for you, since for you this work is too difficult" (121). Bluebeard's housekeeper even establishes a connection between stupidity and moral innocence: according to her, the knight is "simple-minded enough, so that he is almost good" (165). Furthermore, the mentor figure Bernard—who is himself far less intelligent than his antagonist Almida—even ventures into a comparative review of contemporary novels in order to discuss with his protégé Bluebeard the question whether "the main hero is allowed to be an idiot" (188–190).

The superimposition of stupidity upon Bluebeard's cruelty represents a central artistic device of Tieck's reworking of the fairy tale. Due only to this alteration of his predominant attribute can Bluebeard for the first time in the plot's history figure as the hero of the "fairy tale" instead of just its villain; at the same time, the emphasis on his stupidity allows him to be the ironical embodiment of a genuine Romantic desideratum, namely, the critique of the intellect. As Maria Tatar has noted, stupidity is the basic characteristic of almost all the masculine heroes in the Brothers Grimm fairy-tale collection. "'Innocent,' 'silly,' 'useless,' 'foolish,' 'simple,' and 'guileless': these are the adjectives applied repeatedly to fairy-tale heroes in the Grimm's collection."[142] Such heroes would be the least likely to win prizes for "intelligence and good behavior";[143] rather "the fathers of male heroes are eternally exasperated by the unrivaled obtuseness of their sons. To the question, Who is the stupidest of them all? most fairy-tale fathers would reply: my youngest son."[144] This dumbest son, then, is consistently chosen to make his way to fortune, for "in fairy tales all over the world, the one least likely to succeed paradoxically becomes the one most likely to succeed [. . .] fairy tales featuring male protagonists chart the success story of adolescents who lack even the good sense to heed the instructions of the many helpers and donors who rush to their aid."[145]

Tieck's remodeling of Bluebeard under the sign of stupidity thus does not abandon the field of the fairy tale. Instead, it incorporates into the figure of the evil antagonist an auspicious and basic characteristic of the positive fairy-tale hero—and thereby also compensates for the removal of the "proper" heroine of the traditional plot.

Bluebeard's fearlessness in battles and dangerous situations, first demonstrated when he regains his inheritance (109), also at least partially preserves the positive promise of fairy-tale stupidity. If he still ultimately fails, then it is because he lacks by definition a second characteristic that in fairy tales constitutes a condition for the dumb hero's success story: the ability to sympathize, and/or humility.[146] This formal requirement of "soft-heartedness" or "meekness"[147] is directly countered by Bluebeard's cold heart (153, 169), his "heart harder than stone."[148] Thus, on the one hand Tieck mixes the fairy-tale figures of hero and antagonist by virtue of bestowing the quality of stupidity on the serial killer; on the other hand, he splits off, in this very same move, the positive fairy-tale stupidity from its obligatory attendant characteristic.

Through his stupidity, Bluebeard's actions and reflections acquire a comic quality that also has its model in the form of the fairy tale itself: "Heroic feats performed by figures with clear character defects—lack of wisdom and wit—can end by producing comic effects. Blockhead, Numbskull, and Simpleton rush into one hazardous situation after another; they get the upper hand by putting their dimwittedness on display, taking every word of advice that they hear literally."[149] In particular, the conjunction of stupidity and fearlessness—which marks the active masculine hero as opposed to the dumb, softhearted one—guarantees all kinds of burlesque effects already in the fairy tale itself.[150] However, never have genuine fairy-tale heroes themselves been allowed to join in a *laus stultitiae*, in praise of their own stupidity. Here too Tieck's Bluebeard exceeds the limits of the fairy tale by means of articulating them: "The devil take understanding! [. . .] I've noticed you can't be dumb enough in this world if you want to get ahead" (194). While the old fairy does not positively affirm Peter Berner's stupidity, she does so negatively by noting that he is unaffected by the modern sickness and is thus unable to make an excessive use of understanding (140); thus, she lends his deficiency a specifically Romantic seal of approval.[151] Consequently, dumb Bluebeard, as a citation from the fairy-tale genre, may also ironically embody the Romantic wish for overcoming the constraints of modern rationality: the positive deficiency in "common sense" (173) as the motto of the arabesque, which "means nothing" and hence also provides nothing for the understanding, is doubled in an analogical deficiency of understanding in the "psychology" of its heroes. Tieck's protagonist must even expressly thank the fairy "for the good advice" that it is better for him to remain stupid (141). Following Tieck, Friedrich Schlegel demanded an explicit "theory of stupidity."[152] This theory was to have been elucidated in his work entitled "*Arabesken.*"[153] "A dummy and a fool are necessary in the philosophical novel;"[154] once a "certain height" is achieved, they embody "the truly ultimate principle of everything amusing."[155] The model for the Romantic praise of stupidity and foolishness, however, is not Bluebeard but Sancho Panza.[156]

In the wake of stupidity, Tieck finally also brings his protagonist's blue beard into play. Upon receiving from the old fairy the leaden head that is both helper and substitute for his own stupid head, Bluebeard further wishes for a second, purely semiotic supplement to his deficiency. A "proper, decent beard" should let him at least symbolically convey "age," "wisdom, and understanding," which is precisely what the fairy had just told him it is desirable *not* to have. Staying in line with her advice, the fairy tries to talk her protégé out of his wish for the symbolic presence of age and wisdom; for her this wish is just more evidence of his stupidity. Only after he reproaches her for "being herself as old as the hills," the old fairy utters the wounded cry of "impudent dummy!" and finally awards him the wished-for supplement. However, "in order to punish him" it is "completely blue." The "odd appearance" of the beard, however, hardly irritates its simpleminded owner:

> Peter examined himself in the mirror the following day, and since his fate could not be changed, he was satisfied with it. One can't say whether it was because of a lack of vanity or because of wholehearted vanity that he believed, as he continued to gaze for a while into the mirror, that this beard suited him incredibly well, and that, like a red beard being a sign of falsity, so his extremely blue beard, by contrast was proof of an almost excessive magnanimity. He therefore had the beard delicately shorn and gave it good contours so that it would

> grow beautifully and orderly; in brief, he declared this bastard a legitimate child and treated him just the way other gentlemen dealt with their usual beards. (144–145)

Whereas Perrault's fairy tale and Tieck's Bluebeard leave obscure "why the main protagonist has a blue beard" (242), Tieck's arabesque offers in the place of this lack an abundance of motivations. The main protagonist himself explains why he wants a beard and how it came to have its unusual color; fairy and narrator also make their contributions to "understanding" the famous prop. Vanity underlies the wish for the beard and wounded vanity underlies its being granted. Its color is found good "because of a lack of vanity or because of wholehearted vanity." From the fairy's perspective it is a punishment, a stain, or brand with which Peter is marked. Peter by contrast wants and understands it as a "sign" of positive qualities: of "bravery" and "virility," which he had proven in battles; of "age," "wisdom, and understanding," which he lacks; and of "an almost superfluous magnanimity," the meaning of which remains completely obscure unless it is an inversion of Bluebeard's traditional association with gruesomeness. By mockingly intensifying the "wisdom and understanding" interpretation, the fairy exposes a parallel between the beard and the leaden head: both are supplements of his stupidity, one (supposedly) a genuine supplement, the other a deceptive and purely symbolical one that conceals the absence of that which it symbolizes. The critical remark of the old genius figure—"You are simpleminded and even have a blue beard" (188)—supports this interpretation, which works only by means of the three variables stupidity, leaden head, and blue beard. To the extent that the blue beard draws its "meaning" from its opposition to stupidity and its parallel to the leaden head, the explicit interpretation proffered by Tieck's arabesque lacks any relevance for the traditional Bluebeard fairy tale. The conventional fairy tale doesn't even have those two elements (stupidity, leaden head) which in Tieck—as parergonal additions and substitutes—take on the burden of providing a motivation for the blue beard without, however, establishing the least connection to Bluebeard's habitual murders of women.

In the final and quasi-authoritative testimony by the beard's owner himself—that his facial fixture is "proof of an almost superfluous magnanimity"—the "superfluity" of the signified even "flows over" to the level of the signifier itself. Can there be a physiognomic sign for "an almost superfluous magnanimity"? For something that is at once both overabundant and useless but that is also precisely *not* these two things? The adverb "almost" revokes the meaning of superfluity and holds it *below* the line of that superfluity that in fact is the only relatively close definition of the indicated virtue. The paradox of a superfluity that is no superfluity itself redoubles an analogical almost-superfluity of the blue beard itself. Lacking a secure (metaphorical) relation to its owner, the beard is a superfluous sign that terminates in nothing signified: an abundant sign. On the other hand, this sign is yet only *almost* superfluous, for it still evokes reactions and thus propels the plot forward, at least in the "genuine" fairy tale. This functionality for the plot, and thus the "almost" of the superfluity, gets progressively lost in Tieck's arabesque of the fairy tale. Only the first wife—the only one who does not want to marry the knight because she already has a lover—tries to make the "ugly blue beard" an objection to marriage in her confrontation with her father (149). By contrast, all the other women find nothing disturbing in Bluebeard's appearance. They all seem to share the opinion of the second wife: "He looks good" (178), and do not mention anything about the beard's uncommon color. The attribute that gives Bluebeard's story its title vanishes from that very story. The superabundance of proffered motivations is not realized in any plot function: this too is an inverted reflection of the conditions that obtain in the original fairy tale. Thus, the titular attribute of the fairy tale, the blue beard, enters into Tieck's arabesque as itself another arabesque, a decoration along the borderlines of the face, and the superabundance, the overflowing of the borders of its motivations can be read as an arabesque inscription of this arabesque "adornment." The beard ironically presents "meaninglessness" as the central characteristic of the contemporary discourse on the arabesque.

Bluebeard's Wives and Other Women

Just as the blue beard does not live up to its promise [to be a purveyor] of meaning, so, too, does the story's titular subject (*The Seven Wives*) fail to become the subject of the story: these "Wives" are neither its main actors nor its privileged *sujet*. The decisive seventh wife, who drives the plot in the fairy tale, is completely absent from the arabesque discourse, and the first six wives are marked only by a single characteristic respectively.[157] They "appear and disappear again quickly without making the foolish and annoying pretense that they should be kept and developed further" (186); at least in this respect they resemble "genuine" fairy tale characters. Conversely, the one woman whose life story and attitudes are described in detail, and who takes action and tells long stories, is not named by the title. She is not one of the wives; rather, she is Bluebeard's housekeeper. Thus, the story's title assumes the same eccentric relationship to its nominal subject that the "contents" of the arabesque have to its fairy-tale plot.

The conventional Bluebeard fairy tale can be read as an allegory of the patriarchal oppression of women: it divides power, wealth, and knowledge (at least knowledge provided by the magic key) in a strictly asymmetrical way between a masculine monster and his female victims. With regard to this distributive schema Tieck's arabesque calls into question yet another avenue for interpretation and at least potential understanding. His Bluebeard is first and foremost a victim of female power and female knowledge. Bluebeard's "protectoress" (188) turns out to be "an old witch" (147) who calls him an absolute idiot and flatly denies his wish for more common sense. Equally powerless is the stupid hero in the face of the opposing fairy Almida, whose interventions provide a painful conclusion to his "romantic" abduction of Adelheid, his childhood love. Even his housekeeper uses the knowledge she gained from her disobedience to ward off "quite calmly" Bluebeard's attempt to punish her: merely by touching Peter she renders him "momentarily so powerless that he had to let his sword drop" (129).

Regarding the two key semantic differences of the fairy-tale plot—male vs. female and powerful vs. powerless—an abyss of irony opens up at the realization that a halfway plausible "sense" of Tieck's version can be established only at the price of inverting the otherwise symmetrical interrelation of these two "binary codes." Beyond the "witty" play of Romantic "capriciousness," Tieck reveals here the unsettling law of inversion between perpetrator and victim that, in less obvious forms, has defined most of the interpretations of the fairy tale ever since Perrault.[158] Thus, the Bluebeard plot also confirms the suspicion with which the arabesque began, when "thinking" about the word "morality": that the goal of "better understanding" is furthered by inverting what is to be understood (89). In a similar way, the Romantic theory of "(re)presentation" is essentially a theory of the inversion undergone by the (re)presented object.[159] In the "topsy-turvy world" of Tieck's arabesque, the women are ironically exonerated of the "guilt" of "curiosity" by its being provocatively acknowledged as an immutable given of nature (128–129). At the same time, they are assigned a new guilt: their lack of solidarity among each other, their failure to use their considerable power to their own benefit. None of the fairies considers using her power to help Bluebeard's female victims; and the housekeeper, herself magically protected from violent acts, even advances from a loyal accessory to an active accomplice. The "thesis" thus presented, that to a large extent the women themselves perpetuate their own oppression, can certainly be discussed sociologically. However, as an explanation for the Bluebeard plot this thesis so severely distorts what it is supposed to explain that it achieves one thing above all: it compromises, one more time, the reader's need for "motivation," "meaning," and "sense" precisely by fulfilling it in a grotesquely distorted way and thus casting the need back upon itself.

Tieck also uses the exposition of the female characters to refer the reader continually back to the process of reading itself. This becomes quite explicit in his treatment of Bluebeard's second wife. Immediately after mentioning her name (Jakobine) and her chief characteristic (she is domineering), Tieck embarks upon a metahermeneutic reflection about "allusions," "allegories," and the pitfalls of "understanding too well." In this reflection even the function of political criticism, as an "excessive winking" with meanings, falls under the general verdict against the constraint to be meaningful:

> The author requests permission here to make merely a very small remark. Indeed I run the danger here that many readers will entrust me with much too much understanding and acumen and will follow their own acumen in believing that they have made out the whole trick and that they understand me incredibly well. That is, they covertly think that I am groping into allegory and that afterwards I will therefore conclude the whole matter in a way that is both extremely witty but for governments just as dangerous. The girl was naturally called Jakobine not by chance, and one will soon recognize that I (the author, that is) belong to those bright minds, who etc.—Other writers often complain that they have readers who do not understand them; on the contrary, I complain that I am understood far too well by mine [. . .] I always have to laugh, when a writer thinks a great deal of himself, when with cursing and sufficient democracy in his books he reaches the point where the poor innocent reading world declares him to be a dangerous person. In doing so, the readers merely want to express that they have understood his excessive winking; but since, as is well known, no one among the readers is dangerous, how then do things stand with his own dangerousness? (175–177)

"Too much understanding" is thus just as bad for the reader as, according to his fairy, it would be for Bluebeard (141). In contrast to the perceptive reader, dumb Bluebeard runs no danger of stumbling into allegory in his dealings with his wives. The specific properties they represent are at most annoying to him; confronted with the one unchanging question of their obedience, all other questions about them and their behavior lose import. But even for the reader, who must first be brought up to the level of Bluebeard's "positive" stupidity, the "groping into allegory" is orchestrated only to promote awareness about itself. Understanding an allegory that is at once both proffered and rescinded would be understanding precisely "too well," and hence misunderstanding. But simply not reading the allegory—or reading it as a non-allegory—is just as effectively frustrated by Tieck's reflection. Thus, the reader is required to perform a reading of the non-readability of the allegory, an understanding of that positive non-understanding, which is prevented in "too good an understanding."

In the episode with Bluebeard's fourth wife, the rustic "innocent" Magdalene, the play with meanings grows from an instructive trap for the reader into a vehicle for comedy. It evaporates into the Kantian "nothing" of laughter instead of opening an avenue of inexhaustible sense. Just when Peter Berner has decided to marry her, Magdalene comes walking

> across the field, [. . .] pulled her apron apart, and showered the knight with a bunch of beautiful big crabs which she had caught for him. He was amazed and asked what these creatures should mean? They should mean my love, answered Magdalene laughing; just look how big they are.
>
> But normally, Peter said, lovers cover each other with flowers, not with crabs.
>
> What can flowers do? exclaimed Magdalene, I like edible things better; but in remembrance of your name Peter I will go now and pick parsley [*Petersilie*]. Keep an eye on these creatures so that they don't run away. (210)

If crabs need to have their meaning imposed as an imperative—they don't just mean, they "should mean"—then the corny likening of "Peter" to "*Petersilie*" pursues even more rigorously an investment with meaning that consumes itself, producing contingent sense-effects merely as the medium for comic nonsense. These signs for love will be "later in lovely harmony consumed" along with the ingredients of the beloved's own name. However, in their lively materiality, which even includes a latent threat of castration, the "signs" leave the knight literally no peace in which he might abandon himself to their signified: "innocent love." They entangle him in a battle where the signifiers successfully resist being tamed by the signified and its addressees: "I cannot defeat the crabs, they are too strong for me." The imputation of meaning traces a course of deviation within which the signs turn out to be uncontrollable and yet are (to be) consumed; a course of heterogeneous and finite laugh effects instead of an infinite totalization of understanding.

At the conclusion of the narrative, the sequence of *Seven Wives* promised in the title undergoes yet a third eccentric deformation. Not only is the decisive seventh wife absent (at least as a figure "presented" in the narrative); and not only does the woman presented in most detail not belong to the series of the seven wives, but represents a narrative addition outside of the series. This addition generates in turn yet a further addition, one in which—as an arabesque within an arabesque—a fairy-tale heroine finally appears who at the same time is a substitute for the missing positive protagonist. Mechthilde tells Bluebeard's sixth wife (who is the last wife presented in the narrative) a tale of horror. This tale is not only much closer in tone to the genuine fairy tale than its parergonal enframing; upon closer inspection, its narrative elements also seem to be inverse reprises of the Bluebeard fairy tale. Here the evil and childless Bluebeard has been transformed into a good woodsman and father who lives alone with his children in a deep, dark forest. With the formula "the mother had long since died" (231) Tieck marks that transcendental motherlessness of the fairy tale that also affects each of the "seven wives of Bluebeard." This small but significant "correction" of the Perraultian model incidentally also returns in the version of Bluebeard in the Brothers Grimm collection. (In general, the fairy tale has only dead or evil mothers, and Tieck's Bluebeard figure, an orphan raised by a shy "old woman," is as little "socialized" by his mother as his victims are. Thus, he overtly and normatively lacks what Friedrich Kittler regards as a decisive aspect of the discursive system 1800: the "bourgeois" mother who provides her children with proper upbringing and literacy. As if it were confirming Kittler's conjunction between the hermeneuticizing of poetics and the new pedagogical practices, Tieck's subversion of the constraint of meaning is accompanied by a substantive critique of "our modern education" and the "inventors of motherliness."[160] Even the final pillar of Kittler's diagnosis, the role that the interpretation of the "classics" played in the professional education of the "civil servant" and hence of the state, is recognized by Tieck with great acumen. "That's why we have the old classics," concludes a paragraph from his chronicle *Schildbürger* [1796], which tells how "in our time," "the gratitude of the state" as well as "fame and office can be gained" by means of "a treatise on a poem."[161])

In Tieck's horror tale, every year on the same day "a strange racket can be heard around the house [. . .] and the father would warn the children not to go outside." It so happened, however, that once "he had to travel during the week in which that day fell. He gave the strictest orders; but the girl, partly out of curiosity, partly because she had forgotten the day out of carelessness, goes out of the cottage." Bluebeard's command not to go into a specific room finds its negative parallel in this paternal order "not to go outside." Both orders are issued with extreme strictness and on the eve of departure, both are disobeyed, and in both cases "curiosity" is given as the motivating reason. The scene of death that Bluebeard's wife discovers in the forbidden room presents itself to the disobedient girl in the great outdoors: the entire landscape mutates into images of menace and death. Out of the lake "strange, bearded faces" gaze at her suddenly—a reprise of the blue-bearded horror, which is continued in an uncanny bird "with a long beard." "Three bloody, very bloody hands [. . .] pointed with the red index finger to the girl"—just like the bloody key points to the "guilt" of Bluebeard's wife.

Each of the various agents and beings that appear in this horrific landscape poses as a helping figure and at the same time denounces the others as cannibals, child murderers, and other monsters. Hence, wherever the girl looks for salvation, she soon discovers new dangers. Every escape turns into a new trap and intensifies the horror.[162] Finally, through a window of her house "the little girl" sees herself "dancing with a skeleton" and yet at the same time is standing "outside as an age-old woman." At this point the sixth wife stops listening and interrupts the story, horrified. Thus, it remains undecided whether the heroine of Mechthilde's tale ultimately escapes the evil antagonists or not. Before this "dreadful nonsense" can vanish like an evil apparition, before the fairy-tale heroine who is absent in the primary level of the text (which is actually already a secondary level) can find a positive "end," this very lack of sense undergoes an "eternalization" by being arrested, interrupting and suspending the fairy tale's own inner teleological dynamic. However, here once again the escape from horror may continue, inversely, the traditional Bluebeard tale. This tale has, in fact, variants in which the heroine, rather than being saved by her brothers, escapes through magical flight. Equipped with helping objects and animals and helpful instructions, the heroine, each time it seems that she is about to be captured by her pursuer, is able to escape in the nick of time; finally, after numerous episodes of almost getting caught and just barely escaping, she reaches her salvation.[163] Tieck's fairy tale inverts this rhythm of magical escape into an oscillation between merely apparent escape and a repeated recognition of still being trapped within the disaster. Thus, in the framing texts around the absent center of the Bluebeard fairy tale, elements of what is absent seem to return as a further framing text, a digression within the digression, as it were. But if this is so, then it occurs only in the forms of inversion and interruption: an inversion, however, whose further, additional inversion does not recuperate the "original" of the Bluebeard fairy tale; and an interruption that fragments the strictly finalized plot line of the fairy tale and that is able to join in the parergonal frame of the proliferating arabesque only as a horrific and decorative ruin of itself.

Incoherence and Non-meaning of the "Course of Life"

Bluebeard fights "feuds, always feuds, lots of insignificant bagatelles that no one wants to worry about" (189). His other principal activities, marrying and murdering, share with these feuds the characteristic of pure seriality and virtually no "development." The order of the episodes is arbitrary; they also do not culminate in any purpose that would structure them nor in any "lively interest" that could be maintained across them (217). Never does Bluebeard draw a lesson from a specific episode in order to apply it in the subsequent one. In this he exhibits ostensibly a characteristic of the genre from which he has escaped into the arabesque, only to reflect it parergonally: "The characters of the folktale do not learn anything, nor do they gain any experiences."[164] Insinuations by the guide figure to "take up" again an earlier episode and "continue" it—"if only so that your life might acquire a little unity"—are gratefully declined (217–218). In his one attempt in this direction, Bluebeard is "almost beaten to death": for him a strong argument not to pursue the poetics of "unity," "coherence," and "meaning." In refusing to follow this poetics, the evil protagonist, the good fairy Almida, and the narrator turn out to be caught in a surprising liaison. By traversing both positive and negative figures as well as various textual levels (author's and narrator's reflection, plot, narration, protagonists), the critique of "coherence" paradoxically becomes a unifying moment of the "book that has no coherence" (241). Unlike the mechanical repetitions in Bluebeard's own career, however, the meaning of the repeated critique of meaning begins to slide. Its variations are differentiated into a spectrum that becomes self-contradictory; and by means of this self-negating articulation, the critique of meaning lives up to its own concept of non-coherence.

The dumb protagonist attacks the presumption that his career should have unity and meaning with a tirade on the senselessness and purposelessness of human life in general that disarms his guide:

> Why was I born at all? What did they want with me, that I came into the world, and that I live my life, and at some point it's over and gone? Look, there is no common sense in that, and that makes me so depressed. If you think about the fact that you can find no purpose and coherence in a person's whole life, then you'll also gladly give up trying to introduce these things into the course of my life. (193)

Contemporary aesthetic theories, paradigmatically that of Kant, proclaimed the purposelessness of art while also integrating it into a paradoxical "purposiveness" ["*Zweckmäßigkeit*"] without purpose (which in a second reflection also communicated a transcendental meaning to the meaninglessness of purely aesthetic play). Bluebeard puts an end to this aesthetic ideology. He takes the purposelessness seriously: as a sobering insight, shorn of illusion, into the negativity of human existence that comprises only "many broken-off fragments" (220) and that frustrates every hope for a meaningful totalization. This variant of the farewell to "coherence," "purpose," and "meaning" does not aim for a positive conception of poetic autonomy. Rather, it is first and foremost a negative appreciation of the expectations for one's life. Only upon second reflection and only under the "realistic" premise that "poetic composition" should not impose anything on life that it normally lacks (193), does this attitude of resignation also bear on poetics. From this perspective, a poetics of meaninglessness above all does justice to a lack of the "object" to be (re)presented. It does not make any claims to inaugurate a positive aesthetic telos or even a desirable characterization of life.

In the pedagogy and philosophy of the good fairy, the farewell to "unity," "coherence," and "meaning" takes on quite different contours. Rather than acknowledging with resignation the failure of these categories, she advocates deliberately abandoning them out of the wise recognition that they only "spoil" life (105–106). For instead of bestowing sense to what is otherwise "senseless," such "unity," "coherence," and "meaning" only do violence to the "course of one's life" and ruin its best possibilities. From Almida's perspective, then, Bernard's undertaking is not so much futile and unrealistic as it is positively pernicious. Whereas "bad writers," the "precursor and harbinger" of whom is Bernard, "at most spoil good paper" with such a poetics, Bernard would violate "quite healthy careers," "and [you] would receive neither an honorarium nor author's copies for it. Let life take the course it wants to" (106). The categories from Bernard's "classical" poetics are unmasked as an oppressive regime, which in the best case fails but could never establish meaning, let alone "happiness." By contrast, the dismissal of this regime and the related praise of the trivial as "fortunate" meaninglessness opens up the promise of a life that is free to run its own course.[165]

This promise comes true in the figure of Adelheid, whose fairy does not force her into any plan of her own but rather protects her from the violence of other plans. First abducted and then freed with the help of magic, Adelheid comes closest to being a substitute for the absent fairy-tale heroine, even though she is spared the customary trial of obedience. From the perspective of German Romanticism we may therefore see a distinct fairy-tale-theoretical "sense" in the fact that the only character in the arabesque who is both rescued and happily married is also the one whose career is programmatically relieved of, if not "saved" from, motivation and meaning, planning, and coherence. As it becomes true in Adelheid's case, the license of the "most incoherent careers" is invested with the promise that in the end it would result in "a better coherence" (105) than the normative dictate of "unity" and "meaning" ever could. It is, however, almost *per definitionem* that this promise cannot give an account of its own "metaphysical" ground; it does not even try to. For any such attempt would only succumb to that constraint on motivation and meaning against which it is articulated. At best, like Kant's positing of a subjective "purposiveness" of aesthetic purposelessness that forsakes any objective ground, this promise can postulate itself in transcendental reflection—for the sake of its promise in fact. However, Almida as well as her author foregoes this as well. Nevertheless, with its formal structure of self-induced paradox—the better coherence *in* incoherence, sense as an effect of nonsense, "unconstrained" meaning as the promise that comes with the license of the meaningless—Almida's philosophy shares one, if not *the* central rhetorical figure of the aesthetic ideology of Kant, Schiller, and the early Romantics.[166]

The author's (narrator's) reflections weave together Bluebeard's and Almida's diametrically opposed apologies for poetic purposelessness and incoherence into an ironical "synthesis." First of all, the narrator claims for his own part that in his book he has in fact realized the (anti-)features in question by subscribing to "contradictory nonsense" instead of caring about any unity of meaning:

> Not one reader can feel more than the author that (my book) suffers a deficiency of good simplicity, that it has no goal and no purpose whatsoever, and contradicts itself at every moment, that it is only the most trivial nonsense when Bluebeard cannot read and yet cites a passage from Horace. (220–221)

This self-description itself produces what it talks about. The seemingly simple phrase, the book "contradicts itself at every moment," introduces that vertigo of paradoxical self-annihilation that affects even the most lucid slogans of incoherence and meaninglessness. For a book that contradicts itself *at every moment* also contradicts itself at that moment in which it certifies precisely this self-contradictoriness at every moment. In the Romantic theory of the fairy tale and in its poetic anticipation in Tieck's Bluebeard arabesque, the fairy tale's sovereignty over the modern hermeneutical reader's demands for motivating psychology, meaning, sense, and understanding itself accedes to a presentation only insofar as it loses its "innocence" and divides against itself. In the very act of their articulation, the affirmations of meaninglessness and positive non-comprehension miss the pure presence of what they aim at under the categories of absence and lack.

In the author's reflection, the description of the book is followed by two justifications for its lack of coherence. The first takes up Almida's position, the second that of the protagonist. "Why, dear reader, should there not for once be a book without any coherence, since we possess so many with excellent, enduring coherence? Shouldn't that wonderful creature, called writer, not once be granted the privilege of shaking off saddle and bridle?" In the image of the writer as a horse shaking off saddle and bridle there returns both Almida's "repression hypothesis" (the poetics of unity and meaning as a constraint, as an oppressive, subjugating power) and the promise of liberation attached to the license of unfettered diversity and purposelessness. In this case, however, the rhetorical question—as though it were not at all sure of its answer—passes over from an antithesis of attested repression and promised happiness into an argument for realistically diminished expectations:

> Dear reader, who speaks so often of unity and coherence in books, look into your own breast for once and ask yourself: for in the end you live just the way I write, if not worse. Among the life stories of thousands of people—of readers who are both Christian and tasteful—I perceive only torn fragments: no points of rest and yet an eternal standstill; no lively progression of plot despite much movement and running hither and thither; no interest, though much anxious confusion; no originality but affected oddness; no sentiment, but rather bombast or reminiscences from poets from whom the poor people of today have so much to suffer that they no longer are able to feel anything according to their own taste.
>
> If you are so particular about printed books, why not about your own life, which could become such an excellent work, destined for eternity? You examine verses to see whether they will serve posterity, and forget your own immortal soul, the eternal harmony within yourselves, which is destined for times to come. Tolerate my book then, and I will tolerate your lives, as I tolerated and had to tolerate them up to now, even if I didn't want to. (220–221)

Programmatically, Tieck's writing calls into question what Friedrich A. Kittler describes as a central desideratum of the then "new education culture [. . .] in bourgeois German homes and universities": "to reduce the great dice throw of events and discourses into coherent biographies and psychographies."[167] Arno Schmidt's enthusiasm for the "unfortunately downright unknown prose of the *Seven Wives*"[168] is grounded in the same questioning of sense-making discourses. Schmidt takes Tieck's bizarre "miracles of senselessness"[169] and their explicit renunciation of sense literally: for him, such "farce-like" and "crazy 'Romantic irony'" is "simply the witty and bitter imitation of the irony of existence." Indeed, it is "Poetry's long overdue adaptation to life itself [. . .] By 1800 it was really high time that one learned to grasp this avowed 'senselessness' [. . .] as being one of life's typical characteristics."[170] Yet with these remarks Arno Schmidt has merely reformulated the disillusion and resignation hypothesis of both Bluebeard and the author himself. He overlooks the complementary theory that informs the text from the very beginning and returns in the author's reflections: namely Almida's critique of "sense," "meaning," and "unity" as violence against life and reading and the positive promise that inheres in their absence. Still, Schmidt's literary-aesthetic observations open up at least an implicit perspective on what is given short shrift in his conceptual schematization. If the "senselessness" of Romantic prose is at the same time apostrophized as a sequence of "miracles," "about which one can sit and dream, for hours on end,"[171] then the theorem of literature's conformity to senseless life obviously falls short. We are hardly able to dream for hours about senselessness "as a typical characteristic of life," nor do we generally experience it as a bizarre "miracle."

Neither to the protagonist's slogans nor to the author's self-interpretation does Tieck's arabesque grant the power to determine and control the discourse about "meaning," "unity," "sense," and "coherence." This is not only because the affirmation of poetic non-meaning and incoherent sequences is haunted by the irony that such affirmation must present itself as meaning(ful) and establish various forms of coherence. The credibility of this affirmation is further compromised by the particular characters who advocate it in various ways. Bluebeard's "realistic" insight serves above all as a self-legitimization, conveniently allowing him to refuse any demand to follow some kind of a meaningful project that would require effort. It thereby also legitimates indirectly the serial continuation of his murders. Meanwhile, Almida's "idealistic" philosophy of planless letting-things-happen and of a life redeemed from the constraints of unity and meaning is able to fulfill its promise only by means of massive interventions into such a life left unto itself. To this effect, the good fairy acts like a Homeric goddess: descending from the clouds, she promotes the intentionless life of her protégé by helpfully frustrating the intentions of others. Thus, the politics of happy letting-things-happen itself requires what it attacks: planned and decisive action. It secures a space for unplanned and unrestrained life trajectories only by repulsing attacks from the side of third party planning and intentional control. As the intertwining of Bluebeard's and Almida's contrary positions, the authorial reflections even suffer from twofold contradictions. They propagate emancipation into purposelessness and meaninglessness while simultaneously declaring that a planned and meaningful life is impossible anyway. Hence, the author's rhetorical emphasis on making a difference and introducing a new paradigm—the writer as an unbridled horse that finally shakes loose saddle and reins—instantly inverts into poetry's mere conformity to the senselessness of life itself. At the very least, these reflections do not succeed in avoiding the contamination of the meanings of meaninglessness or in establishing a diaeresis of "good" poetic and "bad" mundane meaninglessness.

From a "Lack of Understanding" to the Wondrous

Two dominant "motifs" in the arabesque are guided by perhaps the most obscure prefix of the German language: *Ver*bot [prohibition, taboo] and *Ver*stand [understanding, common sense]. "The original Indo-European meaning of the particle 'away, off'" became differentiated, in a wide variety of ways, in two diametrically opposed directions during the evolution of the German language.[172] On the one hand, the *ver* marks "a going beyond or a leading off paths used hitherto": to lose one's way [*verlaufen*], to lead astray, seduce [*verführen*], to bend incorrectly [*verbiegen*], repress [*verdrängen*], ban [*verbannen*]. The abstract meaning of *ver* as negation, as the inversion [*Verkehrung*] of the simple verb into its opposite, has also developed along this line: to fail [*versagen*], to prohibit [*verbieten*], to refuse [*verbitten*]. "Along the second line, *ver* has the meaning 'onward, until the end,' and thus designates a striding forward, a bringing forward of the activity expressed in the simple [= non-prefixed] verb along the path chosen and to its completion": to use up [*verbrauchen*], to burn, incinerate, cremate [*verbrennen*], to remain, perdure [*verbleiben*], to destroy, eradicate, exterminate [*vertilgen*]. Instead of indicating a deviation or negation, the prefix *ver* in the latter cases signifies an "intensification" and "heightening" of the basic concept. A subclass of this line contains verbs that carry this meaning of completion too far and topple the sense of "too much, too strongly": to oversleep [*verschlafen*], to oversalt [*versalzen*].

None of these opposed semantic lines, however, helps in understanding "to *understand* [*verstehen*] as an expression for the process of mental grasping."[173] "We sense just as little in the substantive as we do in the verb the inner relationship between *Stand* [stand, standing position] and *Verstand*."[174] The word *understanding* is everything but understandable and has driven linguists virtually to confess their *non*-understanding. "(Many peoples) derive their name for the intellectual faculty from standing," says Wachter in his *Glossarium germanicum* of 1727, "the Germans as *Verstand*, the English as *understanding*, the Swiss as *förstand*, the Belgians as *verstand*, even if it is not so easy to grasp what actually that state of the body might have in common with the act of intelligent comprehending or what reason might have moved the ancients to designate the intellect with the word for standing."[175] In the face of such embarrassment, Grimm's dictionary takes a speculative detour for which its precursors had already paved the way. It attempts to understand the word *understanding* [*verstehen*] by substituting the prefix *ver* with *in* and *under*: "in-*standan, in-stân* means 'to stand, rest, be at home in an object,' *under-standen, under-stân* 'to stand in between, e.g., in the midst.'"[176] Certainly, these composita would have been more understandable candidates for the metaphorical meaning of understanding. The questions remain why the incomprehensible *Verstehen* became established rather than these, and how the prefix *ver* was able to take on the meanings of *in* or *under* that are *not* already part of their own large and complex semantic spectrum. About all this the Grimms' dictionary still owes us a convincing explanation.

The meaning of *verstehen* is thus itself displaced, dislodged, disfigured [*verlegt, verschoben, verstellt*]. It is understood at best in its physical meaning, no longer used nowadays, of "blocking the path, blocking entry to a room"[177] or in the equally defunct sense of corruption and decay (*verstandener* wine, *verstandene* horses, *verstandene* pledges).[178] The word "understanding" ["verstehen"] (*mis*)understands [*ver*steht] an understanding of its own form and therefore does *not* understand itself. In Tieck's critique of "understanding" ["*Verstand*"], the negativity as well as the "too much," the "too strong" in the *ver* of *Verstehen* once again becomes audible: as violence against that which is (mis)understood [*ver*standen] in it. The complementary Romantic praise of incomprehensibility [*Unverständlichkeit*] operates along the lines of an *ordo inversus* doctrine with a doubled negation, with an *Un* of the *Ver.* This doubled negation does not, however, lead to a sublation of the first negation and thus back to a pure "prehensibility" ["*Ständlichkeit*"][179] any more than the *un* can be offset without remainder against the negativity of the *ver.* Rather, for the Romantics the field of (re)presentation is the interplay between a first negation (understanding as bringing to a false [*ver*], inverted stand) and a second one (disconcerting, or making understanding itself *un*-understandable), an interplay that neither reaches a stable congruent relationship nor sublates itself.

Regardless of its incomprehensible linguistic form, the noun *Verstand* [intellect, "understanding"] has very comprehensible meanings. While on the one hand, "understanding" designates both a faculty and an operation of a subject who understands by employing his understanding, it can, on the other hand, refer to an objective quality that is ascribed to what is to be understood (*verständig* in the sense of "understandable"). In 18th-century usage, words themselves have an "understanding" [*Verstand*] that "objectively designates 'the sense, the meaning.'"[180] Through this partial synonymy of *sense* and *meaning,* which for their part are also not strictly differentiated,[181] *understanding* is pulled into the critical vortex of a Romantic poetics that understands the fairy tale above all from the perspective of its suspension of "sense," "meaning," and "purpose." Even the affirmation of "incoherence" implicitly promotes the critique of the operation of understanding. This operation entails "recognizing and grasping [. . .] the coherence of the contents of the thought, of speech, of writing,"[182] so that inversely anything "that follows no law of coherence" constitutes for Schleiermacher "the purely incomprehensible."[183] Where there is no coherence, no meaning, no sense, and no purpose, there is also, *per definitionem*, no "understanding" [*Verstand* here meaning an attribute of the words or objects in question], and hence there is also nothing to understand [*Verstehen* in the sense of a subjective operation]. Bluebeard says it directly: the "accidents" that befall him have "no coherence and no normal human understanding [*Menschenverstand*]" (173). To this extent, his stupidity, his subjective "lack of understanding" only doubles the "lack of understanding" that the arabesque claims for itself; the fairy-tale attribute of stupidity thus blends in a Romantic (anti-)poetics. In this space of a twofold "emancipation" from understanding, every process of understanding runs the danger of "understanding too well" (176), that is, of actualizing that meaning of its own prefix that designates "past the goal, too much, too strongly."

Not coincidentally, Bluebeard discovers a lack of "coherence and human understanding" for the first time when confronted with the wondrous "accidents" in the subterranean fairy kingdom. For in 18th-century poetics the suspension of understanding (in the twofold sense) frequently stood under the rubric of a vigorous discussion of miracles, marvels, wonders, and the wondrous. The license of the wondrous and the Romantic exaltation of the fairy tale as "high literature" are interdependent. No other literary form provides such "an ensemble of wondrous things and occurrences" as the fairy tale.[184] Novalis even made a direct connection between the (anti-)poetics of senselessness and incoherence and the character of the wondrous: "In a genuine fairy tale everything must be wondrous [. . .] and incoherent."[185] Tieck's Bluebeard fairy tale anticipates this theoretical conjunction in its literary performance. Prior to being claimed as general characteristics of (every) man's "life story," meaninglessness and incoherence are made the object of discoveries pertaining to the realm of wondrous occurrences in the more traditional sense. So too, it is within the space of a generalized Romantic concept of the wondrous, of existence "without reason (motivation)" and "without coherence," that goblins and ghosts first enter the scene.

Wondrous and fantastic are concepts for phenomena with one common quality: they cannot be understood according to the dominant modern reality principle. Rather, they make possible an experience of the limits of this principle. With the fantastic, the question remains open: whether the phenomena that accost the understanding ultimately conform to its laws, or whether understanding on its part can extend its borders to the point of including these phenomena, or whether it must finally accept something beyond its sphere of dominion before which it is powerless. Due to this suspended hesitation at a borderline,[186] the fantastic performs a permanent sounding of the difference between understanding and non-understanding. The wondrous, by contrast, crosses over the borderline. It eludes by definition our capacity to understand[187] and hence subjects us to an experience of otherness that no longer encourages any hope of its being integrated into our customary reality principle. In the wondrous specific to the fairy tale, customary understanding is so thoroughly left behind that its very claim and impulse fall into complete suspension. This is how the fairy tale, by its very form, achieves the paradoxical effect of turning the wondrous itself into something entirely self-evident. Thus, the fairy tale does not operate according to the fantastic's code of a line of demarcation maintained between understanding and non-understanding. Rather, it assumes the collapse of this difference, as the claim of understanding is confronted by something that is both incomprehensible and self-evident. Yet the moment this collapse is reflected upon as such (which never occurs in fairy tales, but only in their Romantic appropriation), the fairy tale's hermeneutic indifference necessarily approaches the fantastic's critical attention to differentiating between understanding and non-understanding and to delineating their borderline. To this extent, the various combinations of the fantastic and the fairy-tale-wondrous in Romantic narratives follow not just from the ideal of mixing genres but also from the self-reflective nature of the Romantic fairy tale itself.

Tzvetan Todorov defines the fantastic as a hermaphrodite, something that holds the decision between a "natural" and a "supernatural" explanation in suspense. Not coincidentally, this recalls the basic model of Tigges's definition of nonsense as a tension maintained between meaning and non-meaning.[188] Studies on nonsense poetry regularly venture on comparisons with the fantastic and the wondrous, and Ludwig Tieck's poetics of "non-sense" is even largely presented in the medium of partly fantastic, partly wondrous phenomena. Reference to the limits of understanding, and likewise a balancing between two opposed textual tendencies regarding this limit, represent the metaphorical connecting link between nonsense and the fantastic. A disjunctive distinction between both forms, on the other hand, is provided by Todorov's additional criterion concerning the representational function. According to Todorov, the fantastic should not be read either allegorically as a representation of some abstract meaning or "poetically" as a literal and autonomous play of words. Rather, it demands that fantastic narratives, like other fictions, be taken seriously as representation in the sense of referring to, rendering, making present an extralinguistic "reality."[189] Nonsense, by contrast, often recombines and modifies the words of a language in a way that violates the rules governing their possible "sensible" contexts; thus, usually we also deny them any claim to representing reality. (In the field of Tieckian "non-sense," however, the irreality stands side by side with its extreme polar opposite: an intensified claim to reality.) Since the unreality of nonsense should *per definitionem* not allow any allegorical or symbolical interpretation, nonsense belongs, in Todorov's schema, to the field of poetic language. This corresponds with the predominant role accorded by "Nonsense poetry" to playing with sounds, words, and phrases as the material of language itself. However, contrary to Todorov's extremely restrictive definition of poetic language, the language of Nonsense in no way represents a complete disavowal of representation. Rather, it distinguishes itself from a purely self-sufficient wordplay by nonetheless claiming, for every word, the very "reference" that it leaves behind so blithely; indeed, this is what Nonsense must do in order to attain the differential profile of non-sense in the first place.[190]

"Wondrous tones" (134) attract and lead Peter into the realm of the subterranean fairy. There, after a wondrous dinner (135), he is feted with a maximum intensification of the wondrous. A "tournament and jousting" are magically conjured in midair; a "red-spotted parrot" proceeds to unseat a "blue-armored eagle-owl," a woodpecker, a bittern, and two partridges; afterward, a rooster emphatically sings his praises as the greatest hero of all time and as "the one and only subject of speech"—just before "everything disappeared into the airy twilight" (136–139). Were he a genuine fairy-tale character, Peter would hardly be amazed at this captivating show. Instead, he reacts more like the hero of a fantastic narrative when confronted with the "other": with confusion and yet a desperate willingness to discover some "reasonable sense" or "a serious meaning" underlying the striking blows to his reality principle. As if to conform to Bluebeard's search for meaning, the absurd drama is not free of allegorical hints. The red-speckled parrot may recall the bird that accompanied Adelheid's childhood and belongs to the paradigm of positive nonsense and beautiful triviality (104). This allusion to the kingdom of the good fairy Almida becomes clearer when Adelheid is greeted and surrounded by "parrots" and other "red-spotted birds" before her wedding (206). The blue-armored eagle-owl can be interpreted analogously as the blue-bearded hero, the ultimately defeated protégé of the other, adversarial fairy. On the other hand, Bluebeard understands the tournament of airy animal apparitions to be an aping of every "reasonable sense;" to him it seems "ridiculous" (136), "silly," "so ridiculous and false, so childish and terrible at once" (138). It is only when the fairy herself interprets the wondrous manifestations—for her, their unmotivated coming and going without a trace means the "insignificance" of all life plans and goals, a "play of empty space with oblivion"—that Peter acquires an ironical acceptance of their incomprehensibility:

> Very true, answered Peter, very true, but still just as incomprehensible. However, the incomprehensible never harms the truths: the more obscure they are, the better they make their way; like the nightingale

> they prefer to live in the darkness, and so it should be all right with me as well. (139)

Instead of encountering the wondrous as something self-evident, the fairytale arabesque piles up a tremendous amount of ridiculous profundity and sublime nonsense, in order to exhibit an incomprehensibility that is concealed and sealed *within* the fairytale genre's power to treat the wondrous as something self-evident.

The incomprehensible can be recognized as the core of the wondrous for a second time in a scene that displays even more clearly characteristics of the fantastic. Friederike, Bluebeard's first wife, has just entered the forbidden room and made the surprising discovery that "everything was empty," when her gaze falls on the "wondrous wall tapestry," which shimmers with the privileged colors of the fairy-tale genre, "red" and "gold" (166). The figures adorning the tapestry, most of all the horrible-looking King David, seem to "rob" the fearful Friederike "of life and movement [. . . She] expected that at any moment the old king would step out of the wall tapestry and address her, would know everything and say something wondrous and terribly incomprehensible about it" (166–167). Decorating the room's walls, the tapestry whose "life" provokes an equivalence of the wondrous with the incomprehensible, is yet a further figure of arabesque enframing. The "flourish and adornment" coming alive, becoming three-dimensional bodies, and their stepping into the scene even corresponds precisely to the concept of the "arabesque," that Tieck developed "for that gothic, wondrous world" of Shakespeare's dramas.[191]

At first glance, Friederike's terrifying vision of the tapestry justifies neither the predicate "wondrous" nor "fantastic." The vision is explicitly defined as an illusion and moreover allows for a simple explication. The wall covering, that is, portrays exactly what awaits Friederike: "interrogation" and deadly "slaughter." It is only when Bluebeard himself enters the scene and murders his first victim, caught *in flagranti*, that the tapestries get serious:

> Suddenly the tapestry stirred, as though it were being rustled to and fro by the wind. Something was going on inside it, and bustling

> voices were speaking all at once. Instruments sounded from a distance and their wondrous tones came closer and closer. Peter stood still, and didn't know what would come out of all this.
>
> The figures in the tapestry became larger, and grew ever larger before his eyes. Suddenly there was a crackling, as when an ember leaps out of the fire, and all the heroes from the Old Testament strode out of the old tapestry on living legs, the servants and foot-soldiers following them, and only an empty gallery, whose lines and overhead perspectives were badly painted, remained behind. All the figures hovered around the amazed Peter, who didn't know what he should do with such strange company. In his embarrassment he greeted each one, and hardly did a few servants and Moors think it worth their while to thank him.
>
> David stepped up before him and beside him Tobias with his small dog, and all three shook their heads quite seriously. Peter was convinced that, regardless of its moral significance, he had not bought the tapestry to be taught a moral lesson; therefore he did not show the figures too much respect, but in case of emergency relied on his good sword, which he held in his hand.
>
> The colorful retinue circled about him on magical paths, the garments and golden clasps shimmered before his eyes, and he remarked clearly that great Saul's trailing coat was repeatedly stepped upon. What caught his eye most of all was one foot soldier's beautiful helmet, which looked bright and warlike, and for which he finally sensed a deep, incomprehensible desire. He was just about to speak to the fellow when the entire entourage retreated back into their customary restrained position and figured as merely a painting on the wall. The knight consoled himself with the thought that the next day he would wrench that beautiful helmet down off the soldier's head with his own hands. (170–171)

This second tapestry scene also offers hints at a psychological motivation. Friederike's fearful gaze may here be matched by Peter's bad conscience at the murder he has just committed, which produces a spontaneous vision of disapproval through the tapestry figures' becoming alive. To the extent that this interpretive gambit raises doubts about the presumed reality of the wall hanging's apparitions, these may be more properly fantastic than "wondrous tapestries." However, the narrator recounts the strange happenings as an "objective" event without any qualification. He also avoids describing Bluebeard's contact with these phantoms just after committing a murder in a way that follows the conventions of a fantastic encounter. The "fantastic" hero normally would expect the encounter with the Other, for expectation—prototypically at the midnight hour—is the temporal mode for encounters with the fantastic.[192] Yet the tapestry apparition occurs just as laconically and out of the blue as any wondrous event in a fairy tale. Not only is expectation that builds suspense lacking here, but fear too, along with all the other agitated feelings that the fantastic rarely does without. Indeed, after a brief initial astonishment, Bluebeard responds with fearless disapproval of the wondrous "text" and even with a desire to exploit the apparition materially ("one foot soldier's beautiful helmet"). Above all, in fantastic narrative, the experience of the fantastic would decisively stigmatize or support the hero; in either case it would have a strong impact on him. There is nothing of this in Tieck: the apparition causes no experience, no trace of thought or sentiment; it has no prelude and no aftermath in the text and doesn't even lead to the acquisition of the beautiful helmet. The wondrous in fairy tales may occur just as unpremeditatedly and have just as little psychological consequence, but at least it always has a function: to move the objective plot line further along. This too Tieck's ghosts lack. They appear from nothing, vanish into nothing, cause nothing, and mean nothing: a "marvel of senselessness,"[193] in Arno Schmidt's commentary, before he too quotes the apparition in its full length.

Bluebeard himself is therefore permitted to present the diagnosis that the wondrous fulfills the essential features of his antipoetics: "I don't perceive any coherence and healthy common sense in this at all" (173). The entire "thing" he says, is "*Unfug*," something nonsensical, incoherent, out of joint [*Un-gefugtes*]. Just as earlier with the analysis of the "incomprehensible" ["*Unverständliches*"], so too here this anti-idealistic diagnosis of the apparition as "out of joint" comes down to acknowledging the "incomprehensible" ["*Unbegreifliches*"]: "And people come and say, there is absolutely nothing incomprehensible. Well, comprehend all this at once, and you'll be certain to have some hard work on your hands" (173). The imperative to understand is called into question simply by being posed as such. Thus, Bluebeard is still acting in accord with his discovery that there is no "coherence and healthy common sense" when just afterward he hits upon a traditional interpretive gambit of poetics:

> Quiet! I'm getting a thought. The whole thing, and this nonsense, is perhaps what painters always call the life in a painting. I've often enough heard a fool say that a picture looks as though it were talking to you, as though it wanted to climb right down from the canvas. Well then these ones here are really quite exquisite things, for the figures actually do climb down and come forward like I've never found in any Dutch or Italian artist. And then every dilettante must admit that these paintings have much style, indeed they have the best countenance in the world, for they go right back to their proper place once they're done fluttering about with such great liberty. (173–174)

Simpleminded Bluebeard as art connoisseur, explaining the apparitions in his death chamber by means of a poetics of "life" that is rich in tradition: here too a "meaningful" coherence is only touched on in order to be consumed by irony and consigned to "contradictory nonsense." That the animation of the tapestry is a complement and metonymy of a murder (based on the spatial and temporal relations of contiguity), that this animation, in the ghostly leap of life from the corpse to its environment, is a part of an economy of death: this inversion of the conventional model surely introduces en passant, citing "fools" and "dilettantes," the radical modification the poetics of animation and of deceptively lively representations undergoes in the space of the fantastic. However, whereas the fantastic relatives of Pygmalion's statue always exercise a great power that shapes the entire plot, Tieck's tapestry figures remain confined to a powerless and purposeless as well as inconsequential parlor trick. None of the later wives notices them, and they are never mentioned in Bluebeard's numerous visits to his leaden head, regardless of their "wondrous" power of metamorphosis. Through the supplementary removal of any possible plot function, the resistance of the wondrous to understanding is combined with narrative purposelessness, and consequently an essential category of the fairy-tale genre inverts into mischievous, "ill-fitting nonsense" ["*Unsinn*" and "*Unfug*"].

With each staging of wondrous phenomena, certain categories for fantastic-wondrous "nonsense" are "won." However, between the first two and the later two encounters with fantastic-wondrous nonsense, these categories are expropriated from the wondrous in order to be transferred by both protagonist and author to everyday life and to poetics in general. Thus, the metaphorical movement away from the wondrous is followed by its twofold return. In this return the poetics of nonsense will be pushed to extremes that can no longer be covered by the euphoric or the resigned "philosophy" of its acceptance. Instead, it indicates all the traits of a traumatic haunting. In one case, persecution by nonsense inverts directly into fatal insanity; in another, its anxiety-resistant "object," the protagonist Bluebeard, becomes at least so uncomfortably agitated that he wishes never again to encounter this version of his own "philosophy." By also venturing into these traumatic avenues of "nonsense," the arabesque demands and enables a still sharper differentiation of its persistent pattern. In the figure of Catharine, Tieck excludes the correlation of "wondrous," "nonsense," and "madness" from any tincture of "Romantic" nobility. Her stereotypical pathology reveals her to be a prop from the stockroom of the horror novel: "raised in a cloister," "sickly and of weak nerves," suffering from a "gloomy, melancholy fantasy" and regular crying fits, Catharine von Hohenfeld "from her childhood on was occupied with gloomy and strange objects." Thus, she is attracted even from afar to the "peculiar man" Peter, and conversely Peter also wanted "to give it a try with such a woman" (226). As the mistress of Bluebeard's castle she does everything in order to nourish her propensity for "the most wondrous objects":

> Catharine usually arose in the dark of night and looked out the castle's window, seeking to delight in the wondrous forms of the clouds,

to see the stars shining between them and to hear how the damp night wind passed over the lonely heath.

Thus she stood pensively one night and saw from afar a tiny little light moving and creeping along as though bent over the ground. She fixed her attention on it and thought she was also able to make out figures in the distance, swaying to and fro.

Midnight had passed and nature lay under the holiest peacefulness, when far away she heard quite clearly a pitiful whimpering, like a sad dirge. She didn't know what it all meant, and a quiet dread seized hold of her. (227–228)

The midnight hour, the wondrous cloud formations, the damp night wind across a lonely heath, pitiful whimpering in the distance: an ideal gothic novel scene for the entrance of spine-chilling ghosts and ghouls. That "Catharine didn't know what it all meant" does not imply here any legitimization of this deficiency. On the contrary, Catharine assuredly assumes and believes she knows *that* it means something; correspondingly, not-knowing the *what* of this *that* is merely the motor of her hermeneutic intention instead of indicating its reflected interruption. Her presumption of a wondrous meaning is quickly fulfilled: before her eyes unfolds the spectacle of her own burial; no less than "death" himself insists on leading the "black entourage" of the funeral procession, with a lantern casting a bluish light. The citational character of these reliable props and the entire wondrous scene, which causes Catherine to become "crazy" and "mad," could not be clearer. The equivalence of "wondrous" and "hideous" (229) keeps haunting Catharine on the following evening as well. In order to "dull melancholic reality," she asks Mechthilde for "a wondrous fairy tale and poem of fantasy." Instead of the desired sedative, however, she receives the tale of horror and persecution previously analyzed, which offers her ill-fated preoccupations a veritable psychedelic rush. She interrupts the fairy tale being narrated with a cry:

What dreadful nonsense are you piling up here to sink me into ice-cold terror? Talk of realities so that I can return to myself. (233)

Catharine moves in a circle: she wants to escape from ghastly reality into the fairy tale, and to escape from the ghastly fairy tale into realities—and remains everywhere persecuted by the same "dreadful nonsense" that in turn she craves with "an indescribable lasciviousness" (235). Her death comes not from Bluebeard's hand but from a renewed terrifying vision of her own funeral. In the mouth of this ideal victim of gothic novel trappings, the connection between the words "wondrous" and "nonsense" is not just stripped of any positive value while being shaded with the horrible and monstrous. That connection also changes its logical relationship to the theory of incoherence. In the reflections of Almida, Bluebeard, and the narrator, resistance to the category of "sense" goes hand in hand, in fact, is coextensive with resistance to "coherence" and "unity." By contrast, the "nonsense" that haunts Catharine has all the qualities of a coherent persecution complex; it is accompanied by an increase rather than a decrease in "coherence." Stated schematically, the "classical" poetics of coherence and sense thus has two avenues of decomposition in Tieck: one tends toward nonsense as incoherence—the "leitmotif" of the *Bluebeard* arabesque—and another tends toward a "coherent nonsense," which Tieck also classifies as the language of madness in *William Lovell.*[194] Just as Kant distinguishes the "methodical derangement" of madness that produces a "false" coherence from the "tumultuous derangement" of "coherence" altogether in nonsense,[195] so too madness is for Tieck not least of all a madness of sense, a compulsive coherence of sense. It can only be called "nonsense" from an ignorant external standpoint or, as with Catharine, in the interest of gaining relief from its excessive pressure. Yet in no way does madness cast the hermeneutical discourse into question. Catharine and the horror tale she was told therefore do not represent a *mise-en-abîme* of the nonsensical fairytale arabesque. Rather, they polarize nonsense into two opposing extremes[196]—similar to the antithetical relations that Benjamin analyzes between Goethe's novella *Die wunderlichen Nachbarskinder* and the itself novella-like novel into which it is inserted.[197] Bluebeard's, Almida's, and the narrator's devices of turning the defect of nonsense into a positive requirement are obviously supposed to be resistant to the neurasthenic threat posed, in the case of Catharine, by the connection between "nonsense" and delusional "coherence." Yet not only subsequent narratives of Tieck and E. T. A. Hoffmann, but also the second of the last two instances of the wondrous in the Bluebeard arabesque raises doubts whether a strict distinction can be made between positivized nonsense and its dark sides.

It is a goblin who demonstrates to the protagonist how unpalatable his own slogans are. Hardly has Peter explicitly sacked his mentor Bernard and hence all plans and pretensions of meaning, and hardly has the author distilled from this a poetics of the purposeless and incoherent book, when on his way home from a recent duel Bluebeard comes upon a goblin who right away spoils his taste for this "philosophy" by applying it rigorously. The goblin represents an inverse substitution for the genius figure who had just been fired. He offers himself as "servant" instead of "guide;" rather than great plans and a career full of unity and meaning, he promises pointless "spectacles about nothing":

> I bait scholars into having a go at each other, I invent the readings and conjectures over which they subsequently wage such noisy wars, I am the one who hexes up those passages in ancient authors that trip up even the greatest men, I invent the treatises about nothing [. . .] Furthermore I know other arts, continued the goblin, for certainly scholarship is not my only specialty. For example, whatever is on the floor I can carry into the cellar, and conversely I'll gladly carry the casks out of the cellar and lay them on the floor. But my greatest joy is actually creating rumors, so that a spectacle about nothing arises: I make a lot of noise and no one knows what should come of it, and in the end nothing really does come of it except that it roars far and wide into the world and still means absolutely nothing. (222–223)

Using the same rhetoric of senselessness, incoherence, and indifference toward meaning, the goblin's peculiar self-advertisement rephrases practically verbatim what protagonist and author had earlier propagated as their insight into human life and the basis for a new poetics: much "confusion," but without any higher "interest," "much movement and running hither and thither," yet "no lively progression of the plot" (220). Bluebeard, however, does not recognize the word-for-word return of his own ideology in the rasping voice of the goblin and declines the offered services as "unprofitable arts": "So I have no use for you" (222–223). As an unrecognized echo of Bluebeard's "emancipating" life toward not-meaning, the goblin defends the "stupid thing" of his arts even explicitly as a mimesis of the human model:

> To the devil, shrieked the goblin, isn't that enough? What more do you want, and what more do you humans do? I mean I learned this stupid thing from you people, so as to make me popular with you. You are an ungrateful people, and so full of your own wisdom that nothing seems right to you unless you do it yourselves.

The wonderful slapstick episode, into which the goblin then transforms Bluebeard's journey home, once again lacks both psychological motivation and narrative significance. Indications of persecution mania are not only neutralized by the comic style of the narrative but also by the final outcome of the apparition: the seemingly inimical forces bring Peter safely home and reveal themselves to be more like fairy-tale helpers. *As* helpers, to be sure, they are not at all needed, since Bluebeard was in no distress. On the other hand, it remains equally unclear what danger they pose to him in their role as antagonists, and why. The difference between the "normal" and the wondrous journey home consists solely in the degree of discomfort and fatigue endured by the hero. There is no abiding gain or loss, no indispensable function for the history of the hero connected to all this. To this extent, the senseless and pointless "rumor-making" that the goblin claims as his power does indeed represent a "spectacle about nothing," where "in the end really nothing comes of it" and that "means absolutely nothing."

However, Peter is not only too stupid to recognize in this wondrous spectacle a caricature, a fool's contortion of his own tirades against his genius figure, and in the goblin the inverted continuation of his guide. In this strange variation through the goblin, the leitmotiv-like "proposition" of meaninglessness, which winds its way through the arabesque like Kantian foliage or the ornamental flower patterns imprinted on wallpaper, finally comes into open contradiction with itself. For Bluebeard, the poetics of purposelessness and meaninglessness is founded in the very "course" of life itself and justifies the resigned renunciation of planned action. With Almida, this poetics is even linked to an emphatic philosophy of letting things happen. By contrast, the goblin makes this poetics into the purpose and goal of an active project. He wants to bring about what Bluebeard and Almida are content to let happen, and the justification of which—either resigned or utopian—they see precisely in the lack of intention implied in letting things happen. Lack of intentionality itself becomes an intention for the goblin, purposelessness becomes a purpose. Thus, whereas the preceding representations of the poetics of -lessness were haunted against their will by the paradox that they, in turn, create a meaning and a coherence, with the goblin the self-thwarting of the positive deficiency is integrated, as the negative presence of what should be lacking, even into the intentionality of his character.

Yet the more the goblin "gobbles up" Bluebeard's and Almida's "philosophy" in the willful repetition of their categories, the more he tends to agree with the author's own reflections. The author dedicates himself, as does the goblin, to an (anti-)poetics and hence ultimately a *poiein*, a making, an active producing of the pointless and incoherent book. To be sure, Tieck repeatedly tries to save his authorship from this paradox by describing it, in terms of the traditional model of inspiration, as a purely passive occurrence where the author is a mere conduit. Writers proceed without a plan, Tieck explains, and thus are more amazed "than the reader about the incidents that come along" (185–186). The device "One word provides the next, one hero elicits the next, and the German reader reads it and enjoys himself" (186) even propagates a veritable poetics of pure metonymy, a composition in which—without predefined purposes or meanings—each word elicits the next, and syntagmatic elements are effects of relations of contiguity. However, this praise of the "German reader," who "reads" and simply "enjoys" himself without any foolish pretensions of understanding, is itself infected by ironical ingredients and, in view of its context, is not just an apology for writers of popular entertainment literature. Rather, the Romantic concept of authorship resists generally any commitment to the mere "receptiveness" of genius and emphasizes the active caprice of the writer. Accordingly—as we have seen elsewhere—the invocation of -lessness is described as an active emancipating act, a "shaking loose of saddle and bridle" (220) that does not just happen on its own. This act of shaking oneself free unmistakably has a goal, a purpose, and a meaning; yet it is supposed to make possible a work that "has no goal and no purpose whatsoever, and which contradicts itself at every moment" (220). Fantastic-wondrous goblin and Romantic author converge in the intentional submission to a contradictoriness that contaminates itself in and with itself, and that thereby ceases to be a simple contradiction that could be determined and checked from a position external to itself. Only in this way, by permanently thwarting the possibility of being itself without contradiction, can Early Romantic nonsense rescue its own "concept" from a twofold danger: either always working toward some sense yet again; or else sacrificing its borderline nature in order to posit itself as a system of elevated silliness [*Blödeln*].

As a contradiction that also contradicts itself, that is at odds with its own contradictoriness, the poetics of nonsense oscillates "at every moment" undecidably between self-potentiation and collapse. The Romantics called such a figure "hovering" ["*Schweben*"];[198] a suspense and suspension that annihilates what it potentiates and potentiates what it annihilates. It is in this oscillating rhythm of setting loose and (af-)fixing that the "redemptive" power of the fairy tale—which is always also a redemption from (mythic) constraints of motivation and meaning—gets transformed into modern poetry and literature. Indeed, the "wondrous creature called writer" through recourse to the fairy tale attempts "to shake off saddle and bridle" (220), yet he is not granted the chance to become a wild horse (again). As a Red Indian he only remounts the horse that he is himself. The "Wish to Become a Red

Indian," one of Kafka's "fairy tales for dialecticians,"[199] is a continuation of Tieck's wish to be an unbridled horse: "until one let go the spurs, for there were no spurs, until one threw away the reins, for there were no reins."[200] "Whether it is a man or a horse," Benjamin concludes his essay on Kafka's fairy-tale tricks for dealing with the forces of myth, "is no longer so important, if only the burden is removed from the back."[201]

§ 6 Suspensions of "Sense" in Genre Theories of the Fairy Tale

The Romantic poetics of the fairy tale and especially Tieck's parergonal circumscribing of Perrault's *Barbe-Bleue* gravitate around characteristics that hardly belong to our concept of the "folk-tale": incoherence, non-sense, lack of motivation and development, chance, and arabesque patterns. It would seem reasonable to consider this a deviant development of the so-called literary fairy tale [*Kunstmärchen*] belonging more to contemporary Romantic poetics than to the "timeless" poetics of the fairy tale. However, a more careful scrutiny of authoritative theories of the fairy tale results in a different picture. Again and again these theories discover ruptures in hermeneutical understanding and challenges to sense expectations that closely parallel Romantic poetics. Yet just as often they try, by interpretive countermoves, to take the edge off their own findings. This entails, within these theories, considerable discrepancies between descriptive and theoretical statements. Tracing these discrepancies through underlining some intriguing descriptive findings reveals a more than subterranean affinity between recent theories of "genuine" fairy tales and their apparently eccentric conception in Romantic poetics. In what follows, such traces of Romantic elements will be disclosed in the works of Vladimir Propp and Max Lüthi, the leading scholars on the fairy tale. An additional section is devoted to the structuralist critique, modification, and development of Propp's ideas. In this chapter the general hermeneutical problem of sense and understanding receives only indirect illumination, in light of the comparison repeatedly undertaken here between the two genres of fairy tale and myth. The Bluebeard fairy tale serves as the focus of all these genre-theoretical reflections, which therefore also evaluate the various interpretations this specific fairy tale has received.

Formalism, Ethnology, and Hermeneutics: Vladimir Propp's Theory of the Fairy Tale

Singling out 31 functions and applying symbolic formalization, Vladimir Propp's *Morphology of the Fairy Tale* (1928) has designed a unified combinatorial schema underlying all magical fairy tales [*Zaubermärchen*]. Yet with the elaboration of this schema Propp does not lay any claim to interpretation: "Naturally, it is not our business to interpret this phenomenon [i.e., the uniform structure of fairy tales—W. M.]; our job is only to state the fact itself."[1] Instead of an interpretation, Propp suggests that it is possible to generate an indeterminate number of new fairy tales by applying his schema of 31 functions:

> In order to create a tale artificially, one may take any A, then one of the possible B's then a C, followed by absolutely any D, then an E, then one of the possible F's, then any G, and so on. In doing this, any elements may be dropped (except possibly for A or *a*), or repeated three times, or repeated in various forms. If one then distributes functions according to the dramatis personae of the tale's supply or by following one's own taste, these schemes come alive and become tales.[2]

The production of "living" fairy tales by means of a formal text machine recalls those automata of fantastic literature that undo the dualism of "animate" and "inanimate." This fairy-tale machine, according to Propp, always executes the identical sequence of its plot functions not only largely without "motivations formulated in words,"[3] but also in grandiose indifference to the intentions of the tale's characters: "One may observe in general that feelings and intentions of the dramatis personae do not have an effect on the course of action in any instances at all."[4] As a result, there is also no comprehensible connection between the intentionality of the protagonists and their actions. Moreover, the comprehension of such a connection would not conform to the narrative laws of the genre; it would be an ideological incomprehension of the indifference toward (in-)comprehension. Admittedly, many fairy tales themselves produce this ideological "understanding effect" insofar as they superimpose secondary "motivations" on the objective plot schema. To be sure, these motivations "add to a tale a completely distinctive, vivid coloring," but they are also among the most superfluous and "unstable elements of the tale."[5] The majority of fairy tales, however, do not motivate "the actions of a dragon and of very many other villains" at all;[6] most of the encounters with helping figures likewise occur without preparation and completely by chance. "In folklore, reasons, or to use the language of poetics, motivations, are not required for actions [. . .] Quite often the development of the action depends on chance [. . .] Fortuity of events, which determines the course of action and its favorable outcome, would be a defect in terms of realism, but it is not a defect in terms of the folk narrative."[7]

The unmotivatedness of plots makes them incomprehensible only from the perspective of those acting in the plot, but not from the perspective of the plot itself. The plot obstructs only a hermeneutics of the protagonists, but not an interpretation of the plot and the genre per se. In place of the missing "motivation from the front"—psychological motivation from the protagonists—this interpretation offers an all the more rigorous "motivation from behind," an objective performance of the genre's rules oriented toward a fixed goal. Clemens Lugowski has shown how literary prose, in the course of becoming more "realistic," increasingly shifts from the motivation from behind to that of "from the front."[8] This shift conforms to the "spirit" of the hermeneutical view of literature in that it allows the reader to establish a continuum of sense from the psychology of the protagonists to the course of the plot. From this perspective too the Romantic recourse to the fairy tale contains a decidedly "untimely" momentum. It combines the triumph of the novel—and hence of a form that successfully promotes the law of motivation from the front—with the counteracting and retarding element of a genre that obeys an older law. The fairy tale's plot structure, motivated from behind, is far less available to hermeneutic interpretation; literary history based on hermeneutics has not even been able to describe it effectively. Being a reaction formation to the pitfalls of this type of literary history and hermeneutics, it was only Russian Formalism and genre theory between 1915 and 1930 that was first able to describe the forms of "folklore" without measuring them either explicitly or implicitly against the structure of "modern" narratives.

Thus upon closer inspection, Propp's rigorous organizational schema reveals itself not to be the mere opposite of the Romantic motifs of anarchy, incoherence, and incomprehensibility. Rather, his schema gives great space to "chance"—as a complement to its rigid universality. Not only does it permit, it outrightly prescribes the random choice of elements and functions, their triple repetition, omission, or variation, and their random distribution among fairy-tale figures. Furthermore, the schema does not claim that the sequence of functions produces, beyond a typical fairy-tale narrative chain, a coherent nexus of meaning or that it must be motivated in itself. Furthermore, it expressly denies transposing the factual functions and figures of the fairy tale into the ideality of an interpretation. All these elements give rise to the impression that Propp sees the distance his *analysis* takes from conventional interpretive procedures to be in fact inherent in the *object* of his analysis.

The *Morphology of the Folktale*, however, also performs a countermove in which everything that the compositional analysis at first programmatically disregarded returns in the conclusion. At the outset of the book, in the interest of constant plot functions, "the names of the dramatis personae (as well as the attributes of each)" are excluded from the analysis for being mere "variables."[9] Yet in the penultimate chapter they already return in the title: "On the Attributes of the Dramatis Personae and their Significance."[10] The advocate of analyzing plot functions irrespective of their bearers expresses the surprising credo: "The study of attributes [of dramatis personae] makes possible a scientific *interpretation* of the tale"[11]—where "interpretation" means the complementary other to the descriptive compositional analysis. The concluding chapter similarly sketches out for the classified plot functions the prospect of a "question concerning origin and meaning," which would proceed past the separate investigation of all individual elements to the totalizing understanding "of the individual materials."[12]

Thus, for Propp, compositional analysis does not yet unlock the enigmas of the fairy tale. He also does not claim those enigmas to be principally insoluble; rather, he thinks his morphology at best paves the way for a more well-founded approach to interpretation. The answers that he finally gave in his book *The Historical Roots of the Magic Fairy Tale* in 1946 are already prefigured in the *Morphology* of 1928. Quite in line with the brothers Grimm, for whom the fairy tale preserves "*Anschauungen und Bildungen der Vorzeit,*"[13] Propp claims in the *Morphology*: "The tale at its core preserves traces of ancient paganism, of ancient customs and rituals," which "gradually undergo a metamorphosis."[14] In another passage: "It is very possible that there is a natural connection between everyday life and religion, on the one hand, and between religion and the tale on the other. A way of life and religion die out, while their contents turn into tales."[15] After many years of research in this field, Propp sharpens his suggestions into a hard thesis: "Up until now informed opinion has maintained that the fairy tale has incorporated certain elements of primitive social and cultural life. We will see that the fairy tale is comprised of them."[16] With this thesis Propp switches from the formalistic to the ethnological approach to the fairy tale—for him a necessary supplementary move. As an ethnologist of the fairy tale, Propp has written yet another unsurpassed reference work.

The provocative suspension of the sense paradigm that characterizes the *Morphology* is not by any means retracted in Propp's genealogy of the fairy tale. Instead, that provocation is preserved in a twofold way. On the one hand, Propp widely adheres to a positivism that above all inquires into the origin of fairy-tale elements and plots and that only partially transposes the findings of its historical semantics into hermeneutical understanding. On the other hand, a gap opens up between the ethnological genealogy and its concluding totalization, a gap, however, that escapes Propp's own attention: his discovery that the birth of the fairy tale is synonymous with the eclipse of its "origin" and that the fairy tale carries on that origin only by way of displacement and "non-understanding,"[17] critically recoils upon the attempt nonetheless to win an integral understanding of the fairy-tale elements from this always already withdrawn origin. The distinguishing characteristic of the fairy tale, which Propp at once asserts and suppresses in his concluding summary, in the mode of "non-understanding" and the suspension of motivations, leads anew to the specific obstructions that fairy tales throw up against any advance toward their "sense."

In the second half of the 19th century, the ethnological interpretation of fairy tales had developed a specialty that was quickly seen to be misleading. It examined the fairy tale for traces of archaic ideas and rites associated with particular times of the day and the year as well as with special days like new year's and fasting periods. In this context, fairy-tale heroes were preferably considered to be personifications of dawn. As a rule, the recourse to time-related mythologies did not relieve the fairy tales of previously incomprehensible aspects; rather, it merely superimposed a conventionally conceived allegorical meta-narrative upon the otherwise unquestioned elements. Not much was gained for the Bluebeard fairy tale this way. Several authors have identified Bluebeard as the personification of the sun that pursues the dawn, or of the day that pursues the night with his sharp saber. Even a blue-bearded ancient Indian god of weather has been recognized in Bluebeard.[18] None of these associations solve any of the hermeneutical problems of the Bluebeard fairy tale and are far less evident than the narrative they claim to illuminate.

The ethnological approach became more reflective vis-à-vis its own procedures and more productive vis-à-vis the fairy tale, as it combined its efforts to merely identify *personifications* of diurnal or annual times with careful study of the ritual *actions* that were associated with them, and even more as the approach shifted its attention from the rituals associated with the natural course of time to those rituals that organize social life. Pursuing this line, the ethnological study of the fairy tale revealed traces of all the customs and actions that a young man or a young woman had to undergo before he or she were acknowledged as a full member of the community. Propp continues this comparison with rituals of transition and initiation.[19] Although the *Morphology* both initiates and represents the highest achievement of a new direction in fairy-tale scholarship, "only" the latter is true of the *Historical Roots of the Magic Fairy Tale*: it represents the summa, the most authoritative work of an already established approach.

In many rituals of initiation, initiates are temporarily excluded from the community (young women are locked up, young men are sent out on quests). Furthermore, these rituals are often connected with "ideas of a yonder world, of journeys to another world." These two characteristics "quantitatively provide the majority of motifs" of fairy tales[20]—this is the finding Propp's immensely detailed and persuasive investigations end up with. Rites of initiation isolate the initiates and/or banish them temporarily from the community.[21] Something similar happens at the beginning of the fairy tale's plot: "Any motive is suitable that will isolate the hero and turn him into a wanderer."[22] The transcendental solitude of the hero in the modern novel is anticipated by the archaic fairy tale in sharply delineated forms of social isolation: "The blind, the disinherited, the youngest born, the orphan, the errant, these are the true heroes of the fairy tale, for they are all isolated people."[23] Admittedly, the fairy-tale heroes usually do not betray any awareness of an initiatory purpose underlying their isolation. When the father leads his children into the forest, this is merely "a hostile act,"[24] and the fairy tale justifies it if at all with the poverty of the parents or with an evil stepmother.

The path of an initiate through a symbolic death includes circumcision and other forms of bodily mutilation, especially cutting off fingers, causing severe wounds or burns, and visions of being eaten by powerful magical animals. Once again the fairy tale bears the signs of all of these initiatory acts, but not their motivation and significance. When Bluebeard decapitates his wives, when the thieving groom even dismembers and prepares them as cannibalistic fare, there is no higher purpose to be discerned that the victims are lead to acquire through their ordeal. The amputation of fingers, the most common and often the only motivistic relic of these rites, is justified in fairy tales in a highly practical and rational way: robbers hack off a finger because a ring "couldn't be slipped off right away;"[25] witches slice off a finger, "so as to see if the boy was already fat enough;"[26] fairy-tale heroes themselves cut off one of their fingers when they need it as a tool.[27] Unlike the initiates, the dismembered or mutilated fairy-tale heroes do not undergo any "substantial changes." As a rule, they express no pain at all and at the earliest convenience they can be restituted to their former physical intactness without the slightest trace of the mutilation.[28] In the rite of initiation, by contrast, permanent bodily traces also indicate a profound change undergone by the initiate. Nothing could be farther from this emphatic ritual model of experience than Max Lüthi's dry observation: "The characters of the folktale do not learn anything, nor do they gain any experience."[29]

The situation is similar when a character is being eaten or burned. Images and ideas of an initiate being eaten and then excreted again are part of the mythological context of prehistoric rites: "Being in the belly of an animal bestowed upon the person who returned magical abilities, especially power over the animal. The person who returned became a great hunter."[30] The heroes of some myths therefore set about getting themselves eaten in order to receive the special powers. The fairy tale knows both the positive cathexis of man-devouring animals, especially snakes, and the heroes' being devoured, but never does it conjoin these elements with one another. Where fairy-tale heroes—such as *Däumling* or the seven goods—end up in the bellies of wild animals, these beasts are represented as evil adversaries instead of as helping figures. The best that can happen to fairy-tale heroes in this case is that they escape the beast safe and sound with the help of others. The ideas and practices involved in purificatory burning by a helping figure in the forest undergo a similar displacement to the point of unrecognizability: "in the rite the children are 'burned,' in the fairy tale the children burn the witch."[31]

In a highly persuasive way, Propp traces even the extremely concrete and yet complex attributes of the helping figures, destructive figures, and the ambivalent double figures—most of all the witch—back to ethnological data. For the interpretation of Bluebeard, two aspects of initiation rites are particularly important: the prohibition against entering (or leaving) certain rooms, and gaining admittance to previously inaccessible rooms as the means and goal of the rite de passage. Propp tries to map both onto the institution that in ethnology is called the men's house;[32] for women and uninitiated men it is forbidden, yet the initiates who have returned are admitted to it. Maturity rites prototypically establish a young man's ability to marry and result in a procession into the men's house; fairy-tale plots result in marriage and ascension to the throne, consequently in a procession into a new, larger house. However, in most cases the fairy tale destroys the circular movement that is essential to the rite: the fairy-tale hero does not return, as the initiated does, to his ancestral community so as to assume a new social and spatial position within it; the fairy-tale hero instead finds his happiness somewhere in the wide world and stays there.[33] As a consequence of this the fairy tale's counterpart to the men's house—if the large house or the palace, by virtue of its social exclusivity and despite the absence of any gender-specific admission rules, represents such a counterpart—is "transferred" out of the community and "into the forest;"[34] the fairy tale thus exterritorializes: it exiles the men's house out of the context within which it has its specific sense.

In just this respect, however, the Bluebeard fairy tale, like many classical fairy tales of transgression such as *Le petit Poucet*, seems to be an exception. In the brothers Grimm's and several other versions, the heroine, now wealthy with the inheritance of the dead monster, is taken back home by her brothers. However, for the plot only the successful escape is decisive, not the escapee's destination. This is proven by the majority of the Bluebeard versions, in which a destination is not even named and where various magical animals or objects instead of the brothers come to the heroine's assistance. This is also shown in the haste with which Perrault transfers his heroine out of Bluebeard's arms right away into those of a better groom and avoids any mention of returning home despite the brothers' role as helpers. Thus, the parallel that can be drawn between the outcome of both initiation rite and fairy tale is disfigured by a movement that displaces the temporal and spatial circularity of the rite into open, wildly adventuristic lines without return—a displacement that also maps the objects of social relations' spatial symbolism into modified coordinates of space and significance.

Propp's interpolations on the motif of the forbidden chamber and the Bluebeard plot in general offer exemplary testimony to the limits and dangers in relating fairy-tale elements to ancient rites. The parallelism he draws regarding the prohibitions between the men's houses and sacred spaces quickly comes up against its limits. The speculative three-step argument: initiation rites involve actual or imaginary dismemberment; forbidden rooms play a special role in initiation rites; therefore, ideas of dismemberment are associated with forbidden rooms,[35] by his own admission lacks any concrete support from ethnological data. Ethnology has not located any rooms in men's houses that held dismembered human bodies or even just women's corpses. It might indeed be true that in some cultures women could have been killed if they entered men's houses. However, the prohibition on entering did not have the character of an intentional test deliberately and seductively set up by the men, nor did breaking the taboo lead to the creation of "feminine" death chambers in "masculine" houses. The comparison also fails in that Bluebeard's wives are *always already* welcomed into the house of their uncanny husbands and are merely instructed not to enter one particular room in the house. Even the forms of the prohibition diverge in their most important aspect. Ritual prohibitions, no matter how unmotivated they may appear to be, are nonetheless justified by a collective tradition: either through a mythological narrative or through the existence of the rite itself. Bluebeard's prohibition, by contrast, is legitimated solely through his abstract personal will; it is more this particularity than the unmotivated character of the prohibition that evokes its transgression. In the face of all these difficulties, Propp can do no more than refer to a third-rate study by Paul Kretschmer and note skeptically that obviously "the search must go on."[36]

Paul Kretschmer, convinced that the "incomprehensibility" and "inconsistencies" of the Bluebeard plot could "not be original,"[37] presents a variant that is supposedly closer to the original from which the versions à la Perrault later evolved. Kretschmer's "original" narrative also unfolds along a series of women who are married and murdered by a wealthy and rather creepy man. Here, however, the test of obedience does not consist in the prohibition against entering a certain room but in the command to eat parts of corpses while the man is absent. The attempt to get rid of the body parts some other way fails, because when the sinister gentleman calls out, they instantaneously reappear and even speak. In response to their disobedience, the women are then killed, and their corpses collected in a room. The parallel is obvious even if in a strict sense any Bluebeard fairy tale requires the motif of the forbidden chamber (and Kretschmer offers nothing more to its understanding than merely eliminating the motif). Why does this Southern European relative of Bluebeard bring us to its "root"[38] and hence also to a complete understanding of Bluebeard? Because, Kretschmer maintains, Bluebeard's counterpart appears in a Greek version of the tale as the master of the underworld, and Greek mythology elucidates the custom of eating corpses.[39] Bluebeard is, after all, Charon, the Greek demon of death, who also has a betrothed at his side; in a modern Greek folk song, the couple's plates are described as "filled with the heads of small children."

One need not even ask whether Kretschmer's extremely scanty evidence that Greek underworld demons married and practiced domestic cannibalism is sufficient for speaking of "genuinely Greek ideas."[40] The Bluebeard-Charon parallel is in any case spurious. Charon does not force anyone to eat corpses or forbid anyone entry into a locked room while furnishing its key, and he does not murder women serially and stow their corpses in a bloody chamber. On the other hand, even in the version Kretschmer stresses as "original," Bluebeard does not once practice cannibalism but only demands that his victims do. Kretschmer's efforts to come to terms with Bluebeard's "incomprehensibility" thus merely multiply the "inconsistencies" they seek to dissolve. The resolute will to reduce the text to familiar "roots" and meanings leaves behind a rubble heap of uncomprehended signs in the wake of its failure.

Propp's perhaps more desperate than confident reference to Kretschmer's uncritical identifications is all the more surprising since he was aware of a more thoughtful attempt to interpret the Bluebeard tale as modeled on an initiation rite. In 1923 Pierre Saintyves had portrayed the Bluebeard figure as a teacher of magic, his wife as an apprentice figure, and the plot as an initiation into marriage.[41] Although Bluebeard, in possession of immense wealth and a magic key, may easily pass for a magician with a demonic touch, it is hard to know what his wife learns or should want to learn from him. Moreover, a marriage initiation or marriage test that takes place only some time *after* the wedding, is a rather implausible custom, regardless of the fact that Saintyves himself admits that he knows nothing positive about rites of marriage initiation that might illuminate the elements of the Bluebeard plot. Nevertheless, he offers something interesting concerning the motif of the forbidden chamber. He reports on initiation rites during which the initiates broke the prohibition issued by the magician and actually found the decisive helper in the forbidden rooms. The positive transgression of the prohibition is associated with an idea of kairos: it has to occur at the right moment in the maturation and learning process.[42] Both the kairos idea and the discovery of helpers upon entering forbidden rooms exist abundantly in fairy tales—but not in the Bluebeard tale, where the prohibition is absolute and where the forbidden chambers always harbor only murdered wives, not helpers.

Propp's ethnological inquiries thus end up in a highly ambivalent result. To the extent that these inquiries trace back an immense number of fairy-tale elements to analogous phenomena in archaic customs and beliefs, they succeed in proving the hard thesis that the fairy tale has not only incorporated "certain elements of primitive social life" but that it "is comprised of them."[43] However, "comprised of" does not yet imply "comprehended as" since the facticity of the traces is split off from the ideality of their "original" meaning and does not in itself provide any way back to that presumed origin. The emptied out and no longer comprehended signs gather into new configurations, whose rigid narrative regularity is inversely proportional—perhaps compensatorily so—to the demotivation, the resultant formal character of its elements. They survive their former motivation without finding a harmonious new one. The "non-understanding" of which Propp speaks[44] is not an exception or limiting case but rather the rule, and it is precisely this "non-understanding" that first creates the symbolic space proper to the fairy tale.

In his theoretical summaries, Propp repeatedly effaces the limits of his discoveries as they unambiguously can be grasped from his descriptive presentation of positive data. Exemplary of this is the answer he gives at the book's conclusion to his self-posed question: "But what have we found?": "We have found [that] the compositional unity of the fairy tale [. . .] lies in the historical reality of the past."[45] Precisely this claim—that "going back"[46] to a past reality provides an interpretation of fairy-tale plot and figures and an understanding of "the fairy tale as a whole"—is not substantiated by the material analysis. The path back to the origin is not only compromised by a counteracting movement but is already extremely fractured itself. There is a hopelessly aporetic quality to the past reality. The rites in which Propp searches for the "key" to understanding the fairy tale do not in themselves reveal their "sense" but only indicate the need of yet another key: "the study of the rite does not provide us with any key to its understanding; it is the myths accompanying the rite that give us this key." These myths, however, so long as the rite was alive and they were recounted during the initiation, represent "an extremely well guarded mystery":

> Only initiates knew them, they were not recounted openly and not communicated to Europeans. They were first recorded in a time when the narratives had fallen away from the rite, they were recorded late and by Europeans from peoples who had already lost the living connection to the rite [. . .] In other words, we possess only fragments of the myth that with the loss of its sacred character was already beginning to lose its form.[47]

The key to the rite, which in its turn should serve as the "key to the fairy tale,"[48] is thus constitutively displaced. Either it is secret and we can only guess at its existence or it is accessible to us, but then it is only a fragment of its former self, irrecoverably removed from the rite whose "sense" and "understanding" it should disclose. In view of the mythological narratives that elucidate the rite, this problem of the key may only be a methodological aporia inherent in the ethnological research of later times. However, in the fairy tale it concerns "the thing itself." For the fairy tale, at least according to Propp's hypothesis, arises at precisely the moment when the rite has waned and when only profane remnants of the beliefs accompanying it remain. "The moment of this dissolution from the rite is the beginning of the history of the fairy tale, whereas the syncretism with the rite represents its prehistory."[49] The origin of the fairy tale is thus precisely its displacement from an origin that is no longer recoverable and in any case uncomprehended. The contingent historical fact that the fairy tale has its "birth" in the irreversible loss and occlusion of an origin of whose traces it is comprised, becomes a "transcendental" condition from the internal perspective of the fairy tale: it has no chance of peering beyond the limits of its "dissolution from the rite" that is at once its "birth" and the loss of its origin. The fairy tale not only hands down remnants and fragments of past customs and beliefs, but the becoming-remnant of these remnants, the becoming-fragment of these fragments is the precondition, trajectory, and substance of its very emergence. In the mythical "vestiges" of the fairy tale, Wilhelm Grimm had already seen a movement of dispersion, a figure of defiguration: the shattering of a gem into small pieces.[50] If one pushes Propp's analysis beyond his own conclusions, Grimm's simile has to be read with the additional stipulation that the unity of the gem itself—the transcendental signified of the intact figure—is constitutively inaccessible to any originary perception.

Propp's historical-genetic "derivation" of the fairy tale powerfully describes the derealization of archaic social practices as well as the defunctionalization and decomposition of myths. However, the derivation does not explain why these processes are recounted in the form of the fairy tale and thereby fails in its attempt to provide understanding. Propp clearly acknowledged that the evidence of "sources of particular motifs" and even of their "coherence" does not yet explain why they were recombined into narratives and repeatedly recounted for centuries.[51] Here too Propp is far ahead of almost all other ethnological studies of the fairy tale. His speculative answer to the question "what does the oldest stage of storytelling look like?" once again bears only on that "reality" of the "rites" the fairy tale left behind from the very beginning:

> From the preceding we already know that something was narrated to the young men during the initiation. But what was it? The agreement between the composition of myths and fairy tales with the sequence of events that took place during the initiation suggests that what happened to the young man is the same thing that was narrated; however, it was not narrated about him, but rather about an ancestor, a father of the clan and founder of customs who, born in a wondrous way, entered into the realm of bears, wolves, etc. and brought back fire, magical dances (the same that the young men learned), etc. Originally these events were not so much narrated as dramatically performed in a stylized way. They also were portrayed in the visual arts. One cannot understand the wood-carvings and ornaments of many peoples without knowing their legends and "fairy tales." The sense of the actions that are performed upon the initiate is revealed to him here. The narratives equated him with the protagonist whose doings they narrated: they formed part of the cult and were placed under taboo.[52]

This theory, persuasive as though it may seem, obviously falls flat as soon as it is applied to the fairy tale. The fairy tale is neither a "part of the cult" nor "placed under taboo." It doesn't elucidate, explain, or accompany anything. Indeed, by definition it lacks the rite that its predecessor explains, and in a clear contrast to the myths, it exhibits no axiological structure deriving a social custom or a belief about nature from a mythic past. Even more: instead of explaining or even "revealing the sense" of a rite, the fairy tale distorts and obscures the eclipsed rite by holding fast to its remnants and fragments without understanding them. It conveys traces, indeed is comprised of traces, that it no longer reads, that narrators and listeners also (can) no longer read, traces whose virtual unreadability nonetheless is the constituent of the fairy tale's form and the condition of its readability—traces, to sum up, that do not so much lead to a reference to be discovered but rather dissolve themselves from that reference without ceasing to be traces. The fairy tale objectively preserves a memory of something that it subjectively cannot recall nor enable the reader to recollect, since this fall into oblivion opens up its symbolical space.

In view of Propp's own findings, therefore, the decisive question would be: why does the fairy tale inherit and pass on with such surprising constancy the remnants of mythological narratives, when it shares their axiological function and structure just as little as their references to real rites and when it does not understand their details anymore? Propp's book suggests at best two answers of broad and unsatisfying generality: that "beliefs," even uncomprehended ones, generally can "live longer" than realities[53] and, secondly, that the fairy tale "ventures into the free space of artistic creation."[54] In their abstractness these observations describe numerous literary genres, but they do not provide the genre of the fairy tale with an a priori of form and a function specific to it.

Yet in this regard Propp merely shares the persistent perplexity that plagues scholarship when contemplating the pragmatic function and intentional effects of the fairy tale. This unresolved enigma is all the more striking since related small forms like sagas and legends allow for very distinct pragmatic definitions. "The saint's legend [*Legende*]," says Max Lüthi, "is an attempt to make converts or to confirm a faith. Migratory legends [*Sagen*] draw attention to events that are extraordinary or remarkable; they are intended to shock or to teach a lesson. But what is the aim of the folktale? Simply to entertain, as has been claimed for too long?"[55] The hypothesis of pure entertainment, which after all derives from an all too simple consideration of nursery tales, is not easily reconcilable with the peculiar seriousness of the conflicts encountered in fairy tales or with the magical enchantment through its stylistic gestures. However, even the other possibilities of the classical triad of rhetorical effects—*delectare, docere, movere*—obviously do not do any more justice to the fairy tale. With the often observed lack of affect among its characters and its representational form, the fairy tale works against raising intense emotions. As to *docere*, it is hardly possible to perceive a gesture of instruction that could be said to underlie the fairy-tale genre as a whole, disregarding the fact that the "lessons" of many fairy tales are extremely questionable from a moral point of view. Propp ultimately formulates a variant of the *docere* hypothesis for the prehistory of the fairy tale, in that the archaic narratives explain the reality of the rite and "reveal its sense;" yet by contrast he denies the fairy tale itself this function without giving it any other.

To the extent that it sees the fairy tale spring out of cult and migrate "into the free space of artistic creativity," Propp's ethnological inquiries merely seem to lend support, even though with unprecedented detail, to an assumption repeatedly maintained well before Propp: that art emerges from cult and in the form of free play continues what was originally a social and religious practice. In all arts—dance, visual arts, music, narrative forms—this theory has an immense amount of evidence in its favor. Yet its generality leaves much to be desired. Does art at some point really occupy *the place* of cult in the fictive household of all human forms of expression? Or does the evolution of art rather lead *away from this place* in order to form a "system" of its own with its proper laws, contents, and functions, whereas the place of cult is abandoned, surviving only ever more rudimentarily in art or being inherited by everyday practices (as much in late capitalism suggests[56])? Propp's study of the fairy tale leaves these general questions regarding the theory of art and cult unanswered. The more directly and the more concretely the study relates the fairy tale to a past "reality," the more pressing becomes the question outlined above: how can a narrative genre constitute itself out of fragments of anachronistic customs and beliefs so exclusively, so enduringly, and so successfully, although it does not understand them (anymore) and—this is decisive—can neither (or not fully) accommodate them to the new historical reality, but instead leaves them untouched in their otherness, as citations?

Perhaps this question can only be answered if one replaces the "although" with a "because." In this case, the fairy tale would once again be diametrically opposed to myth: the same realia and plot sequences that the myths explain and expound are carried on as alien, unelucidated elements and are recombined without explanation into a non-axiological narrative structure by the fairy tale. Displacement and incomprehension would then be the conditions of possibility and, to a certain extent, the medium and connective tissue of this recombination. On the one hand, they would neither irritate the reader nor prove to be a merely temporary challenge to his understanding, because the fairy tale—in contrast to the riddle or enigmatic poetry—does not demand any effort on the part of the reader to solve the tale's partial incomprehensibility. On the other hand, displacement and incomprehension would be positively indispensable: they contribute to generating the effect that has repeatedly been called the mystery of those very fairy-tale plots that at the same time are so simple and clear. Above all else, the characteristics in question would have to account for the peculiar quality of "the wondrous" that shapes a preeminent "stylistic" effect of the fairy tale. The wondrous transcends our possibility to render an explanation based on the customary reality principle. The fairy tale, now, does not explain the wondrous from some other principle but simply posits it as something beyond comprehension. Moreover and paradoxically, the fairy tale makes use of the wondrous as though it were completely self-evident, consequently without soliciting any efforts on the part of the reader to understand it. As opposed to the way mythological narratives answer a need for explanation and a demand to understand, the fairy tale's sovereign intransigence vis-à-vis any hermeneutic reduction of its wondrous phenomena and stylistic mystery effect may even serve a need to *suspend* the imperative of understanding—a need whose role in the household of the human soul has been little investigated.

Propp's *Morphology* suspends the comprehension of the fairy-tale elements and their totality in order to make that comprehension possible in the first place. The theoretical statements of his second great book on the fairy tale claim to provide the "key" that turns this possibility of comprehension into a reality. However, the book's material descriptions, contrary to its theoretical statements, result in a renewed suspension of understanding. They lead to a structure that not only refuses to open up to this "key" but that fundamentally compromises the will to understand, which requires a "key." As a result, then, and conforming to Novalis's reflections, the fairy tale tends to drive the will to understand to the point of acknowledging a positive "non-understanding" and a positive "incomprehensibility."

The Comparison Between Myth and Fairy Tale in Structuralism: Claude Lévi-Strauss and Eleasar Meletinsky

Claude Lévi-Strauss has tried to reduce drastically Propp's contrasting definitions of myth and fairy tale.[57] His analyses of myth claim to provide in themselves and ipso facto a theory of the structure of fairy tales. Yet one looks in vain in Lèvi-Strauss's work for a closer treatment of the fairy tale. "Professor Lévi-Strauss," Propp could therefore sharply note, "is not at all interested in the folk tale nor does he attempt to become acquainted with it."[58] At least, Lévi-Strauss's analysis of Cinderella [*Aschenbrödel*] may be considered an exemption to this criticism: Lévi-Strauss reads the ambiguity of this figure as a "parallel phenomenon" to mythical "trickster" figures. As a "kind of logical tool" designed to mediate cosmological oppositions like death and life, nature and culture, or human and superhuman, myth operates by means of a spiral of repetitions. It replaces the strictly dichotomous "concepts" "with no intermediary [. . .] by two equivalent terms which admit of a third one as a mediator; then one of the polar terms and the mediator become replaced by a new triad, and so on."[59] The figuration of elements that intrinsically combine opposing characteristics is of preeminent significance for this procedure. Thus, the analysis of myths of the Zuni Indians distills the triad "Agriculture—Hunting—Warfare" and "Herbivorous animals—Carrion feeders—Beasts of prey" as a sequence of weakened repetitions of the initial doublet "Life—Death." With this logical structure, Lévi-Strauss is able to solve the "riddle" of why, almost throughout all of North America, the role of the so-called trickster is ascribed to the coyote or the raven: because both, as consumers of carrion, combine characteristics of beasts of prey (they only eat other animals) and of herbivorous animals (they don't kill what they feed on).[60] Fairy-tale heroes like Ash-boy or Cinderella exhibit a similar mediating structure: they overcome the opposition between beautiful and ugly, establish connections between opposites such as nobility and retinue, and rich and poor, and so forth. In both cases the mediating hero preserves "something of that duality that his function overcomes."[61]

This parallel, for all its suggestiveness, neglects an important difference in structure. What only a complex structural analysis can decipher in the case of the raven, is in the case of Cinderella a basic semantic pattern—one that directly defines the story's content and not just its "supersignification."[62] This accords with a second structural difference: whereas the mythical tricksters usually "mediate" the (homological) initial opposition only indirectly, that is, by detour through their weakened, displaced substitutions, and thus are mediators "of the second and third degrees," in the figure of Cinderella the basic opposition of the fairy tale is directly articulated and undergoes a transition from one pole to the other.

Algirdas Julien Greimas simply declared a logical schema he extrapolated from Propp's fairy-tale functions to be the very schema of all "mythical narrative."[63] By contrast, Lévi-Strauss at least sketchily distinguishes the structures of contradiction in myths and fairy tales. These distinctions, however, are still in line with the critique Lévi-Strauss directed against Propp's comparative definition of the two genres. "Nearly all societies," admits Lévi-Strauss, "perceive the two genres as distinct," and "the constancy of this difference" without doubt has "a reason." But this reason can be reduced from a difference in essence

> to a difference of degree which is twofold. In the first instance, the tales are constructed on weaker oppositions than those found in myths. The latter are not cosmological, metaphysical, or natural, but, more frequently, local, social, and moral. In the second place—and precisely because the tale is a weakened transposition of the myth—the former is less strictly subjected than the latter to the triple consideration of logical coherence, religious orthodoxy, and collective pressure. The tale offers more possibilities of play, its permutations are comparatively freer, and they progressively acquire a certain arbitrary character. But if the tale works with minimized oppositions, these will be so much more difficult to identify.[64]

The very genre differences that Lévi-Strauss concedes already compromise his attempt to reduce them to merely distinctions of degree. If fairy tales are "miniature myths" operating with diminished oppositions, do they really still use "the same oppositions transposed to a smaller scale"[65] or doesn't the material redeployment of the oppositional pairs also entail a fundamental change in the logical structure of the contradiction? The cosmological oppositions of myths such as "death—life" elicit a highly complex process of mediation, not least of all because between them any kind of reconciliation seems impossible.[66] The impossible is achieved by the very miniaturization of oppositions that in the case of fairy tales is a given feature from the outset. Lacking the myth's cosmological "initial pair," the fairy tale lacks the specifically contradictory (impossible) element of mythic opposites. The fairy tale has always already evaded this impossibility. It doesn't so much miniaturize the myth's contradictions as prescind their first level. Meletinsky moreover has shown that many of the oppositions characterizing the fairy tale are in fact proper to it and not miniaturized versions of the oppositions that occur in myth.

For Lévi-Strauss, in contrast to Propp, the relationship between myth and fairy tale is not one of "before and after, from original to derivative," but rather one of synchronic co-existence in which each form needs the other to preserve its "balance." However, the epoch of the genres' co-existence, whose material alone is said to provide a reliable object of research,[67] conceals a characteristic of fairy tales that for Propp is particularly revealing: its ability to radically asymmetricalize the "balance" postulated by Lévi-Strauss. Myths survive the disappearance of their original contexts—at least as a living *oral* tradition—for a relatively short time only; by contrast, the fairy tale's enduring narrative integrity and its ease of cultural transmission are not so much threatened as made possible by the loss and forgetting of its (allegedly) original meaning. Admittedly, even Lévi-Strauss asserts of the fairy tale: "Only its form survives, while its content has vanished."[68] In his ingenious "theory of the fairy tale" (1796), Wilhelm von Humboldt had already established the "completely formal" character of the genre as its "law" and even accorded this "ideal of mere form [. . .] a certain emptiness."[69] By contrast, Lévi-Strauss, on the one hand, regards this mere formality as an impediment to thorough research: "the tale lends itself imperfectly to structural analysis."[70] On the other hand, he sees even a deficiency in the form itself: "the tale [. . .] suffers from subsisting alone"[71]—without the complement of the myth that accompanied the fairy tale like an older brother in archaic societies. Propp locates the fairy tale's "origin" precisely in this deficiency: in its becoming pure form, its derealization, and its inability to understand itself anymore. Propp has also provided strong arguments against the thesis of a synchronous complementarity of myth and fairy tale:[72]

1. "All the folklore" of the most archaic peoples has an "exclusively sacred and magical character" that categorically excludes the fairy tale. Only in a later period do myth and fairy tale coexist as the "believable" and holy on the one hand, "fabrication of reality" and "lie" on the other.

2. In the "moment" of their coexistence, the *sujets* of myth and fairy tale are both diverse and belong to diverse compositional systems. For instance, classical antiquity knew "both folk tales and

myths," but never does one at the same time and in the same place find the myth of the Argonauts *and* the fairy tale of the Argonauts. When their *sujets* are the same, then the myth always precedes the fairy tale. (According to this logic, those fairy tales that do co-exist with myths yet differ in subject matter should be aligned genetically less with their contemporaries and more with the older, already "vanished" myths, making even the synchrony of both a simultaneity of the nonsimultaneous.)

3. The compositional system of myths and fairy tales—which for Lévi-Strauss is admittedly only of secondary interest—in a few instances actually coincides, "yet this observation absolutely lacks the character of universal validity. A whole series of ancient myths, indeed the majority of myths, has absolutely nothing in common with this system, and that is all the more true for myths of primitive peoples."

Thus, with regard to the comparative definition of the fairy tale, structuralism runs the danger of going too far with its reductions and homologizations, to the point of leveling out essential differences. It is Eleasar Meletinsky's achievement to provide the first structural study of the fairy tale that, for all it owes to his structuralist predecessors, is less rigidly reductive and renders more justice to Propp's works than Lévi-Strauss and his follower Greimas do. Meletinsky's works offer a network of oppositions more finely tuned to the fairy tale; they deepen the analysis of individual motifs and attain a considerably more differentiated comparison of myth and fairy tale (that doublet of oppositional genres that permeates the Proppian and structuralist discourse as much as it was a focus of Benjamin's thought).

Meletinsky constructs a first sequence of oppositions by making the distinction, as Lévi-Strauss did, that the fairy tale lacks contents involving collective beliefs. Whereas the actions of mythical heroes are mediated with the fate of the community, the fairy-tale hero's endeavors affect only his own progress. This opposition of "collective vs. individual" is reflected in the different degrees to which the hero forms the center of the story. In fairy tales, "the class 'hero' is contrasted to all the other classes, since all the functions are defined according to it."[73] By contrast, in myth other "classes"—like the community and the gods—can assume functions that are similarly important for the progress of the entire plot. The unusual role of marriage in the fairy tale emphasizes this difference. Marriage, as the goal of all action and the end of the narrative, is foreign to myth.[74] Mythical heroes use marriages or amorous relationships usually only in order to come into possession of the holy mead (Odin) or the hammer (Thor). By contrast, in the fairy tale this occasional technique for the transfer of goods becomes an almost exclusive end in itself. Being given, on top of the daughter, half the royal kingdom represents only an extra "personal" premium for the hero and not a communicative exchange of goods between social groups.[75]

Just as much as fairy tales, myths are essentially about transfers of power, displacements, and exchanges of positions of power. However, once again very different forms of a similar process characterize the genres. Mythical heroes receive a supernatural power by initiation or actions similar to initiations. Fairy-tale heroes do not enjoy such benefits. They are instead provided with externalized, "fantastic" substitutes of their own power: magical helping objects or helping figures that act in place of the heroes. In a complex rhythm of gain and loss, the mythical hero fulfills his destiny only when he bestows to his community the goods he has acquired or found and abandons his superhuman role in order to be reintegrated into the community that has benefited from his deeds. Myths can begin with the hero's gain just as well as his loss of power, and in general they end with the transfer of the acquired goods to the community. By contrast, fairy tales always begin with a loss or lack of power but allow the hero himself to possess and enjoy what he acquires.

On the level of logical analysis, for Meletinsky all these elementary differences in plot are not transcended into the unity of a constant structure. Rather, in the transition from myth to fairy tale, there also occur displacements in the system of oppositions.[76] In myths semantic oppositions function as "universal classifiers" and are usually recruited from the basic coordinates of the world's mythological "physics" and "mechanics": for example, dry—damp, raw—cooked, fresh—rotten, hard—soft. In fairy tales these physical and mechanical oppositions play only a minimal role. The set of oppositions is rather drawn from *interactions* and especially the representation of *conflicts* between hero and antagonists. In contrast to myths, these oppositions are much more subjectively and ethically shaded: "as indicators of the value movement from a negative condition to a positive condition."[77] The fundamental opposition "own—foreign," which characterizes myths as much as fairy tales, in the latter is completely focused upon the relationship between the hero and his antagonists, that is, the distinction friend/foe (well-disposed—ill-disposed) and therefore overlaid with the opposites good—bad and especially high—low.[78]

Thus, the quantitative miniaturization of mythical oppositions in the fairy tale, which for Lévi-Strauss was the fairy tale's sole characteristic, is joined by a wealth of qualitative distinguishing criteria in Meletinsky's work. Based on this more refined and differentiated procedure, the subsuming of the fairy tale under Lévi-Strauss's concept of mediation in myth must also begin to crumble, even when Meletinsky continually tries to conceal this. First, the fairy-tale hero only seldom has the traits of the mythic mediator hero. This is demonstrated in those fairy tales whose heroes most strongly resemble mythical mediators: fairy tales like "Frog Prince," where the hero along the appearance—reality axis belongs to two different worlds, or Lévi-Strauss's example of the Cinderella figure, who personifies the opposition between beautiful and ugly (pretty figure vs. ugly clothes) and the other oppositions associated with it. All of these fairy tales proceed to a conclusion in which the initial oppositions are not mediated (as in the mythical raven) but are actually *de*-mediatized [*ent*mittelt]. The Frog Prince loses everything frog-like about him when his magic spell is broken and is only pure prince, young, and handsome. At first through a temporary magical transformation, then permanently by hypergamy, Cinderella casts off the burden upon her beauty: her ugly clothes and her ugly everyday life.

The negative beginning of a fairy tale is thus not related to its positive conclusion like an unmediated opposition to a mediated one; rather, the transition from one to the other eliminates the negative elements for the benefit of the unadulterated triumph of the positive. This demonstrates the power of the fairy tale's tendency to valorize all oppositional pairs along the good—bad contrast, a contrast that is clearly too simplistic to characterize mythical oppositions like death—life or nature—culture. This also confirms the structural significance inherent in the fact that fairy-tale heroes, unlike their mythical counterparts, usually do not return to their social starting point and hence the world of initial opposition, but instead completely abandon it for the sake of making their fortune elsewhere—a non-return that entails an abstract negation and ultimately a complete erasure of the heroes' origins. This transfer, this "complete separation of the hero from his initial situation"[79] imparts traits of *de-mediatization* [*Entmittlung*] to the fairy tale's movement of mediating oppositions, that is, traits of complete effacement and removal of one pole of the oppositions.

On the level of more abstract structural schematization, Meletinsky, by remaining closer to the material, avoids the extremely "hard" theorizations à la Lévi-Strauss and Greimas. His studies of motifs and his comparative formal analyses are more prolegomena to a yet unfinished theory of the fairy tale than the theory itself. Those particular elements of this theory that have already received more detailed elaboration predominantly offer variations of Lévi-Strauss's theory. Thus, it reads for instance, "The fairytale herewith appears on a very abstract thematic level as a distinct hierarchic structure of binary terms, the last one or pair of which has to have positive meaning."[80] Applying further steps of abstraction, Meletinsky distilled from formulae of this sort the single "universal" principle that he stipulates in summarizing his findings: "the principle of tale balance." "Everything in the system of oppositions which organizes the tale world and structures each episode rests on action and reaction, forming paired elements with opposite characteristics."[81] In the thin air of this universal principle, the differences between myth and fairy tale are just as leveled out as the differences between pairedness and logical opposition. At the same time, an addendum is required in the form of a second universal principle that would explain why the balance of oppositions does not produce a mere zero-sum game of pole and anti-pole but instead unfolds in a telos-oriented course of events.[82]

Nonetheless, Meletinsky's extremely abstract principle of balance touches upon the challenge to understanding that many fairy-tale elements issue to their reader. In view of the figures' specific rules of behavior, this principle succeeds at least inchoately in making incomprehension reflexive and in incorporating it into the theory. Thus, for instance, the strict rule according to which the hero or heroine violates every prohibition and follows up on every positive command or suggestion to act, be it even from the part of the antagonist, represents for Meletinsky one of the numerous "rules of the game" that obey the general rule of balance. To be sure, acceptance is not as plausible a balancing counterpart to a suggestion or command to act as transgression is to prohibition; for carrying out the action rather intensifies and reinforces the command instead of balancing it out with a counterweight. Nonetheless, it appears to be legitimate to speak of a "certain formalism in the system of behavior," anyway.[83] Even when in many cases secondary motivations are superimposed upon it, this formalism in the behavior of the protagonists provides further indication that the fairy tale is myth's sense-indifferent complement. Whereas the behavioral rules in myths are wholly characterized by social customs and beliefs, in the fairy tale they are precisely detached from such collective motivations and "have the character of rules of the game to a much higher degree than in myth."[84] Thus, on the one hand, the behavioral rules are less constrained: vis-à-vis reality and its norms; and on the other hand, they are more constrained: by the laws of the narrative form itself.

Game rules are pure positings. They are a medium and effect of the performative force of a genre; as such, they need not be interpreted but rather are simply carried out and imitated. To the extent that the fairy tale is characterized by an inherent formalism of its form as an index of its "emancipation" from mythical motivations, the narration and reception of the fairy tale create enduring difficulties for hermeneutical understanding. However, in a second reflection, even game rules are accessible to a hermeneutical inquiry into their "projection of a world" or their characteristic "intellectual activity" (Jolles). In view of the fairy tale, this leads to the problem of understanding the non-understanding and the very emptying out of meaning. Meletinsky offers here a historical model (the relation between myth and fairy tale) as well as a structural model (the principle of balance). Both at least tangentially and indirectly touch upon the Romantic formulation that freedom from sense is the particular "sense" of the fairy tale.

Hermeneutics and the Description of Style: Max Lüthi's Generic Definition of the Fairy Tale

Vladimir Propp occasionally spoke of a hypothetical "third volume" of his research on fairy tales.[85] Its field of focus was to include the "choice of linguistic means." For Propp "this highly rich area is not subject to the morphologist's study."[86] However, since "the folk tale is not a work of art only because of its composition,"[87] Propp concluded, "the *style* of the fairy tale is a phenomenon that must be studied separately."[88] This is exactly what Max Lüthi undertook in his brilliant study *The European Folk-tale—Form and Essence*, published in 1947. Admittedly, it is not only written without familiarity with Propp's works (for neither of Propp's books were yet available in a Western language), but it also approaches the problem of style at a "deeper" level: in Propp's first level instead of his third. For Lüthi the style of the fairy tale is itself of morphological relevance rather than merely lending an individual color to the preexistent compositional schema: both "form and essence" of the genre are therefore to be disclosed from the style. The analysis Lüthi carried out fulfills this claim to a considerable degree.[89] First, at the descriptive level, it classifies stylistic gestures and effects of the fairy tale into five fundamental representational devices. It is only in the concluding sixth chapter that the question is explicitly raised concerning the "significance" of the stylistic characteristics that have been analyzed. As in Propp's case,

Lüthi's concluding theoretical statements slip back behind the achievements of his descriptions and forcibly construe an ideal, indeed an ideological, common denominator that attests much more to a traditional need for synthesis than to the ability to satisfy it. However, within his descriptive chapters he implicitly articulated a meta-hermeneutical problematic that in its radicalness nearly meets Romantic formulations and in its refinement supersedes Propp's similar meditations.

The hero of the fairy tale, by contrast with the hero of legend or the initiate, interacts with supernatural powers and wondrous helpers without any shyness, inhibitions, or second thoughts. The "gap separating the everyday world from the world of the supernatural," the feeling of "an other dimension," is missing.[90] This "one-dimensionality" of the fairy tale is a reflection of its general "flat, surface-like character": "In its essence and in every sense, the folktale lacks the dimension of depth. Its characters are figures without corporeality, without inner and exterior worlds." The same holds for the fairy tale's world of "flat" or even "linear objects": in these "staffs, rings, keys, swords, rifles, animal hairs, feathers," a "corporeal extension" is hardly perceptible. By contrast, the legend with its kettles, pans, pitchers, mugs, plows, cow bells, and loaves of bread exhibits "objects of pronounced spatial depth." Along with spatiality, the fairy tale's objects also lack temporal and social dimensions of depth: "They do not bear the signs of active daily use; they are not embedded in the living space of their owner but remain isolated in themselves."[91] Similar things can be said about the fairy tale's figures, who hardly express feelings and whose bodies resemble "paper figures from which anything at all could be cut off without causing a substantial change."[92] When it does come to changes in these dimensionless objects and figures, the transformations happen "mechanistically and suddenly, [. . . they] do not give rise to a sense of development, of a process of becoming, growing, or vanishing, a sense of any passage of time."[93] Time is punctuated into leaps within a surface, every continual "interrelation and succession is magically transformed into a static juxtaposition."[94] This game of "surfaces" without "depth"[95] produces the fairy tale's "abstract style" that Lüthi expounds very nicely through a comparison with painting:

> The exterior of a body [in sculpture] constantly informs us of a hidden interior, whereas a flat surface is isolated in and of itself. A painting can either obscure or intensify the unrealistic character of the pure plane. It can simulate curves, three-dimensionality, and reality, and it can make the flat surface appear to have a depth. But a painting can also permit the flat quality to stand by itself and can emphasize it by means of geometric lines and stark colors. The folktale follows this latter approach.[96]

The fairy tale takes this course: by preferring "inflexible material" with "sharp contours" and a metallic or mineral shine—"gems and pearls, or metal rings, keys, or bells, or golden gowns, hair, or feathers occur in almost every folktale;" by spreading "clear, ultra-pure colors" on its surface (gold, silver, red, black, white); and by unfolding the "plot-line" as well "with sharpness and definition."[97] This sharp contouring, which employs rigid forms and extreme contrasts, can be found in a number of plot elements—for example, in the precise correspondence between a difficult task and magic help, the strict prohibitions as well as the severe punishments, the rigid formulae as well as the stark oppositions between good and evil, rich and poor, and giant and dwarf. "Miracles" are the "quintessence" and "most pointed expression" of this abstract style[98] as a schematism that without effort and with mechanical suddenness brings the dead to life and makes the blind see or lets the gravest desperation turn into complete happiness.

All of these elements lend the fairy-tale sharpness, definition, clarity, and ease but by no means an increased intelligibility of the figures and actions. On the contrary, the intention of the form toward depthless clarity and definition means that the figures and many contexts become rather opaque and obscure in their superficiality. The clarity of the exterior becomes dissociated from any clarity of an "interior" that in any case is absorbed into the one-dimensional surface. This applies all the more as the fairy tale merely names and posits its most wondrous elements and agents "without ever revealing the basis and nature of their existence."[99] The fairy tale "does not motivate or explain anything"; it leaves the threads that lead to the respective plot elements in obscurity; Lüthi therefore speaks "of a fundamental obtuseness of all fairy-tale motifs."[100] The external clarity and definition in shape that characterize both elements and plot lines of fairy tales therefore correlate with their lack of motivation, reason, and (hermeneutic) definition. To put it paradoxically: the more unfounded and unmotivated, the clearer and the sharper the fairy tale unfolds its line. Lüthi's basic definition, according to which the fairy tale levels the (metaphysical) opposition between this world and the world beyond, between corporeal or psychological surface and depth, pushes both the ritual model of initiation and the hermeneutic model of understanding to their limits. Initiation bridges the gulf between the two worlds: the initiate journeys into another world and returns from it transformed. In a similar vein, the business of hermeneuts is largely understood as a journey from the surface, from the signs of a text, to the "depth" of its meaning and its sense. Although he himself does not draw this conclusion, Lüthi's concept of a surface without depth subverts both these models.

Propp had already recognized that the figures' intentions have no influence on the course of the plot and hence are nothing but elements of the tale's phenomenal surface instead of bearing on any dimension of depth underlying that surface. Beyond that, Lüthi observes that in a completely non-psychological sense, "the unity of the protagonist is split" by the definiteness of the individual plot sequences. Attributes are given almost at random, discarded, or forgotten without the slightest concern about consistency—not because of "lack of representational skills or clumsiness" but because of the "highly developed sense of form" underlying the "isolating style that permeates everything":

> The fairy tale isolates people, objects, and episodes, and each character is just as foreign to himself as the individual characters are to one another. What the princess did or desired at another time and in another context, need not play the slightest role in what she does and desires now.[101]

The isolation of the figures thus not only characterizes the beginning of the plot but is a structural characteristic of the genre's elements in general, a condition for the sharp—because abstract—connections and divisions that account for the far-reaching plot line of the fairy tale: "Only that which is not rooted anywhere, neither by external relationships nor by ties to its own inner being, can enter any association at any time and then just as easily break it off again. Conversely, isolation acquires its meaning only through the ability to form connections in every direction."[102] By virtue of this structure, the fairy tale dissociates itself radically from the archaic social structure characterized by strong external and internal bonds—the social structure within which the fairy tale arose. Lüthi's description accords better with the modern metropolitan life of abstractly free individuals and the electronic combination of "visible isolation" and "invisible interconnection of all things"[103] in computer networks than it does with any ethnological construction of archaic societies.

In view of these general results of stylistic analysis—one-dimensional flatness, unfounded positionality, unmotivated clarity, and isolating syntagmatics—there is nothing surprising for Lüthi in the scandal encountered by ethnological studies of the fairy tale: that the fairy tale no longer understands the elements of which it is comprised, but rather "empties" them out and eludes understanding. This scandal only uncovers in a negative perspective what positively defines the self-constitution of the form: "The folktale no longer understands its own symbols (or, better, the symbols that it employs) [. . .] Those who tell or listen to the folktale usually do not understand it, either."[104] Nor do they need to understand them: this is precisely the relief that Lüthi's genre theory offers. Only ethnology is able "to discover" the "old rites, customs, practices"—whose omnipresence in fairy tales as proven by Propp admittedly was unknown to Lüthi. Ironically, this very discovery makes ethnology *mis*read the fairy tale. To the extent that it retraces the displaced and discarded material contents to its presumably original form and meaning, it runs the danger of missing the fairy tale's essential form of non-understanding: "When a fairy tale hero is locked into a chest, a trunk, or basket, this may well derive from a rite of initiation. But there is no immediate sense of all this in the fairy tale. Towers, chests, trunks, and extreme tasks all function again as elements of the fairy tale's abstract style."[105] Lüthi does not compensate for the intransigence and insouciance that the fairy tale and its reception betray vis-à-vis the non-understanding of its symbols; he does not care about recovering their forgotten "origins" or revealing any new symbolic meaning. Rather, he leaves them in their insensible materiality—as tower, box, trunk, difficult task—and in this "pure surface quality" devoid of meaning reads them as functions of the fairy tale's stylistic a priori. Thus, is the non-understanding once again understood? Is it subjected to understanding? No, to the extent that the emptied-out relics and citations are not laden with a new symbolic cargo. Yes, to the extent that their "emptiness" and incomprehensibility are thus displaced from the level of the semantics of individual elements to the symbolic level of style: that the sting of non-understanding vanishes, or better, that the de facto absent provocation by this non-understanding doesn't even appear as a problem anymore. The fairy tale's irrevocable displacement from its (supposed) origins and the evacuation and derealization of its archaic relics were recognized well before Lüthi by scholars of the genre such as Friedrich Panzer[106] or Friedrich von der Leyen,[107] but only in negative terms. It was Lüthi's stylistic analysis that was first able to explain the same phenomena in positive terms, as the means to obtain a specific clarity of a sort that is even promoted by non-understanding. Wolfgang Mohr has translated Lüthi's findings into a more semiotic terminology:

> Regardless of whether we want to investigate the etymological origins of the fairy tale in myth, heroic saga, or something else, it has abandoned these origins like a word that is restrained to a gesture of signifying which no longer arrives at any "meaning," and being devoid of meaning asks to be taken as a pure form, like a foreign word that seduces us into repeatedly pronouncing it.[108]

The most appropriate interpretation of this depthless, clear, and opaque fairy-tale surface is to repeat it in narration (or reading)—

not only for reasons of social pragmatics but because of the particularities of the form itself. In Plato's *Ion*, acts of declamation from memory, of recollective repetition of the "pure form," were also called ἑρμηνεία. Modern hermeneutics' universalized will to understand encounters in this ἑρμηνεία its particularity and limitation. In this sense Novalis was at the cutting edge of fairy-tale scholarship and did not need to consider only his own or Tieck's fairy tales when he defined the genre by its critical relationship to basic categories of hermeneutical theory (understanding, sense, coherence).

Redirecting all attempts at comprehension to performing repetitively a mere "surface," the fairy tale's both sign-like and meaningless materiality indeed limits and particularizes the hermeneutical "intention" but does not exclude it entirely. This is because the "superficiality" of the pure surface, which refracts the hermeneutical intention, is also refracted in itself; it has more of a paradoxical than a plane nature. Its "clarity" is not based on the transparency of its elements but is in harmony with the opacity of these elements, which no longer understand themselves. It is just as little an effect of a thoroughgoing, meaningful coherence. Rather, it coexists with manifest deficiencies in "sense" and "coherence." This clarity is not all-illuminating and pure luminosity, but in the opacity of its elements and its syntagmatics preserves something unsolved: it is "clarity and mystery [. . .] in one."[109]

A mystery is negatively related to its revelation, to the discovery of what it conceals within itself: once it is solved or deciphered, it is no longer a mystery. Moreover, if it can be solved, then it never was a mystery but a riddle, a game of hide-and-seek, or something similar. According to Benjamin, a mystery is defined precisely by its unrevealability. Its "veil" prevents penetrating to whatever lies within or beyond it; indeed, the mystery *is* precisely this "veil" *in* its "unavailability to being unveiled."[110] Thus, in the context of mystery we remain on the surface just as much as in the one-dimensional superficiality of the fairy tale. This sticking to the surface is, however, charged with tension. In its resistance to unveiling and understanding, the mystery necessarily evokes an attempt of "getting behind" it, a hermeneutic effort—even if, as long as the mystery remains one, it just as necessarily frustrates this effort. The hermeneutical structure of mystery is this hovering, this suspension of the will to understand between the temptation or even the task of unveiling and its frustration by the impossibility of unveiling—a frustration that not only negatively amounts to a failure but also positively entails an acknowledgment of the mystery's "unavailability to being unveiled." Certainly, through its style the fairy tale lessens the impulse to seek revelation, to "get behind" the veil, because it is able to posit the mystery and the wondrous phenomena, for all the challenge to understanding they might entail, "as though they were completely self-evident."[111] However, one could not speak of the mysterious quality of the fairy tale's clarity if it did *not at all* participate in this hovering tension that feigns a difference between the veil, the surface, and the mystery itself just as necessarily as it prevents the positive uncovering of something underneath the veil. In this refraction and limitation, the hermeneutical "intention" remains a necessary moment in the repetition of the fairy tale's pure surface. That follows at least implicitly from Lüthi's definition of the fairy tale's surface as "clarity and mystery [. . .] in one."

In the concluding sixth chapter, Lüthi asks explicitly about the "function and significance" or the "meaning" of the described form.[112] The answers he offers do not maintain or even come to terms with the radicalness of his implicit hermeneutical reflection; they even partially destroy it. At the beginning, Lüthi ventures a formulation that in view of the fairy tale's surface quality and its abstract style, its indifference to dogmatic or realistic "bonds"[113] is quite logical, even if it fundamentally contradicts the expectations of an "archaic" narrative form: that the fairy tale "is a pure, purposeless literary mode."[114] Although Lüthi's numerous fairy-tale studies strongly resist concessions to "fashion," several of his basic definitions—the depthless surface of elements and words, the structure of isolation and random abstract relations, the poésie pure of the whole—surprisingly recall theories of modern literature and thereby invite to a comparative reflection. Lüthi himself did not articulate these associations nor did he pursue them. The dictum of "pure, untendentious literature" is for him no answer to the question of the "function and meaning of the fairy tale," but only a transition point, another way to pose the question:

> What function does an entity of this kind have in the context of human existence? [. . .] All other narrative forms can be traced back easily and without constraint to a basic need of the human soul, a unified "intellectual activity" [*Geistesbeschäftigung*], to use André Jolles's term. The fairy tale outgrows them all; its function is not immediately evident.[115]

Even today, its function remains as unknown as the question of the narrative form's age remains unanswered.[116] Lüthi's attempt at an answer clearly lags below the level of his stylistic description. This weakness is partly due to the fact that the critical attention devoted to Jolles conceals the positive wealth of Lüthi's own stylistic findings. Indeed, Jolles had ascribed to the fairy tale a unified "intellectual activity." According to him the fairy tale answers the question "how should things be in the world?;" it opposes the "immorality of reality" with a world of justice and naive morality.[117] All these categories play no role in Lüthi's stylistic analysis, but they all share the characteristic of being irreconcilable with Lüthi's findings. If the fairy tale presents a world of what should be, of morality and wish fulfillment, then its surface is dominated and regulated by an ideality, a dimension of depth that for Lüthi is impossible because of the genre's pure surface quality. Well before Lüthi, fairy-tale scholarship had acknowledged that naive morality does not always come off too well in fairy tales. Furthermore, Lüthi correctly notes that the model of anti-realistic compensatory satisfaction is fulfilled better by the trivial "pseudo-realistic narrative" with a "happy ending" than by the fairy tale.[118] Just as the wish-fulfillment tendency cannot be overlooked, neither can the "fading out" of the fulfillment itself: for in contrast with wish fulfillment in dreams, fairy-tale plots almost exclusively offer a hyperbolic presentation of the impossibility of fulfillment and break off at precisely the moment when the fulfillment begins.[119] Nevertheless, Lüthi does not break free of Jolles's influential definition but remains negatively bound to it. His definition of the genre's function and meaning relies less on his own than on Jolles's categories and merely makes an inverse use of them:

> The fairy tale does not have its origin in a desire to transfigure the world or make it more beautiful. Rather the world transfigures itself for the fairy tale all by itself. The fairy tale *sees* the world just as it depicts it [. . .] The fairy tale does not show us *a* world that is in order; it shows us *the* world that is in order. It shows us *that* the world is the way it should be.[120]

What does this have to do with Lüthi's refined stylistics? At least this much: the leveling of the opposition between is and ought, between seeing the (real) world and outlining the (narrative's) world, rescues the one-dimensional superficiality of the fairy tale. If the fairy tale sees the real world just as it outlines its own, if its narrative identifies the world that is with the world that ought to be, then the fairy tale's pure "surface" does not need to be investigated in respect to any difference to itself, toward any "depth." Then the narrative representation means nothing more and nothing other than what it names and posits with its formula-like words. However, this overlapping of a one-dimensionality of the presentation itself and a one-dimensionality of the presented world not only commits a tacit equivocation in the concept of presentation, it even destroys the structure whose function and meaning it is attempting to determine. With this, the fairy tale's surface quality, its clarity despite its not understanding its own elements, turns out to be precisely what it should not be, namely, a sign with a meaning: it means that it doesn't need to mean anything in order to portray the world both as it is and as it ought to be. In this way, the mere delineating of the fairy tale's world in itself attains a dimension of deeper meaning and ceases to be a pure "surface." To be sure, it does not "motivate," "explain," or "interpret," but it does mean a "deeply pleasing"[121] agreement with the world. Even the talk of a "vision of the world that demands nothing of us, neither faith nor avowal"[122] cannot hide the fact that this "view" no longer rests on the pure surface, sharp lines, harsh contrasts, and isolated elements but rather falls on a phenomenality that is transparent to an ideality and hence is directly accessible to a hermeneutical intention, indeed even to an immediate understanding. The unique "transparency"[123] of the fairy tale, which assertedly co-exists with the hermeneutical opacity of its elements and does not require any ground or abyss to "appear" behind this opacity, cedes to a traditional transparency that lucidly opens onto a depth, onto something else.

Thus, in the end Lüthi stumbles into the trap of aesthetic ideology: the trap of stipulating an intuitive agreement between the fairy tale's surface and its worldview. The fairy tale's "world of events that is blissfully self-sufficient"[124] is interpreted as a sign of the world's being in order, as a sign of an ideality (in the sense of immaterial meaning) that is ideality itself (in the sense that the world of "is" coincides with its ideal of "ought"). The study's summary appeases the world as it does the hermeneutical intention, that had been questioned and critically suspended by the stylistic analyses. However, the "material" part of the study, the first five chapters, is not completely resolved by the "ideal" part (chapter 6). The former stands in relation to the latter more as a corrective than as a precondition, and preserves a critical remainder that must further prove its worth in fairy-tale scholarship.

"Obscured Sense" and Interpretation Failing: The Reception of the Bluebeard Fairy Tale

The article on Bluebeard by Karl Voretzsch in the *Handwörterbuch des deutschen Märchens* provides an elaborate survey of the interpretive attempts directed at the fairy tale and the problems they faced.[125] At the beginning Voretzsch states that "sense and origin of the fairy tale are obscured." In regard to "sense," Voretzsch does not advance beyond that finding. Rather, he simply plays through the untenability of various "explanations":

> The moralizing explanation "female curiosity punished" fails from the outset: death for mere curiosity would be an incomparably severe

> punishment, the murderer is not the appropriate, legitimate judge, and he himself encourages his wife by word and deed to violate the prohibition [. . .] Likewise the historical derivation should be considered disproved: Gilles de Rais, executed in 1440, was only married *once* and did not murder women but children, whom he abused for ritual and sadistic purposes. The fact that in his homeland he is the subject of local legend and occasionally, in the Breton tradition, is confounded with Bluebeard, is of no consequence for the origin of the fairy tale. J. Grimm's idea that the murderer had wanted to cure himself by bathing in the blood of virgins is mere supposition: the murder of one maiden alone would have sufficed for that intention, and moreover he makes no use whatsoever of the blood of his victims. Even less valid is the mythical explanation: that the intruding dawn = the curious wife, the day that consumes the dawn = the knight Bluebeard. For the derivation from the vampire legend there are no clues provided. An explanation of the tale as a myth of death would principally be possible [. . .], but cannot be proved with the cannibalistic variants that surely are not original.

The author does grant some plausibility to Pierre Saintyves's comparison with rites of initiation (Propp's book on this subject appeared only after the handbook article). Yet here Voretzsch immediately reveals the incongruence between the ethnological material and the characteristics of the fairy tale. He underscores the lack, conceded by Saintyves himself, of cultic parallels for the specific syntagmatics of Bluebeard's "rite" (the connection between winning a bride/wedding, test of obedience by prohibition, transgression, murder, and collecting dead women in a bloody chamber) and therefore rejects a direct explanation of the tale from an ancient rite. He concludes therefore on a skeptical note: "There must be a connection here—but certainly not in the way Saintyves thinks." No other attempt to reveal the fairy tale's "sense" is discussed in more positive terms, and Voretzsch himself suggests no other possibility. His article henceforward is limited to some reflections on the historical "origin" of the tale whose obscurity in sense it takes for granted.

Today, more than 60 years after Voretzsch's article, to his catalog of interpretive attempts must be added above all one new variant:

the Bluebeard fairy tale as an allegory of patriarchalism and the oppression of women. It lends support to the feminist thesis of the "male gaze" that this obvious aspect of *Bluebeard* was "discovered" by scholarship only in the very last decades. The demand for obedience, for unconditional submission to male will, physical violence against women, and the one-sided distribution of economic power—these elements of the gender relationship that have been "valid" for centuries, if not millennia, unmistakably constitute an essential experiential content of the plot. Since in *Bluebeard* the wife ultimately emerges as the "victor in the struggle for life and death" and is "even furthermore rewarded" by inheriting riches (which admittedly is much less "realistic" and more along the principle of "wish"), Hartwig Suhrbier sees in "Perrault's La Barbe-Bleue already a feminist fairy tale."[126]

Yet readings following this interpretive approach also face considerable resistance from the text—even where they don't equate feminism with a victorious heroine. Almost all Bluebeard fairy tales are written (narrated) from the perspective of the wife.[127] Bluebeard's last wife, and not Bluebeard himself, is the heroine of the fairy tale; this distribution of the narrative's roles dethrones the male title figure from the very beginning, not just at its conclusion. From this distribution of narrative roles, however, only few Bluebeard variations have drawn the consequence—as is the case with Maurice Maeterlink's *Ariane et Barbe-Bleue* (1901) or Ernst Lubitsch's *Bluebeard's Eighth Wife*—to make the female protagonist the title figure. In Maeterlink the reconfiguration of the title directly derives from an ideologization of the content. In fact, he makes his heroine into a glorious women's liberator who quite openly declares war against Bluebeard and upon victory is even sovereign enough to spare the life of the pathological male. She must then, however, observe that her entire act of liberation was in vain, for her "sisters" from Bluebeard's forbidden chamber prefer to care for the wounds of the downcast monster than begin a new life. Yet neither the female perspective nor the fairy tale's conclusion can be read as an indication of a quasi-feminist critique of patriarchy without complications. Because of their genre a priori, their narrative laws and stylistic gestures, *all* fairy tales privilege the role of the isolated, banished, poor, or powerless figure—*regardless* of gender—and for the same reasons regularly bring them to a wealthy and happy conclusion.

Certainly, this "objective" form a priori is colored by additional motivations in each particular fairy tale, but great care should be taken in essentializing them into the ground or contents of a fairy tale. A study of the "motivations and functions of deadly threats in the Grimms' tales" concludes that death, murder, and the threat of murder in fairy tales "usually have an epic function, and form a fixed component of its frame. The misdeeds hardly serve to characterize the enemies," for example, Bluebeard, as a representative of patriarchy. They are "for the most part only *movens*, movers of the plot," and "arise from the fairy tale's preference for intensification into extreme limit-cases."[128] The fairy tale is as little interested in the psychology of perpetrators as it is in the victims "as sensitive persons with vulnerable bodies and psyches. No matter how horrible the deeds are that they undergo, their body and their soul are done no lasting harm. They happily continue on their life's course, whether they be turned into stone or mistreated, whether they had to sleep a hundred years or persevere in the shape of an animal. We never learn that they suffered from psychic illnesses due to deplorable relationships in their parents' house."[129] Both aspects—the absence of scars in the victims and the disinterest in the character and motivations of the perpetrators—hardly predestine the fairy tale to portray the oppression of women under patriarchy.

In the Perraultian variation of the Bluebeard fairy tale, it is the "good" brothers who cut down the murderous groom. The final sentence of the tale presents yet another gratifying representative of masculinity: Bluebeard's *nouvelle riche* ex-wife right away marries "un fort honnête homme, qui lui fit oublier le mauvais temps qu'elle avait passé avec la Barbe-Bleue."[130] Thus, there is no generalized critique of patriarchal masculinity at all: helpful brothers rescue their sister, a loving husband helps her to forget everything. Even the strange color of his beard serves to exclude Bluebeard from the circle of "normal" men more than to stamp him as their epitome and representative. By its hyperbolic disfiguration, the beard particularizes more than it asserts a generally valid pathology. If one follows Max Lüthi's genre theory, then the fairy tale's abstract style, which also includes the extreme contours and harsh contrasts, produces not an abstractness of what is universal but rather an abstractness of what is particular and isolated in itself.

Yet there is no need at all to make a decision about whether the color blue attaches a particular, if not deviant, or a general value to the beard's bearer. In order to be a "canonical" patriarch and head of family, Bluebeard not only has too much, namely, the superfluous blue of the beard. He also has too little: he lacks fatherhood and paternal authority. He has no family he could treat as his dominion: neither parents nor relatives nor his own children. It is no coincidence that none of Bluebeard's wives becomes pregnant before he puts them to the test and kills them. Lack of children is in fact such an essential part of this figure that the idea of a Bluebeard with children is a self-contradiction. Married couples in fairy tales either have children or (vainly) wish for them; by contrast, when Bluebeard destroys his wives, he is also destroying the possibility of children, family, and hence also his own paternity. He is just as much a child murderer as he is a wife murderer.[131] For the "classical" patriarch, to the contrary, children are not only quite natural, they are also indispensable in order to secure his power and chain his wife to the role of mother. For this reason too, Bluebeard can hardly count as *the* man, as a prototype of patriarchal oppression of women. Regardless of the fact that his violence tends to be a general pattern of gender relations, he obviously does not live up to the general role he is supposed to be exemplifying.

Furthermore, there is a fairy tale that provides a direct female counterpart to Bluebeard: Turandot, the murderer of men, who is called "Meerhäschen" in the Grimms' tales.[132] This cruel beauty and proud princess puts her suitors to the test, stipulates that all who fail shall lose their heads, and the somber trophies are mounted on poles and publicly exhibited. In one variation she even follows up on the sinister idea to cover a tower in the palace square completely with male organs.[133] A number of differences from Bluebeard remain obvious, though: the test takes place before marriage—which fits much better with an initiation model; the test is not forced upon the candidate; rather, he voluntarily undergoes it; the deadly sanctions explained above are not performed or concealed within a secret chamber but presented ostentatiously and provocatively to the public; the killing of men, in contrast to the uxoricides, is not considered illegal and itself deserving death but only a subjectively cruel variation of a structurally accepted power relation (in this sense, Turandot personifies *the* woman more than Bluebeard does *the* man); for that reason, Turandot is not punished unless that means that she must cease her bloody ways and marry the hundredth candidate. Does the fairy tale, in view of this, criticize male and female violence with equal severity?

It criticizes neither but simply uses them equally as appropriate "raw material" for the abstract stylization, for producing the contrasts and effects that characterize fairy tales as a genre. The fairy tale has nothing to do with a general critique of social role models. Rather, it accepts the traditional social positions like father, mother, son, daughter, king, and vassal as universal givens and directs its critical energy solely to the question of whether these "objective" roles are subjectively "well" or "badly" fulfilled by the individual figures. No matter how much the fairy tale imagines a social permeability that permits a peasant's son to become king, the hierarchical structure itself, of the kingdom as well as the patriarchy, is largely sacrosanct.

Compared to reading the Bluebeard tale as an hyperbole of patriarchal oppression of women, other interpretive gambits are far more particular and consequentially just as incapable of disclosing a coherent "sense" of the whole. Is Bluebeard perhaps impotent, and does he kill his wives because they make him aware of his incapacity and are witness to it? Certainly, the motif of impotence accords with the barrenness and inconsequentiality with which Bluebeard's lineage, with him as its last progeny, falls into oblivion. Or does the fairy tale issue a warning to young girls not to consent to marry a (repugnant) man in anticipation of great wealth? Obviously, this motif of blindness and obsession with external wealth also belongs to the symbolic "surface" of the fairy tale. Or does the story of the forbidden chamber evocatively support the prudent psychological maxim that each person should be allowed his secrets—even in marriage[134]—and that it is wrong and dangerous to intrude into a person's privacy against his will? Or do the corpses in the cellar represent Bluebeard's own repressed femininity, which perhaps he unconsciously even hopes to recover through his wives—while the helping brothers in a complementary fashion symbolize his wives' own masculine part?[135] There is almost no limit to the wealth of interpretive ideas—unless it be this: these sparks of inspiration cannot produce any totality of "sense" but only a "chaos" of particular fragments of meaning.

Drawing on psychological and educational patterns, Bruno Bettelheim has provided the most extreme allegorical reading of the fairy tale to date.[136] A striking misreading of one of the genre's general characteristics serves as the basis for a puzzling psychosexual interpretation. Although fairy tales in virtue of their stylistic laws tend toward extreme punishments and often enough to execution even for insignificant offenses, Bettelheim believes that "the nature of the betrayal may be guessed by the punishment: [. . .] In certain parts of the world in times past, only one form of deception on the female's part was punished by death inflicted by her husband: sexual infidelity."[137] Thus, a false postulate of commensurability (that the punishment must fit the crime) and a dubious postulate of realism regarding the extreme punishment lead to the conclusion that in his absence Bluebeard's young wife "had sexual relations. Therefore we can understand her anxious fantasy which depicts corpses of women who had been killed for having been similarly unfaithful."[138] Sexual symbols to support this interpolation are ready at hand: the key can be associated with the male sexual organ, its becoming bloody with defloration. Bettelheim avoids raising even the most obvious questions about the fairy tale's specific logic of this symbolism: is Bluebeard's wife supposed to have remained a virgin from the time of the wedding until her husband's departure? What does the irremovable bloody stain symbolize of the male organ? And above all: why was the misdeed of the wife so thoroughly distorted when fairy tales otherwise don't hesitate to portray female vice very bluntly in all its varieties—including infidelity?

Bettelheim diametrically inverts the distribution of the narrative roles of victim and perpetrator. Accordingly, he sees the tale as providing the following lesson: "Women, don't give in to your sexual curiosity."[139] Nonetheless, this doesn't result in a justification for the cuckolded Bluebeard's vengeance. Rather, Bettelheim "believes" that "the child at a pre-conscious level" is able to draw a lesson for male behavior that aims as much at moderation as does the one for the female side: "The story tells that although a jealous husband may believe a wife deserves to be severely punished—even killed—for this, he is absolutely wrong in such thoughts [. . .] Marital infidelity [. . .] is something to be forgiven."[140] One will look in vain for lessons in this sort of moderation in fairy tales, unless one plants them there as one's own "opinion."

In explicit contrast to Bettelheim, Maria Tatar has provided a more cautious and more balanced psychological interpretation. Her book too is based on a "realistic" thesis: the often observed fact that "fairy tales deal with family conflict" is used "as an interpretive clue to the text's core."[141] By underscoring that family conflicts form the material contents of fairy tales, Meletinsky had avoided such a hasty jump to their truth contents, and, in fact, doubts can arise whether such direct essentialization by dint of psychoanalytical hermeneutics does justice to the fairy tale's elements and plot functions. To be sure, fairy-tale heroes are regularly mistreated or cast off by their stepmothers, and they run their course from abandoning one family to founding a new one. However, at the same time, the concrete substrate of the family conflicts relates in an extremely unrealistic fashion to the social correlate of the fairy tale: the pre-modern if not archaic family structures. The preeminent characteristic of these structures, namely, the tight network within larger groups, is fully absent in the fairy tale. Grandparents, uncles, aunts, and their families are almost never mentioned. Instead, there are "post-modern" singles like Bluebeard—who apparently lives completely alone and without any family—and lots of isolated "modern" nuclear families, composed of father, mother (stepmother), and zero to three children. The latter case (three children) is in most instances already considered "overcompleted."[142] If one also considers that tolerably good mothers are mentioned at most only when they're already dead, and that the "solution" of family conflicts almost always lies in radically "break[ing] up"[143] and irrevocably forsaking the family, then it becomes highly questionable to what extent the standardized family constellations in fairy tales can be taken for real ones whose conflicts require psychological interpretation.

Against this background, Maria Tatar offers a two-fold reading of Bluebeard's forbidden chamber: "With its terrifying display of carnality, it could be said to give vivid shape to what children perceive as nightmarish aspects of human sexuality. But the carnage that meets the heroine's eyes could just as well be viewed as a horrifying emblem of human mortality, in which case the story might give us the heroine's recognition of death."[144] The second reading imputes a lesson to the Bluebeard fairy tale that is foreign to the genre altogether. Irrevocable death is encountered in the genre at most as a punishment for the antagonist. By contrast, the heroes are able to return from temporary deaths and even to bring other figures back to life—thus, in the Bluebeard variant *Fitchers Vogel*, the youngest sister resuscitates her murdered older sisters and rescues them from the deathly chamber—and at the end of fairy tales, the figures are released into a future of possible immortality.[145] Thus, the fairy tale rather negates and denies "the recognition of death" and "human mortality" instead of positively instilling it through terror. The first reading is less precise, while at the same time more plausible. However, like Bettelheim's study, it suffers from privileging the child's perspective within and upon the fairy tale. This perspective represents, as Maria Tatar herself has acknowledged, a later implantation into a narrative genre that "originally" or at least predominantly was cultivated in the circle of "adults." Furthermore, the Bluebeard fairy tale has proven in its numerous reworkings an attraction that predominantly lies beyond children's imagination, an attraction that without doubt is bound up with the spectacular and enigmatic-incomprehensible combination of violence, death, and gender relations.

Besides the forbidden chamber of death, other elements of the Bluebeard plot are subject to psychological explanations as well. Bluebeard's command, for instance, is explained "from a murderer's need to conceal the evidence of his crimes."[146] As clearly as the narrative function of the prohibition stands out—namely to provoke its transgression and thereby to drive forward the plot—so inextricably does Maria Tatar's psychological motivation entangle itself in logical obscurities. If Bluebeard were only concerned "to conceal the evidence of his crimes," he would hardly keep the corpses in his house but rather secret them away somewhere else: in the woods, under a field, in a lake. Apparently he wants both: to prohibit their discovery and also to keep open that very possibility, indeed even negatively to offer it. Maria Tatar's overall portrait of how the women perceive Bluebeard likewise does not fit too well with the tale's exposition of the figure: "The heroine's discovery that even the most exalted and noble personage can prove capable of beastlike behavior stands as the central horror of the tale."[147] This reading is not only at odds with most of the fairy tales of the Bluebeard type, in which the murderer from the outset is identified as a robber or an evil magician; it also fails the Peraultian *Barbe-Bleue* that it was meant for. Even here Bluebeard from the very beginning is suspected by the women of some kind of sinister and deviant behavior, and he is fearfully avoided by the rest of his entourage rather than considered "the most exalted and noble personality."

Voretzsch's finding, the "sense" of the Bluebeard fairy tale is "obscured," thus loses none of its validity in view of more recent interpretive gambits that ignore him. His explanation though, including the very terminology of "obscurity," remains dependent on the ideology of an originally transparent sense. Therefore, it is only the chaotic trajectory of the fairy tale's oral tradition that is blamed for disfiguring any unified sense of the whole by obscuring it with stark modifications and numerous secondary accents. However, since tradition is the fairy tale's originary mode of being and since, in the strict sense, the one "original" fairy tale exists just as little as the one and only genuine myth, the question arises: whether the "obscuring of sense" proper to the tradition and dissemination is not ipso facto proper to the fairy tale itself, a constituent of its "origin." Voretzsch admittedly does not pose this question, but in his reflections on the fairy tale's historical origin he comes to a conclusion that affirms it. His speculations on the tale's origin take their starting point from a dissection of the plot into two heterogeneous narrative kernels:

> Our fairy tale contains two nuclei, that are connected to each other only in a makeshift way: the idea of the wife-murderer who himself becomes the victim of the last wife he brings home [. . .] and the idea of the forbidden chamber that comes from another type of fairy tale. Originally, each has nothing to do with the other.

Evidence shows that these two nuclei of the fairy tale existed independently of each other: as a ballad widely disseminated from the Middle Ages onward "of a blonde-haired sex killer, who is finally killed during his last attempt," and as an element of oriental fairy tales (see the forbidden chamber in "History of the Third Mendicant" in the *Tales of 1001 Nights*). From this Voretzsch draws the following quite plausible thesis on the fairy tale's origin: the Bluebeard fairy tale emerged from the combination of a European ballad about a murderer with an oriental fairy-tale motif. "Presumably," Voretzsch adds with somewhat less confidence, the Old French word *bloi* = "light blond" only had to be confused, as it occurs in the *Song of Roland*, with *blo* (*bleue*) = "blue" and "also the name *Barbe-Bleue* is explained in this way." If one hypothetically follows this speculative historical puzzle, there results a complicated "origin" that is everything but a simple and pure source: the Bluebeard fairy tale "arises" from the misreading or misunderstanding of a word and from the "makeshift combination" of two elements each of which "originally has nothing to do with the other." The connection which makes up this origin is a fragile one from the very beginning. To be sure, it does provide a relatively stable narrative syntagmatics of the two heterogeneous elements—

violating the prohibition becomes the cause or pretext for murder—but it provides no persuasive and unified "sense" for the plot as a whole. It is both illuminating and obscuring at once. The "obscuring" of its sense thus has always already begun; indeed, without that obscurity it is perhaps impossible to think the "origin" of any fairy tale.

August Wilhelm Schlegel therefore took his review of Tieck's Bluebeard drama as an opportunity to polemicize against the assumption of a sense hidden below the surface and against the labor of "interpreting" devoted to it: "Adults usually already have too much in their heads to give themselves up to a wholly uninhibited play of fantasy. They cannot imagine that it is done with a mere, simple fairy tale; and so they allegorize it, interpret it, because they believe there must indeed be something hidden behind it."[148]

Reference Matter

Notes

Chapter 1

1. Immanuel Kant, *Critique of Judgement*, p. 319. Pluhar, p. 188. All citations from this work are referred first to the German *Akademie* edition and subsequently to Werner S. Pluhar's English translation (quoted as Pluhar).

2. Novalis, *Schriften*, vol. 3, p. 572.

3. Ludwig Tieck, *Schriften in 28 Bänden*, vol. 9, pp. 219, 220, and 223.

4. Tieck, *Phantasus*, p. 513.

5. Kant, *Anthropologie in pragmatischer Hinsicht*, pp. 214–215. Dowdell, p. 112. Translation modified. All citations from this work are referred first to the German *Akademie* edition and subsequently to Victor L. Dowdell's English translation (quoted as Dowdell).

6. Kant, *Critique of Judgement*, p. 190. Pluhar, p. 30. Translation modified.

7. Ibid., p. 244. Pluhar, p. 97. Translation modified.

8. See Kant, *Critique of Pure Reason*, p. 69.

9. Johann Gottlieb Fichte, *Grundlage der gesamten Wissenschaftslehre*, p. 227.

10. See Sigmund Freud, "Project for a Scientific Psychology," pp. 324 ff.

11. See on this Friedrich A. Kittler's works *Discourse Networks 1800–1900*, "Vergessen" and "Autorschaft und Liebe." See also Hans Ulrich Gumbrecht, Karl Ludwig Pfeiffer (eds.), *Materialität der Kommunikation.*

12. Michel Foucault, *The History of Sexuality*, vol. 1, pp. 95–96.

13. "Deconstruction" has uncovered in the idealizing element of understanding a metaphysical remainder, a reductive preference for "logos." Kittler's studies on the other hand focus more on the historical-social and technical forces that are inscribed into the hermeneutical field. The topic and strategy of the following readings are indebted both to the deconstructive and to the discourse-analytical work upon the hermeneutical paradigm. However, they offer no synthesis of the two "approaches" but rather select several of their elements and integrate them into a poetological and genre-theoretical analysis that as a whole is neither discourse-analytical nor deconstructive.

14. The German genre *Märchen* is henceforth rendered in English as "fairy tale" and distinctions from related genres such as the *Feenmärchen* [more strictly—"fairy tale"] will be noted in the text when appropriate.—Trans.

15. Friedrich Nietzsche, *Sämtliche Werke. Kritische Studienausgabe*, vol. 12, p. 97.

16. See Susan Stewart, *Nonsense. Aspects of Intertextuality in Folklore and Literature*, p. 51.

17. Gilles Deleuze, *Logique du sens*. The way Deleuze addresses nonsense largely depends on the specific linguistic features to be found in Lewis Carroll. Given the different literary devices and theoretical references of romantic "nonsense," Deleuze's findings seem to me inapplicable in the context of my study.

18. Walter Blumenfeld, *Sinn und Unsinn*, p. 110.

19. Stewart, *Nonsense*, p. 88.

20. See ibid., pp. 13, 60–61.

21. The word "absurd" is here understood solely in its colloquial sense; no scholarly definition of the relations between nonsense and absurdity is implied. On this question, see Wim Tigges, *An Anatomy of Literary Nonsense*, pp. 125–131, and Deleuze, *Logique du sens*, p. 49.

22. See Hans Blumenberg, "Wirklichkeitsbegriff und Möglichkeit des Romans," pp. 13–14.

23. See Gilbert Keith Chesterton, "A Defense of Nonsense," esp. pp. 9–11; Alfred Liede, *Dichtung als Spiel*, vol. 1, pp. 18–19.

24. Stewart, *Nonsense*, p. 206.

25. Blumenfeld, *Sinn und Unsinn*, p. 88.

26. See Freud, *Jokes and the Unconscious*, pp. 11, 34–35.

27. See Tigges, "An Anatomy of Nonsense," esp. pp. 42 and 45. Even the immense popularity of nonsense-making societies in the 19th century,

Kommersbücher [fraternity's book of drinking songs], student pranks, and the nonsense jokes playing on the stupidity of dignitaries [*Honoratioren-Blödsinn*] can be interpreted as a complementary phenomenon—though with a very different aesthetic dignity (see Liede, *Dichtung als Spiel*, vol. 1, pp. 145–165 and vol. 2, pp. 279–306).

28. Arno Schmidt,"'Funfzehn,' Vom Wunderkind der Sinnlosigkeit."

29. An exception is the excellent study that appeared after completion of this manuscript and with which the reading of *Bluebeard* in chapter VII below shares several resonances: Christoph Brecht, *Die gefährliche Rede*, pp. 55–68. See also Bernhard Greiner, *Die Komödie*, pp. 262–278.

30. See Émile Cammaerts, *The Poetry of Nonsense*, pp. 24–25; Liede, *Dichtung als Spiel*, vol. 1, pp. 27–72, 113–124; Dieter Petzold, *Formen und Funktionen der englischen Nonsense-Dichtung im 19. Jahrhundert*, pp. 55–58, 182–189; Klaus Reichert, *Lewis Carroll. Studien zum literarischen Unsinn*, pp. 14–15; Peter Christian Lang, *Literarischer Unsinn im späten 19. und frühen 20. Jahrhundert*, p. 107; Tigges, *An Anatomy of Literary Nonsense*, pp. 234–239.

31. To be sure, Romantic poetry also indulges in sound and word play; but precisely these can only with great effort be found in Romantic Nonsense Poetry.

32. Tigges, *An Anatomy of Literary Nonsense*, p. 51.

33. Ibid, p. 47.

34. Friedrich Schlegel, "Gespräch über die Poesie," in *Kritische Friedrich-Schlegel-Ausgabe*, vol. 2, p. 338.

35. See Lewis Carroll, *Through the Looking Glass*, pp. 10–11.

36. See Liede, *Dichtung als Spiel*, vol. 1, pp. 165, 370, 386–387.

37. Petzold, *Formen und Funktionen der englischen Nonsense-Dichtung im 19. Jahrhundert*, pp. 16–19. Wim Tigges, in contrast, considers any serious comparison of nonsense and fairy tale to be futile, but he presupposes a concept of fairy tale that is hardly tenable (*An Anatomy of Literary Nonsense*, pp. 90, 134, 137). A further weakness of his book lies in the comparison he draws with "fantasy," where the literature of the fantastic, "fantasy" and the fairy tale are hardly distinguished at all (ibid., pp. 107–111).

38. See Liede, *Dichtung als Spiel*, vol. 1, p. 386 and Annemarie Schöne, "Humor und Komik in 'Alice's Adventures in Wonderland' und 'Through the Looking-Glass'".

39. Rolf Hildebrandt has ventured anticipatory comments on this aspect, once again from the perspective of Nonsense Poetry (*Nonsense-Aspekte der englischen Kinderliteratur*. Diss. Hamburg 1962, p. 72). In the

later published version of his study (Berlin, 1970), Hildebrandt however removed these comments.

40. In his studies on nonsense poetry, Alfred Liede also addresses Tieck's literature of "nonsense," but the discussion occupies only one single page of an 800-page publication (*Dichtung als Spiel*, vol. 1, pp. 121–122). Moreover, Liede remains within the orbit of the older critique of Romanticism when he characterizes the related phenomena in Tieck as "vacuous play," "small-scale irony," "without consequence," and the passing whims of "harmless citizens and artists."

41. Blumenfeld, *Sinn und Unsinn*, p. 25.

42. See §14 in Edmund Husserl, *Logical Investigations*, pp. 522–529. Further Husserl citations in the following pages all come from this paragraph. Translation partly modified.

43. This quotation from the first edition of Husserl's *Logical Investigations* is not included in the English translation, which is based on the second edition. See Husserl, *Logische Untersuchungen*, vol. 2, p. 343 (footnote).

44. See Carroll, *Through the Looking Glass*, pp. 28–30.

45. Gottlob Frege, "[Ausführungen über Sinn und Bedeutung]," pp. 133–134. See also Frege's article "Über Sinn und Bedeutung."

46. Jacob und Wilhelm Grimm, *Deutsches Wörterbuch*, vol. 12 (= vol. 25 of the reprint 1984), col. 1542.

47. Ibid. pp. 32–46.

48. Ibid., p. 56.

49. Ibid., pp. 59–61.

50. Ibid., pp. 63–65.

51. Ibid., p. 53.

52. Liede, *Dichtung als Spiel*, vol. 1, p. 6.

53. See Carroll, *Through the Looking Glass*, p. 147 and Elizabeth Sewell, *The Field of Nonsense*, pp. 44–54.

54. See Clemens Lugowski, *Die Form der Individualität in Roman.*

55. See Wilhelm Vosskamp, *Romantheorie in Deutschland*, p. 186.

56. See Günter Oesterle, "Arabeske und Roman," p. 255, and *Kritische Friedrich-Schlegel-Ausgabe*, vol. 2, pp. 330–332 and 337.

57. Ibid., p. 337.

58. Schmidt, "'Funfzehn.' Vom Wunderkind des Sinnlosen," p. 247.

Chapter 2

1. Kant, *Critique of Judgement*, p. 315. Pluhar, pp. 183–184. Translation modified.

2. Ibid., p. 313. Pluhar, p. 181.

3. Kant, *Reflexionen zur Anthropologie*, nos. 932–934. See Giorgio Tonelli, "Kant's Early Theory of Genius (1770–1779)," p. 116.

4. Kant, *Reflexionen zur Anthropologie*, no. 949.

5. Kant, *Critique of Judgement*, p. 314. Pluhar, p. 182.

6. Ibid., p. 251. Pluhar, p. 108.

7. Ibid., pp. 308 and 319. Pluhar, pp. 175 and 188.

8. Ibid., p. 306. Pluhar, p. 174.

9. Ibid., p. 307. Pluhar, p. 175. Translation modified.

10. Ibid. Pluhar, p. 174.

11. Ibid. Translation modified.

12. Ibid., pp. 307–308. Pluhar, p. 175. Translation modified.

13. Ibid. (both instances of "must" my emphasis—W. M.)

14. Ibid., p. 319. Pluhar, p. 188.—In a version of this chapter published separately, I examined in greater detail the conflict between taste and genius, especially in its complex relation to the claim of their "fortunate" relationship. See Winfried Menninghaus, "Kant über 'Unsinn,' 'Lachen' und 'Laune.'"

15. Kant, *Critique of Judgement*, p. 313. Pluhar, p. 181. Translation modified.

16. Ibid., p. 319. Pluhar, p. 188. Translation modified.

17. Ibid., pp. 311–313. Pluhar, pp. 179–181.

18. Ibid., p. 319. Pluhar, p. 188.

19. Ibid., p. 320. Pluhar, pp. 188–189.

20. Grimm, *Deutsches Wörterbuch*, vol. 11 (reprint vol. 24), col. 1384.

21. Johann Christoph Adelung, *Versuch eines vollständigen grammatisch-kritischen Wörterbuchs der hochdeutschen Mundart*, vol. 4, p. 1276.

22. Kant, *Critique of Judgement*, p. 274. Pluhar, p. 135.

23. Ibid., p. 275. Pluhar, p. 136.

24. Ibid., p. 272. Pluhar, p. 133. Translation modified.

25. Ibid. Pluhar, p. 132.

26. Ibid., p. 273. Pluhar, p. 134.

27. Ibid., p. 272. Pluhar, pp. 132–133. Translation modified.

28. See Plato, *Phaedrus* 244a–245a, *Ion* 533d–534e.

29. See Jochen Schmidt, *Die Geschichte des Genie-Gedankens in der deutschen Literatur, Philosophie und Politik 1750–1945*, vol. 1, pp. 98–101 and 475.

30. Cited from Schlapp, *Kants Lehre vom Genie*, p. 251.

31. Kant, *Reflexionen zur Anthropologie*, no. 812.

32. Kant, *Anthropologie in pragmatischer Hinsicht*, p. 202. See Dowdell, p. 98. See also the *Reflexionen zur Anthropologie*, no. 487: "frenzied: an untamable insane person" and no. 503.

33. Kant, *Anthropologie in pragmatischer Hinsicht*, p. 225. See Dowdell, p. 124.

34. Kant, *Reflexionen zur Anthropologie*, no. 487.

35. This move certainly presupposes, however, that the poles of nonsense and madness do not in themselves undergo a semantic change at the moment when the notion of genius is shifted from one pole to the other.

36. See Kant, *Reflexionen zur Anthropologie*, nos. 487, 488, 499, 503, 504, 521, 1505, 1506.

37. Ibid., no. 504.

38. Kant, *Anthropologie in pragmatischer Hinsicht*, pp. 214–215. See Dowdell, p. 112.

39. See Tieck, *Schriften*, vol. 9, p. 220 and Novalis, *Schriften*, vol. 3, p. 572.

40. Kant, *Critique of Judgement*, p. 183. Pluhar, p. 23.

41. Ibid., p. 184. Pluhar, p. 23.

42. Kant, *Reflexionen zur Anthropologie*, no. 1505 (p. 809).

43. Kant, *Critique of Judgement*, p. 242. Pluhar, p. 93.

44. Ibid., p. 203. Pluhar, p. 43.

45. Ibid., p. 242. Pluhar, p. 93.

46. Kant, *Reflexionen zur Anthropologie*, no. 1497 (p. 770).

47. Jean Pierre de Crousaz, *Traité du Beau*, p. 45.

48. Liede, *Dichtung als Spiel*, vol. 1, p. 11.

49. Kant, *Critique of Judgment*, p. 320. Pluhar, p. 189.

50. Ibid., p. 314. Pluhar, p. 183. Translation modified.

51. Ibid., p. 327. Pluhar, p. 198. Translation modified.

52. Ibid., p. 332. Pluhar, p. 202. Translation modified.

53. Kant, *Reflexionen zur Anthropologie*, no. 806.

54. Kant, *Critique of Judgement*, pp. 321–322. Pluhar, p. 191.

55. Ibid., p. 328. Pluhar, p. 198.

56. Ibid., p. 332. Pluhar, p. 202.

57. Ibid. Pluhar, p. 203.

58. Ibid. Pluhar, p. 203. Translation modified.

59. Stewart, *Nonsense*, p. 13.

60. Tigges, *An Anatomy of Nonsense*, p. 27.

61. Kant, *Critique of Judgement*, p. 333. Pluhar, pp. 203–204. Translation modified.

62. Ibid. Pluhar, p. 203.
63. Ibid., p. 334. Pluhar, p. 205. Translation modified.
64. Ibid., pp. 334–335. Pluhar, pp. 205–206. Translation modified.
65. Ibid., p. 206. Pluhar, pp. 47–48. Translation modified.
66. Ibid., pp. 244–245. Pluhar, p. 98. Translation modified.
67. Ibid., p. 196. Pluhar, p. 37. Translation modified.
68. Ibid., pp. 330–331 (my emphasis—W. M.). Pluhar, p. 201. Translation modified.
69. Ibid., p. 298. Pluhar, p. 165.
70. Ibid., p. 273. Pluhar, p. 134.
71. Ibid., p. 334. Pluhar, p. 205.
72. Tieck, *Schriften*, vol. 9, pp. 98–99.
73. Tieck, *Phantasus*, pp. 85–88.
74. Tieck, *Schriften*, vol. 6, p. XXV.
75. Kant, *Critique of Judgement*, pp. 335–336. Pluhar, pp. 206–207. Translation modified.
76. See Grimm, *Deutsches Wörterbuch*, vol. 6, cols. 344–347.
77. Ibid., col. 345.
78. Ingrid Strasser, *Bedeutungswandel und strukturelle Semantik. 'Marotte, Laune, Tick' im literarischen Deutsch der Gegenwart und der Frühen Goethezeit*, pp. 180–181.
79. Christoph Martin Wieland, *Sämtliche Werke*, vol. 4, p. X.
80. Kant, *Critique of Judgement*, pp. 335–336. Pluhar, p. 206. Translation modified.
81. Ibid., pp. 307–308 and 319–320. Pluhar, pp. 175 and 188.
82. Kant, *Reflexionen zur Anthropologie*, nos. 812 and 922.
83. Ibid., no. 931.
84. This was first shown, with special attention to the examples, but also to several of the remarks by Jacques Derrida in his brilliant study "Parergon."
85. See Robert Stockhammer, *Leseerzählungen* and Jochen Hörisch, *Die Wut des Verstehens.*
86. Foucault, *The History of Sexuality*, vol. 1, p. 96.

Chapter 3

1. *Kritische Friedrich-Schlegel-Ausgabe*, vol. 16, p. 475.
2. Novalis, *Schriften*, vol. 3, p. 280. The German *Zusammenhang*, from the verb *zusammenhängen* [to be connected, coherent, contiguous]

is here translated as "coherence," "connection," or "context" depending in turn on its context.—Trans.

3. Ibid.
4. Ibid., p. 438.
5. Ibid., p. 449.
6. Ibid., p. 454.
7. Ibid., p. 572.
8. Tieck, *Frühe Erzählungen und Romane*, p. 604.
9. Ibid., pp. 378 and 627.
10. Ibid., p. 136.
11. Ibid., p. 193.
12. In his fairy-tale comedies, Tieck's poetics of nonsense has a fundamentally different genre-theoretical and literary-historical signature (one that will not be investigated in this study) than in his prose texts. Whereas in Tieck's prose the popular horror and chivalric novel play a double role as ironized background and positive source of motives, its analogon in the dramatic form—the theater of Iffland and Kotzebue—gives way completely to humorous (self-)mockery. Conversely, the prose fairy tales could not draw—as Tieck's dramas did—on powerful precedents such as the staging of playful-burlesque nonsense in Carlo Gozzi's *Fiable* and also in Shakespeare. Nonetheless, what unites the fairy-tale comedies with the *Bluebeard* tale is the following: not only do they articulate most clearly Tieck's poetics of caprice and nonsense; compared with most of Tieck's other *Volksmärchen*, they also hold to a more rigorous concept of the fairy tale in their literary models, which without exception were taken from Perrault's *Contes*. From the viewpoint of the Romantic as well as today's theory of the fairy tale, this coincidence loses the appearance of mere chance.
13. Tieck, *Phantasus*, p. 513.
14. Greiner, *Die Komödie*, p. 275.
15. Ibid., pp. 274–275.
16. Kant, *Reflexionen zur Anthropologie*, no. 812.
17. Tieck, *Schriften*, vol. 6, p. XX.
18. See Grimm, *Deutsches Wörterbuch*, vol. 6, cols. 2783–2787.
19. See Tieck, *Phantasus*, pp. 497 and 623.
20. Tieck, *Schriften*, vol. 9, p. 220.
21. Ibid., p. 219.
22. Ibid., p. 223.
23. Ibid., p. 193.
24. Ibid.
25. Tieck, *Frühe Erzählungen und Romane*, p. 498.
26. Ibid., pp. 146–147.
27. Ibid., pp. 76–77.

28. See Michael Voges, *Aufklärung und Geheimnis*, pp. 551–563.
29. Tieck, *Frühe Erzählungen und Romane*, p. 907.
30. Ibid., p. 898.
31. Ibid., pp. 889, 890, 894, 908.
32. Novalis, *Schriften*, vol. 3, p. 280.
33. Ibid., p. 454.
34. Ibid., vol. 2, p. 558 and vol. 3, pp. 280 and 454.
35. Ibid., p. 639.
36. See Klaus Lankheit, "Die Frühromantik und die Grundlagen der 'gegendstandslosen Malerei,'" pp. 55–90; Manfred Dick, *Die Entwicklung des Gedankens der Poesie in den Fragmenten des Novalis*, pp. 397–414; Winfried Menninghaus, *Unendliche Verdopplung*, pp. 262–265; Barbara Naumann, *"Musikalisches Ideen-Instrument,"* pp. 218–236.
37. *Kritische Friedrich-Schlegel-Ausgabe*, vol. 2, p. 323.
38. I am grateful to Christoph Brecht for this observation.
39. Greiner, *Die Komödie*, p. 270; see also ibid., pp. 265–272.
40. See Liede, *Dichtung als Spiel*, p. 5.
41. See Heinrich Bosse, "The Marvellous and Romantic Semiotics," pp. 218–222.
42. Novalis, *Schriften*, vol. 3, p. 558.
43. Ludwig Tieck, "Shakespeare's Behandlung des Wunderbaren" (1793), in Tieck, *Kritische Schriften*, vol. 1, p. 65.
44. Novalis, *Schriften*, vol. 3, p. 454. On the poetics of the marvelous in the field of the fairy tale, see the still definitive study by Gonthier-Louis Fink, *Naissance et apogée du conte merveilleux en Allemagne 1740–1800*.
45. Novalis, *Schriften*, vol. 3, p. 441.
46. Ibid., p. 449.
47. Ibid., vol. 2, p. 573.
48. On the Romantic poetics of chance and contingency, see the discussion in H. R. Jauß (ed.), *Poetik und Hermeneutik I*, pp. 210–219.
49. *Kritische Friedrich-Schlegel-Ausgabe*, vol. 2, p. 312.
50. G. W. F. Hegel, *Aesthetics. Lectures on Fine Art*, p. 308.
51. Ibid., p. 586. Translation modified. (Hegel's concept of the Romantic is certainly not limited to the epoch of Romanticism.)
52. See Werner Busch, *Die notwendige Arabeske*, pp. 42–55.
53. Kant, *Critique of Judgement*, p. 307. Pluhar, p. 174.
54. Kant, *Reflexionen zur Anthropologie*, no. 823.
55. Ibid.

56. The surprising affinity between "nature and chance" that Kant construes in the concepts of beautiful art and genius (*Reflexionen zur Anthropologie*, no. 823) nonetheless remains concealed in the third *Critique* in three ways. Firstly, the decisive statements on nature and art avoid mentioning their mediator "chance," and instead speak of the lack of "intention." Secondly, throughout the third *Critique* the concept of nature is bound to a regulative principle of purposiveness as a condition for the possibility of a coherent experience. Thirdly, every reader of Kant almost unavoidably hears in the concept of nature its association with necessity in the series of phenomenal appearances, as it forms the basis for the opposition between nature and freedom in the *Critique of Pure Reason*.

57. J. A. Bergk, *Die Kunst zu denken*, p. 172.

58. F. D. E. Schleiermacher, *Hermeneutik und Kritik*, p. 203.

59. See Willy Michel, *Ästhetische Hermeneutik und frühromantische Kritik.*

60. See Fr. Schlegel, "Über die Unverständlichkeit," in *Kritische Friedrich-Schlegel-Ausgabe*, vol. 2, p. 370.

61. Similarly, hermeneutics' generalized suspicion of incomprehensibility serves as a technical maxim, in virtue of which hermeneutics is prone to treat every passage of a text as though it were an "obscure" or "corrupted" passage. Even this concession or, more precisely, this allocation of incomprehensibility has the primary function of activating and engaging the machinery of understanding in an all-encompassing way: it does not restrict the understanding, but instead enormously expands its responsibility and supposed competence, in that it undertakes "to find a mediation for this entire area of the incomprehensible" (Schleiermacher, *Hermeneutik und Kritik*, p. 203).

62. Tieck, *Frühe Erzählungen und Romane*, p. 974.

63. Heinz Schlaffer investigates and develops the two-fold possibility of exoteric and esoteric readings as a thorough-going "politics" in Goethe's novels: "Exoterik und Esoterik in Goethes Romanen."

64. Goethe, letter to Schiller, Sept. 26, 1795, in *Goethe's Briefe*, vol. 10, p. 304.

65. Goethe, diary entry, June 24, 1816, in *Goethes Tagebücher*, vol. 5, p. 391.

66. Goethe, "The Green Snake and the Beautiful Lily," in *Goethe's Fairy Tale of the Green Snake and the Beautiful Lily*, p. 30.

67. Ibid., p. 13. Translation modified.

68. Ibid., p. 36.

69. Ibid., p. 16.

70. Schiller, letter to Goethe, Aug. 29, 1795, in *Schillers Werke. Nationalausgabe*, vol. 28, p. 36.

71. Schiller, letter to Cotta, Sept. 28, 1795, in ibid., p. 64.

72. Christian Gottfried Körner, letter to Schiller, Nov. 6, 1795, in *Schillers Briefwechsel mit Körner*, part 2, p. 178.

73. Charlotte von Kalb, letter to Goethe (November 1795), in *Goethe-Jahrbuch* 13 (1892), pp. 53–54.

74. Goethe, letter to Charlotte v. Kalb, in *Goethes Briefe*, vol. 10, p. 333.

75. Goethe, letter to Schiller, Dec. 23, 1795, in ibid., pp. 353–354.

76. Schiller, letter to Goethe, Dec. 25, 1795, in *Schillers Werke*, vol. 28, p. 142.

77. Schiller, letter to Goethe, Dec. 17, 1795, in ibid., p. 132.

78. Goethe, note to Goethe's letter to Prince August von Gotha, Dec. 21, 1795, in *Goethes Briefe*, vol. 10, p. 427.

79. Goethe, letter to Prince August von Gotha, Dec. 21, 1795, in ibid., pp. 351–352.

80. Goethe, letter to Schiller, Nov. 24, 1795, in ibid., p. 336.

81. Goethe, letter to Schiller, Dec. 15, 1795, in ibid., p. 348.

82. Goethe, letter to Schiller, Dec. 26, 1795, in ibid., p. 355.

83. Goethe, *Xenien*, p. 213.

84. *Journal des Luxus und der Moden*, vol. 11, pp. 143–144.

85. Goethe, diary entry, June 24, 1816, in *Goethes Tagebücher*, vol. 5, pp. 392–393.

86. Goethe, diary entry, March 9, 1809, in ibid., vol. 4, p. 15.

87. Goethe, diary entry, July 19, 1810, in ibid., p. 141.

88. Thomas Carlyle, letter to Goethe, May 23, 1830, in *Goethe's und Carlyle's Briefwechsel*, p. 95.

89. Marianne Willemer, letter to Goethe, January 1830, in *Briefwechsel zwischen Goethe und Marianne v. Willemer*, p. 268.

90. Goethe, letter to Schiller, Aug. 17, 1795, in *Goethes Briefe*, vol. 10, p. 286.

91. W. v. Humboldt, letter to Schiller, Dec. 4, 1795, in *Briefwechsel zwischen Schiller und Wilhelm v. Humboldt*, p. 232.

92. J. F. Reichardt, "Notiz von Deutschen Journalen—Die Horen, erstes Stück," p. 63.

93. Karl Grün, *Über Goethe vom menschlichen Standpuncte*, pp. 159–160.

94. Wilhelm v. Humboldt, letter to Goethe, Feb. 9, 1796, in *Briefe an Goethe, Hamburger Ausgabe*, vol. 1, p. 218.

95. A. W. Schlegel, *Sämmtliche Werke*, vol. 10, p. 86.

96. Ibid., p 88.

97. Ibid.

98. Tieck, *Phantasus*, p. 106.

99. Ibid.

100. Ibid., p. 108.

101. G. G. Gervinus, *Geschichte der deutschen Dichtung*, vol. 5, p. 645.

102. Reichardt, in *Deutschland*, vol. 1, p. 377.

Chapter 4

1. This change in title, however, is due less to a disrespect vis-à-vis the original title than to pragmatic motivations. The majority of the Perrault editions since the end of the 18th century print the earlier fairy tales in verse together with the *contes* in prose. The title *Contes (de fées, du temps passé)*, which encompasses both productions, therefore represents an editorial compromise.

2. See Paul Delarue, "L'œuvre d'un enfant de Paris: Les Contes merveilleux de Perrault et la tradition populaire" and Michèle Simonsen, *Perrault. Contes*, pp. 20–27.

3. This thesis indeed assumes what has not been proven and what probably can never be proven: that in Perrault's time there already existed fairy tales that accord with the generic descriptions of Propp and Lüthi.

4. Charles Perrault, "La Barbe Bleue," in Perrault, *Contes*, pp. 123–129. For the English translation see *The Complete Fairy Tales of Charles Perrault*, trans. Neil Philip, pp. 35–44. All citations from Perrault's "Barbe Bleue" refer to the above-mentioned pages. Neil Philip's translation has in some cases been modified.

5. A third model, which is able to bring ugliness even as a "malheur" into an inner relation to ethical 'character,' is in general not an issue in fairy tales. Ugliness could, one might assume, not be the sign for a presupposed bad character but instead produce such a character: Bluebeard is "par malheur" ugly, and therefore women unjustly find him repulsive, with the result that he becomes embittered and finally truly evil in his hatred of the other gender. To assume such an inner development would be not only highly speculative in light of the scarce information provided in the text; it also contradicts the fairy tale's tendency to portray the protagonist's attributes always as givens, as mostly resistant to change and

indifferent to experience, not as the result of an evolution and as open to inner change.

6. For instance, when the ugly and evil wolf eats chalk and paints his claws white or disguises himself in order to devour the seven goats or Little Red Riding Hood, the figure of disguise that enables him to perform his evil deeds is a fairly simple one: in his outer appearance, the wolf simply becomes not-wolf, becomes a sheep or the grandmother. He does not acquire another nature and the trust of his victims while remaining the same in appearance. Perrault's Bluebeard, on the contrary, in the eyes of his bride successfully generates an impression that makes a difference from his ugly and fearful appearance, without negating this appearance.

7. From a non-literary point of view, a good razor would suffice to remove the scandal. But this is exactly what is impossible in accordance with the laws of the literary genre (and therefore is never suggested to Bluebeard): for whatever can cause offense in the fairy tale must, in fact, cause offense.

8. Vladimir Propp, *Morphology of the Folktale*, p. 78.

9. See Max Lüthi, *The European Folktale: Form and Nature*, pp. 60–62.

10. See ibid., pp. 17 and 64–65 as well as Propp, *Die historischen Wurzeln des Zaubermärchens*, pp. 97 ff.

11. See Lugowski, *Die Form der Individualität im Roman*, pp. 68–69.

12. See Lüthi, *The European Folktale*, p. 75.

13. Freud, *Totem and Taboo*, p. 18. Translation modified.

14. Ibid., p. 21. Translation modified.

15. Tieck, *Schriften*, vol. 9, p. 125.

16. Ibid., p. 166.

17. Ibid., p. 215.

18. Freud, *Totem und Taboo*, p. 21.

19. Lutz Röhrich, *Märchen und Wirklichkeit*, p. 146.

20. Lüthi, *The European Folktale*, p. 35. Translation modified.

21. Ibid., p. 31. Translation modified.

22. Röhrich, *Märchen und Wirklichkeit*, p. 128.

23. Delarue, *Le Conte Populaire Français*, p. 197; see also Marc Soriano, *Les Contes de Perrault*, pp. 164–166.

24. See Lüthi, *The European Folktale*, pp. 29–30.

25. See Jacques Derrida, "Survivre."

26. See Delarue, *Le Conte Populaire Français*, p. 197.

27. See Saintyves, *Les Contes de Perrault et les Récits Parallèles*, pp. 383–387.

28. Novalis, *Schriften*, vol. 2, p. 246.
29. Louis Marin, *Études Sémiologiques*, p. 300.

Chapter 5

1. See Letter to Reimer, Sept. 12, 1817, in *Letters of Ludwig Tieck*, p. 79.
2. See A. W. Schlegel, *Sämmtliche Werke*, vol. 11, pp. 136–140.
3. See Karl Wilhelm Ferdinand Solger, *Nachgelassene Schriften und Briefwechsel*, pp. 468–469.
4. See Käthe Brodnitz, *Die vier Märchenkomödien von Ludwig Tieck*, pp. 48–72; Adriana Marelli, *Ludwig Tiecks frühe Märchenspiele und die Gozzische Manier*, pp. 96–128.
5. Except for Arno Schmidt's portrait, Ernst Ribbat and Christoph Brecht have paid the greatest attention to the Bluebeard tale to date. See Ernst Ribbat, *Studien zur Konzeption und Praxis romantischer Poesie*, pp. 132–136 and Christoph Brecht, *Die gefährliche Rede*, pp. 55–68.
6. Arno Schmidt, "Die 10 Kammern des Blaubart," p. 246. See also his comments on the Blaubart tale in Arno Schmidt's "'Funfzehn.' Vom Wunderkind der Sinnlosigkeit," p. 247.
7. Letter to Reimer, Aug. 12, 1817, in *Letters of Ludwig Tieck*, p. 79.
8. It cannot be ruled out that this title comes not from Tieck himself but from his publisher, Nicolai. See Tieck's similar remarks about the "Muslim date" in the first edition of *Gestiefelter Kater* (*Schriften*, vol. 1, p. XX).
9. Joh. Fr. Penther, *Ausführliche Anleitung zur bürgerlichen Bau-Kunst, Erster Theil*, p. 6a.
10. My presentation of rocaille follows completely the authoritative work by Hermann Bauer, *Rocaille. Zur Herkunft und zum Wesen eines Ornament-Motivs* (here esp. pp. 8–9 and 19–22).
11. See Alois Riegl, *Die spätrömische Kunstindustrie*, p. 327.
12. Bauer, *Rocaille*, p. 63.
13. Ibid., p. 70.
14. Ibid., pp. 63 and 75.
15. See the critique by Winckelmann's friend Reifstein (1746), by Cochin fils (1754), J. Gg. Fünck (1747), and Krubsacius (1759), which Bauer presents (ibid., pp. 42–45 and 63–65).
16. See Bauer, Rocaille, pp. 66–68.
17. Johann Joachim Winckelmann, *Gedanken über die Nachahmung der griechischen Werke in der Malerei und Bildhauerkunst*, pp. 37–38.

18. See esp. three excellent studies by Günter Oesterle: "'Vorbegriffe zu einer Theorie der Ornamente.' Kontroverse Formprobleme zwischen Aufklärung, Klassizismus und Romantik am Beispiel der Arabeske;" "Arabeske und Roman;" "Arabeske, Schrift und Poesie in E. T. A. Hoffmanns Kunstmärchen 'Der goldne Topf.'" In the pages that follow I rely often on Oesterle's work; however, my treatment, taking its cue from Kant and Tieck's Bluebeard tale, diverges principally in that it emphasizes a characteristic of the arabesque that is hardly mentioned by Oesterle: parergonality, the character of the frame. On the discussion of the arabesque before Oesterle, see as well: Karl Konrad Pohlheim, *Die Arabeske. Ansichten und Ideen aus Schlegels Poetik*; Erwin Rotermund, "Musikalische und dichterische 'Arabeske' bei E. T. A. Hoffmann;" Raymond Immerwahr, "Die symbolische Form des 'Briefs über den Roman;'" Gunnar Berefelt. "Verzierungen mit Einsicht und Sinn—Notizen um Ph. O. Runge;" Jörg Traeger, *Philipp Otto Runge oder die Geburt einer neuen Kunst*; Werner Busch, *Die notwendige Arabeske*, pp. 13–55.

19. Busch, *Die notwendige Arabeske*, pp. 131–132.

20. Adolf Riem, "Ueber die Arabeske," no. II, p. 128.

21. Ibid., p. 28. See Oesterle, "'Vorbegriffe zu einer Theorie der Ornamente,'" p. 133.

22. Karl Philipp Moritz, "Einfachheit und Klarheit," p. 149.

23. Moritz, "Die Säule," p. 110.

24. Oesterle, "'Vorbegriffe zu einer Theorie der Ornamente,'" p. 126. (My exposition of Moritz wholly follows this study.)

25. Moritz, "Arabesken," p. 211.

26. Moritz, "Die Säule," p. 110.

27. Oesterle, "'Vorbegriffe zur einer Theorie der Ornamente,'" p. 132.

28. Goethe, "Von Arabesken," p. 85.

29. Moritz, "Spielarten des Geschmacks," p. 212.

30. Moritz, "Einfachheit und Klarheit," p. 150.

31. Tieck, *Volksmärchen*, vol. 1, pp. vi, vii, xvi. This feature of the labyrinthine can also be traced back to the rocaille ornament insofar as the latter transforms the spatial impossibilities and thus the labyrinthine moment of the grotesque. On this, see the outstanding study by Friedrich Piel, *Die Ornament-Groteske in der italienischen Renaissance*, pp. 51–54; and Bauer, *Rocaille*, p. 12.

32. As to the dialectic of this function of framing, see Karsten Harries, *The Broken Frame*, pp. 64–89.

33. Kant, *Critique of Judgement*, p. 229. Pluhar, pp. 76–77. Translation modified.

34. Ibid., p. 207. Pluhar, p. 49. Translation modified.

35. Another meaning of *à la grecque* came into use only after the appearance of the *Critique of Judgement*: neo-classicist, free-flowing garments (Tunica) were called "republican" in opposition to the "royalist" fashion. Applied to these garments, *à la grecque* no longer designated the ornamental trim only. This different use of the concept, however, still maintained the criteria of freedom and frivolity that Kant emphasizes in the "free designs *à la grecque*," the arabesque decorations and the foliage for frameworks. For indeed the à la grecque fashion was distinguished from the previous fashion by its "free and frivolous manner." On this, see Jacob Falke, *Die deutsche Trachten-und Modenwelt*, pp. 308–311, and Wolfgang Bruhns' article on "à la grecque." (The citation above comes from this article, p. 323.)

36. Jean Paul, *Hesperus oder 45 Hundposttage*, p. 375.

37. Kant, *Critique of Judgement*, p. 232. Pluhar, p. 80.

38. Friedrich Schiller, *Kallias oder Über die Schönheit*, p. 395.

39. It is a subordinate question here whether these concepts in an art-historical perspective do justice to the arabesque. One might easily object that even the production of fully non-representational ornamental patterns imply, if not a concept, then surely an intentionality. However, even if Kant in the idea of a "pure," i.e., completely intentionless, art was primarily pursuing a phantom sprung full born from his philosophical system, this phantom has nonetheless exerted an enormous influence upon modern art.

40. Kant, *Critique of Judgement*, p. 244. Pluhar, p. 97. Translation modified.

41. See Moritz, "Arabesken," p. 211.

42. Kant, *Critique of Judgement*, p. 225. Pluhar, pp. 71–72. Translation modified.

43. See Falke, *Die deutsche Trachten-und Modenwelt*, p. 309.

44. Kant, *Critique of Judgement*, p. 323. Pluhar, p. 193.

45. Ibid., pp. 229, 299. Pluhar, pp. 76, 166.

46. Ibid., p. 229. Pluhar, p. 77.

47. Ibid., p. 233. Pluhar, p. 81.

48. See Derrida, "Parergon."

49. Kant, *Critique of Judgement*, pp. 229, 347, 349. Pluhar, pp. 76, 221, 224.

50. Ibid., p. 306. Pluhar, p. 174.
51. Ibid., p. 311. Pluhar, p. 179. Translation modified.
52. Ibid., p. 310. Pluhar, p. 178.
53. Ibid., pp. 306–307. Pluhar, p. 174. Translation modified.
54. Ibid., p. 327. Pluhar, p. 197.
55. Both the "analytic" and the "deduction" do offer, however, another line of thought vis-à-vis the "impurity" of aesthetic judgments concerning works of fine art: the recognition of this impurity. This recognition attempts to understand the "impairing of beauty's purity" not simply as a lack, but rather as a "gain" for "the *entire faculty* of representation" (ibid., pp. 230–231; Pluhar, pp. 77–78, translation modified). "When we judge artistic beauty," i.e., a beauty, which according to Kant is necessarily linked to a purpose, we shall consequently "have to assess the thing's perfection as well" (ibid., p. 311; Pluhar, p. 179)—thus a quality of which pure beauty should be "wholly independent" (ibid., pp. 226–229; Pluhar, pp. 73–75). Yet such a connection between beauty and what is "actually" foreign to it (ibid., p. 231; Pluhar, p. 78) is also present in the "ideal" of beauty of nature itself: in man (ibid., pp. 232–233; Pluhar, pp. 80–81). Just as in man, the "impurity" of beauty in art—its inextricable connection to "perfection," which demotes it to a "merely adherent beauty" (ibid., p. 229; Pluhar, p. 76)—is not simply a deficit but rather a paradoxical mode of intensification by means of contamination. When Kant legitimates the impure beauty of art, he explicitly refers to the analogous impurity of the aesthetic judgment regarding the beauty of man (ibid., p. 311; Pluhar, p. 179).
56. Also in the discourse on the sublime, when the question of the "artistic presentation" of the sublime arises, Kant once again resorts to beautiful accessory works: "The sublime is not an object for taste, but rather for the feeling of emotion; however, the artistic presentation of the sublime in description and embellishment (in accessory works, parerga) may be and ought to be beautiful"(*Anthropologie in pragmatischer Hinsicht*, p. 243; see Dowdell, p. 146).
57. Kant, *Critique of Judgement*, p. 315. Pluhar, p. 183.
58. Hans Sedlmayr, *Die Revolution der modernen Kunst*, pp. 46–47.
59. Ibid.
60. Niklas Luhmann strictly separates this double movement, which, on the one hand, revalorizes and, on the other hand, devalues the ornament. Conforming to the interpretation of 20th-century non-representational art as absolute ornament (*Die Kunst der Gesellschaft*, p. 360), he un-

derstands the development of the modern system of art *entirely* as the development into a pure combinatorics of forms. Under pre-modern conditions the ornament was that upon which this combinatorics could be "as it were practiced," in order subsequently, in an evolutionary step, to progress from a "preadaptive advance" into the standard of art. Luhmann can therefore only condemn the "parallel" phenomenon of a "devaluation of the ornamental as mere decoration" for being a mere conceptual error in the "self-description" of the system of art, or being a lack of consistency that "sabotages the possibility of denoting the unity of art itself, for what could this unity be if beauty as perfection [of ornamental combinations of form—W. M.] still required a supplement?" (p. 353). Even though Luhmann otherwise likes to insist on distinctions in contexts where they aren't made—for example, the distinction between code and program in the "self-description" of the system of art—in this case he does not want to grant validity to a distinction that has been maintained with a certain insistence, namely, "the distinction between artwork and ornament." Contrary to Luhmann and in agreement with the "tradition," I find this processing and ambivalent transformation of the difference between ergon and parergon to be quite interesting. Already at the "origin" of aesthetic autonomy it indicates an awareness of the precarious nature of art's self-grounding—an awareness that Luhmann allows for only in later phases of art's self-exhaustion, as wrought by an incessant and purely internal pressure of innovation. Moreover, I doubt that for the understanding of any artwork, it suffices to define it as a purely ornamental combination of forms, if that combination means nothing other than that "differences accord with [previously made—W. M.] differences," and if the only rejoinder to the "code value" of Beauty that this definition can offer is an extremely boiled-down version of the venerable doctrine of "harmony" (p. 286). Luhmann refrains from offering any criterion for such "harmony" (when does a difference "accord" or "fit" with another and when *not*?) while at the same time stripping it of every metaphysical or transcendental significance (in the sense of the ancient doctrine of cosmological harmony or the Kantian interplay of mental capacities).

61. See Polheim's chapter on "Das Wort Arabeske vor F. Schlegel" in his book *Die Arabeske*, pp. 17–21.

62. The non-mention of the word "arabesque" can be read, on the one hand, as pointing to the lack of a need to mention it explicitly: given the numerous treatises on the arabesque that preceded the appearance of Kant's third critique, Kant could presume that his contemporaries were

familiar with the locus of his intervention. On the other hand, a strategy of conflict avoidance may also be involved here. By forgoing the use of the word "arabesque," Kant could avoid an open conflict with the Enlightenment condemnation of the arabesque that was so eloquently formulated by Adolf Riem in 1788.

63. An exception is Harries, *The Broken Frame*, pp. 82–83. In a very interesting article, which appeared after completion of the present study, Harries addresses again, and this time more comprehensively, the problem of ornament in Kant's third *Critique* ("Laubwerk auf Tapeten"). Several of my elaborations coincide closely with Harries's article. Harries, however, seems to be unfamiliar with the arabesque debate in the 1780s and 1790s, the scholarly work done on this debate, as well as with Derrida's confrontation with Kant's parergon; at least he does not mention them at all. Rather, without taking into account the classicist positions (like those of Moritz or Goethe), he relates Kant's examples directly and exclusively to the art of the rocaille. One consequence of this strategy is Harries's tendency to underemphasize the parergonal element in Kant's examples. Yet in contrast to rocaille's undoing the difference between ergon and parergon, Kant maintains a clear and essential distinction between border and center, despite effacing the hermeneutical relationships between them. This is true not only for the "picture frames, or garments on statues, or colonnades around magnificent buildings" (*Critique of Judgement*, p. 226; Pluhar, p. 72, translation modified); it is also true for Harries's titular example of the "foliage on wallpaper," which in the context of the contemporary debate should be seen more as a parergonal ornamentation of rooms rather than as an absolute decorative pattern. If one adds the construction of parergonal ornaments in nature in Kant's animal examples as well—which is completely overlooked by Harries because of his exclusive concentration on the wallpaper pattern—then Kant's examples attain a considerable, indeed almost uncanny, rigor and are surely not, as Harries surmises, "probably adduced without much reflection" (p. 96). Likewise Harries's observation that "Kant uses as examples of pure beauty not paintings or sculptures, but something like foliage on wallpaper" (p. 94) seems to miss the logic underlying the series of Kant's examples: the foliage, as a parergonal part of the art of adorning rooms, is an exact parallel to the "picture frames, or garments on statues." The primary distinction, therefore, is not being made between wallpapers as decorative patterns, on the one hand, and paintings or sculptures on the other, but between the parergonal series—

wallpaper, picture frames, statue's drapery—and the ergonal series—room, painting, statue.

64. See Derrida, "Parergon," pp. 64–71 and 111–113.

65. See Ulrike Dünkelsbühler, *Kritik der Rahmen-Vernunft*, pp. 50–62. Dünkelsbühler often considerably overstrains the wording of the third *Critique* in her endeavor to see "the identity principle of Western provenance per se" undermined in the Kantian parergon. She attempts to complicate Kant's exclusion of the "golden frame" (*Critique of Judgement*, p. 226; Pluhar, p. 72) from the paradigm of "purely" beautiful "frameworks" with the comment that Kant after all concedes a "pure" beauty of "simple colors" and that gold is just such a pure color (p. 52). Yet the aesthetic "impurity" of the gold frame rests for Kant clearly on the "charm" and the interest entailed by the *costliness* of the *material* gold independently of its form and color. Also the "*like*" in Kant's exemplificatory expressions, such as "like picture frames, or garments on statues," can hardly be read as "*not completely like*" or, as Dünkelsbühler holds, as "a kind of translation or metaphorization." Partly because of these two forced and skewed distinctions, Dünkelsbühler loses sight of the aesthetic locus of the Kantian determinations.

66. Friedrich Schlegel, *Literarische Notizen 1797–1801*, no. 2086.

67. Ibid., no. 313.

68. *Kritische Friedrich-Schlegel-Ausgabe*, vol. 2, p. 319.

69. Schlegel, *Literarische Notizen*, no. 1743.

70. *Kritische Friedrich-Schlegel-Ausgabe*, vol. 16, p. 310.

71. Ibid., p. 247.

72. Ibid., p. 295.

73. Ibid., pp. 330–331.

74. I focus here exclusively on those elements in Schlegel's theory of the arabesque that can be read as following and radicalizing the Kantian argument.

75. See Bauer, *Rocaille*, p. 77.

76. See Benjamin, *The Concept of Criticism in German Romanticism*, p. 177.

77. *Kritische Friedrich-Schlegel-Ausgabe*, vol. 2, p. 318.

78. Ibid., p. 319.

79. Schlegel, *Literarische Notizen*, no. 1804.

80. *Kritische Friedrich-Schlegel-Ausgabe*, vol. 2, p. 319.

81. Ibid., vol. 16, p. 247.

82. See J. G. Herder, *Briefe zur Beförderung der Humanität*, p. 43.

83. Quoted in Oesterle, "Arabeske und Roman," pp. 238–239.
84. Herder, *Adrastea*, pp. 285–286.
85. See here Erwin Rotermund, "Musikalische und dichterische 'Arabeske' bei E. T. Hoffmann," pp. 51–54, and Oesterle, "Arabeske, Schrift und Poesie in E. T. A. Hoffmanns Kunstmärchen 'Der goldne Topf,'" pp. 72–92.
86. Schlegel, *Literarische Notizen*, no. 1065.
87. *Kritische Friedrich-Schlegel-Ausgabe*, vol. 2, pp. 357–358.
88. Ibid., p. 245.
89. Citations from Tieck's *Die sieben Weiber des Blaubart* will henceforth be given in parentheses and refer to volume 9 of the 28 volume *Schriften* of 1828.
90. Tieck, *Phantasus*, p. 540.
91. Tieck, *Kritische Schriften*, vol. 1, p. 162.
92. Ibid., p. 119.
93. Ibid.
94. Letter to Goethe, Feb. 9, 1796, in *Briefe an Goethe*, vol. 1, p. 218.
95. Kant, *Critique of Judgement*, pp. 313–317. Pluhar, pp. 181–186.
96. Tieck, *Kritische Schriften*, vol. 4, p. 246.
97. Tieck, *Schriften*, vol. 28, p. 457.
98. Ibid., vol. 6, p. xxiv.
99. Ibid.
100. Ibid., p. xxv.
101. Ibid., pp. xxiv–xxv; see also Tieck, *Kritische Schriften*, vol. 1, p. 167.
102. On the figure of the reader in Tieck, see Achim Hölter, *Ludwig Tieck. Literaturgeschichte als Poesie*, esp. pp. 67–77.
103. See Hölter, "'Die sieben Weiber.'"
104. At the beginning of *Peter Lebrecht* (1795), Tieck had already quoted a similar textual sequence and stylized it explicitly as a simulation of a popular novel: "In order to win your [the reader's—W. M.] favor, I had to commence my narrative roughly in the following manner: 'The stormy wind rattled the windows of the old castle Wallenstein.—Midnight stretched darkly over the fields, and clouds chased each other through the skies, as Sir Karl von Wallenstein on his black charger, etc.'" (*Frühe Erzählungen und Romane*, p. 75.)
105. See Heinz Schlaffer, "Roman und Märchen. Ein formtheoretischer Versuch über Tiecks 'Blonden Eckbert,'" p. 453.
106. Freud, "The Uncanny," pp. 245–246.

107. Ibid., p. 274.

108. See Hansjörg Garte, *Kunstform Schauerroman*, p. 85.

109. The same, together with similar critical comments, is said of *William Lovell.* See Tieck, *Frühe Erzählungen und Romane*, p. 375.

110. See here Lüthi, *Das Volksmärchen als Dichtung*, pp. 46–52.

111. Letter to Goethe, Feb. 9, 1796, in *Briefe an Goethe*, vol. 1, p. 220.

112. This opposition can at least be seen in the two recognition songs that are sung by the old tutor as representative of the old fairy, on the one hand (134), in the kingdom of Almida, on the other (205–206).

113. Tieck structures the first configuration of this poetics as an attempt to enforce the laws of the idyll in the field of the non-idyllic. This occurs when the beautiful fairy Almida, *outside* of her genuine dominion, the idyllic-paradisiacal island, encounters the contrary legislation of Bernard and his old tutor. To that extent, the results of this conflict, the praise of the trivial, no longer belongs simply to the field of the idyll, but rather reflects and supplements the project of the idyll outside and beyond the idyll.

114. See Marianne Thalmann, *Der Trivialroman des 18. Jahrhunderts und der romantische Roman*, pp. 94–104.

115. Ibid., p. 100.

116. Ibid., p. 97.

117. Ibid.

118. Ibid., p. 57.

119. Ibid., p. 95.

120. On the opposition between the fairy tale and the mythical spell and hence fate, see Ernst Bloch, *Heritage of Our Time*, pp. 164–168; Benjamin, "Franz Kafka," p. 118, as well as Benjamin, "The Storyteller," p. 102.

121. See Paul Groth, *Die ethische Haltung des deutschen Volksmärchen*, p. 41; Dietz-Rüdiger Moser, "Theorie- und Methodenprobleme der Märchenforschung," p. 62; Maria Tatar, *The Hard Facts of the Grimm's Fairy Tales*, pp. 85–133.

122. See here Groth, *Die ethische Haltung des deutschen Volksmärchen*, pp. 42–47; Lutz Mackensen, "Das deutsche Volksmärchen," pp. 316–317; Kurt Ranke, "Betrachtungen zum Wesen und zur Funktion des Märchens," p. 651.

123. Tieck, *Schriften*, vol. 7, p. 202 (my emphasis—W. M.).

124. Benjamin, "Fate and Character," p. 203.

125. André Jolles, *Einfache Formen*, pp. 238–246.

126. See Lüthi, *Das Volksmärchen als Dichtung*, p. 156.

127. See ibid., p. 160.

128. Kant, *The Metaphysics of Morals*, p. 109.

129. See Lutz Röhrich, "Mensch und Tier im Märchen."

130. Lüthi, *The European Folktale*, p. 84.

131. Max Lüthi has also suggested the humanity vs. inhumanity of the protagonists as a further oppositional characteristic distinguishing fairy tale from myth. The fairy tale is nearly always concerned with the fortunes of human heroes; by contrast in myth "human beings in fact need not even appear, the players can be limited to god and demi-gods [. . .] very much in contrast to the fairy tale" (Lüthi, *Das Volksmärchen als Dichtung*, p. 152). Also in the folk *saga* not the human being, but "the forcible entrance of the Wholly Other [stands] in the center" (ibid.).

132. Tieck, *Schriften*, vol. 6, p. xx.

133. Grimm, *Kinder- und Hausmärchen*, p. 39.

134. By the way, the paronomasia in the team of hero and helper (in the term of the fairy tale) or hero and genius (in the terms of the popular novel) also suggests the Romantic *topos* of *Doppelgänger* and split ego.

135. Admittedly, helping figures sometimes are able to lend magical objects whose powers work more generally, beyond a concrete situation—for instance, an unending cornucopia [*Tischlein-deck-dich*] or a magic lamp, but such objects are almost never actively wished for by fairy-tale figures, but only passively received.

136. However, the genius figure, derived from the gothic novel, misunderstands the wish that the *consciousness* of mortality be effaced—"that I *would forget* my mortality and thus can live *as though* today *would* always remain today"—misunderstands it as a wish for the conscious overcoming of mortality itself.

137. A purely negative consciousness of temporality and mortality also characterizes the "philosophy" of Bluebeard's protectoress, the subterranean fairy: "With a rough, merciless hand the future sweeps everything before it, and wipes it away, like erasing an insignificant, incorrect calculation from a blackboard: then that which at bottom never was is in fact gone, and the empty space plays its game with oblivion, where once earthly dreams resided" (139). With this prosopopoeia of the future that effaces all wishes, the fairy, who herself enjoys several powers and objects from the world of the fairy tale, articulates a consciousness of empty time and empty space that is diametrically opposed to the "transcendental aesthetic" of the fairy-tale genre.

138. See F. Schlegel, "Gespräch über die Poesie": "Such a theory of the novel would itself have to be a novel" (in *Kritische Friedrich-Schlegel-*

Ausgabe, vol. 2, p. 337). One year later Tieck formulated a similar project, "to write a novel" as a characteristic of Shakespeare or only "on the period of Old English poetry" (*Kritische Schriften*, vol. 1, pp. 147–148).

139. Tieck, "Ritter Blaubart," in *Volksmärchen*, vol. 1, p. 147.

140. See Thalmann, *Der Trivialroman des 18. Jahrhunderts und der romantische Roman*, p. 290.

141. See Benjamin, *The Origin of German Tragic Drama*, pp. 147–150.

142. Tatar, *The Hard Facts of the Grimm's Fairy Tales*, p. 86.

143. Ibid., p. 88.

144. Ibid., p. 87.

145. Ibid.

146. See ibid., pp. 88–95.

147. Ibid., 94.

148. Perrault, "Bluebeard," p. 40.

149. Tatar, *The Hard Facts of the Grimm's Fairy Tales*, p. 96.

150. See Tieck's remarks on the comical and the connections between the terrible and the ridiculous in *Shakespeare's Behandlung des Wunderbaren*, pp. 56–60.

151. Similarly, the antipodal fairy Almida guards her protégé Adelheid "from too big an understanding, which only presupposes a lack of understanding" (106).

152. *Kritische Friedrich-Schlegel-Ausgabe*, vol. 18, pp. 455–456.

153. Ibid., vol. 16, p. 260.

154. Schlegel, *Literarische Notizen*, no. 612.

155. *Kritische Friedrich-Schlegel-Ausgabe*, vol. 2, p. 332.

156. See ibid., vol. 16, pp. 197–198, and Schlegel, *Literarische Notizen*, no. 427. Jean Paul's early *Lob der Dumheit* (*Praise of Stupidity*, 1781/82) by contrast extols "stupidity" and "nonsense" only in the satirical sense and hence still remains bound to Enlightenment semantics.

157. The first woman, Friedericke, is entirely attached to the sphere of "sentiment," "heart," "love," and "suffering" and to the discursive reflection about it; she already loves a poor bourgeois man but is forced by her father to marry the wealthy knight. The second woman, Jakobine, is typified by domineeringness and jealousy; in a twofold contrast to the first wife, she loves Bluebeard, and must realize her love against the will of her father. The third wife, Caroline, craves admiration, likes to spend money, and prefers to orchestrate large gatherings of women with the exclusion of her husband. She is succeeded by the "nature child" Magdalene, a shepherd's daughter, who pushes her rustic innocence so far as to billet her former lover in the forbidden room. With the fifth woman, Sophie, "even with the sharpest eye one can perceive no character: she wanted nothing, she knew nothing, she was indifferent to everything"

(225). If Mechthilde had not helped, she would have passed the test "out of stupidity" (226)—a combination of stupidity and success that is reserved for the masculine heroes of fairy tales. The sixth wife, Catharine, combines poor health and neurasthenia with a melancholy predilection for everything that seems abnormal, strange, and fantastic, and she dies, without any assistance from Bluebeard, of one of her own horrific visions.

158. See Tatar, *The Hard Facts of the Grimm's Fairy Tales*, pp. 157–167.

159. See Manfred Frank, Gerhard Kurz, "'*ordo inversus*.'"

160. See the discourse regarding mothers and literacy and the "new pedagogues" in the framing conversation to *Phantasus* (pp. 39–41), in *Die verkehrte Welt* (ibid., pp. 627–629), and the similar remarks on education in *Peter Lebrecht* (*Frühe Erzählungen und Romane*, p. 79).

161. Tieck, *Schriften*, vol. 9, pp. 5–6. See also ibid., pp. 53–54.

162. In *William Lovell* Tieck alludes to a similar tale of persecution: "Do you know the fairy tale in which a boy is chased incessantly by a horrible monster? always escaping him and then running into him again?" (ibid., vol. 6, p. 190).

163. See Pierre Saintyves, *Les Contes de Perrault et les Récits Parallèles*, pp. 383–387.

164. Lüthi, *The European Folktale*, p. 38.

165. Through its quotation of idyllic patterns, this promise admittedly oscillates between wise self-deflation by its advocate and slight mockery by the author. See Brecht, *Die gefährliche Rede*, p. 64.

166. In this respect, Almida's philosophy prefigures the recovery of incoherence via a higher coherence, which characterizes the "hieroglyphic" investment of the Romantic fairy-tale narrative and arabesque from 1798 onward. Yet Almida does not draw on allegorical figures.

167. Kittler, "Authorschaft und Liebe," p. 154.

168. Schmidt, "Die 10 Kammern des Blaubart," p. 246.

169. Schmidt, "'Funfzehn.' Vom Wunderkind der Sinnlosigkeit," p. 247.

170. Ibid., p. 240.

171. Ibid., p. 247.

172. Grimm, *Deutsches Wörterbuch*, vol. XII, I (reprint vol. 25), cols. 54–55.

173. Ibid., col. 1665.

174. Ibid., col. 1523.

175. Ibid.

176. Ibid., col. 1665.

177. Ibid., col. 1700.

178. Ibid., col. 1696.

179. The author's thematic-programmatic wordplay can be rendered in English only with egregious difficulty: Standard German has "unverständlich" and "Unverständlichkeit," literally "ununderstandable" and "ununderstandability" but translated "incomprehensible" and "incomprehensibility" as in Friedrich Schlegel's famous "On Incomprehensibility" ["Über die Unverständlichkeit"]; there is no German "ständlich" "Ständlichkeit," literally "standable," "standability," and by analogy, rendered above "prehensible," "prehensibility."—Trans.

180. Ibid., col. 1542.

181. See Schleiermacher, *Hermeneutik und Kritik*, p. 101.

182. Grimm, *Deutsches Wörterbuch*, vol. XII, I, col. 1674.

183. Schleiermacher, *Hermeneutik und Kritik*, p. 203.

184. Novalis, *Schriften*, vol. 3, p. 454.

185. Ibid., p. 280.

186. See Tzvetan Todorov, *The Fantastic*, pp. 24–58.

187. Except in religious worldviews, where miracles are "understood" as integral manifestations of divine rule and do not cause any rupture in the reality principle. On the comparison of the poetics of the fantastic and of nonsense, see Tigges, *An Anatomy of Nonsense*, pp. 32–33.

188. Todorov, *The Fantastic*, pp. 25–27.

189. See ibid., pp. 32–34 and 58–61.

190. On this see Jacqueline Flescher's remark: "Reality remains implicit behind every manifestation of nonsense, but is never explicitly represented. The nonsense world is a world of fantasy which shies clear of reality, yet indicates its existence." ("The Language of Nonsense," p. 141.)

191. Tieck, *Kritische Schriften*, vol. 1, p. 162.

192. See Louis Vax, *La séduction de l'étrange*, pp. 173, 201–203.

193. Schmidt, "'Funfzehn,' Vom Wunderkind der Sinnlosigkeit," p. 247.

194. Tieck, *Frühe Erzählungen und Romane*, p. 361.

195. Kant, *Anthropologie in pragmatischer Hinsicht*, pp. 214–215. See Dowdell, pp. 112–113.

196. Here I disagree with Christoph Brecht, who reads the horror tale as a paradigmatic fulfillment of "the intention of the *Bluebeard* narrative as a whole" (*Die gefährliche Rede*, p. 67).

197. Benjamin, "Goethe's Elective Affinities," pp. 319–333.

198. On this see Menninghaus, *Unendliche Verdopplung*, pp. 132–142.

199. Benjamin, "Franz Kafka," p. 117.

200. Franz Kafka, "Wunsch, Indianer zu werden," in Kafka, *Erzählungen*, p. 44.

201. Benjamin, "Franz Kafka," p. 140.

Chapter 6

1. Propp, *Morphology of the Folktale*, p. 106.
2. Ibid., pp. 111–112.
3. Ibid., p. 76.
4. Ibid., p. 78.
5. Ibid., p. 75.
6. Ibid., p. 76.
7. Propp, "Folklore and Reality," pp. 25–27.
8. See Lugowski, *Die Form der Individualität im Roman.*
9. Propp, *Morphology of the Folktale*, p. 20.
10. Ibid., p. 87.
11. Ibid., p. 90.
12. Ibid., p. 115. Translation modified.
13. Grimm, *Vorrede* (1819) to the *Kinder- und Hausmärchen*, p. 36.
14. Propp, *Morphology of the Folktale*, p. 87.
15. Ibid., p. 106.
16. Propp, *Die historischen Wurzeln des Zaubermärchens*, p. 36.
17. Ibid., p. 286.
18. See the critical survey of these associations presented by Hyacinthe Husson, André Lefèvre, and Frédéric Dillaye in Saintyves, *Les Contes de Perrault et les Récits Parallèles*, pp. 362–363.
19. A survey of this research approach is provided by Bengt Holbek, "Interpretation of Fairytales." For a qualification of the assumption widely held in ethnology that initiation rituals and their characteristics are almost omnipresent, see the two studies by Alice Schlegel and Herbert Barry III: "Adolescent Initiation Ceremonies: A Cross-Cultural Code" and "The Evolutionary Significance of Adolescent Initiation Ceremonies."
20. Propp, *Die historischen Wurzeln des Zaubermärchens*, p. 451.
21. Ibid., pp. 97 ff.
22. Lüthi, *The European Folktale*, p. 16.
23. Ibid., p. 61.
24. Propp, *Die historischen Wurzeln des Zaubermärchens*, p. 99.
25. Grimm, *Kinder- und Hausmärchen*, p. 241 ("Der Räuberbräutigam").
26. Propp, *Die historischen Wurzeln des Zaubermärchens*, p. 108.
27. Grimm, *Kinder- und Hausmärchen*, p. 173 ("Die sieben Raben").

28. Lüthi, *The European Folktale*, p. 13.

29. Ibid., p. 38.

30. Propp, *Die historischen Wurzeln des Zaubermärchens*, p. 286.

31. Ibid., pp. 87 and 118–124. However, such direct inversions of individual elements do not yet prove in themselves a temporal descent of the fairy tale from the de-realized myth. They also occur in the transformations that myths undergo when crossing spatial thresholds—from a population to a neighboring one—and do not automatically result in myths ceasing to be myths. Only the connection of such inversions and, even more, the demotivation of individual mythical elements with the narrative law of their recombination allows for a definition of the relationship between myths and fairy tales. See chapters X and XIV in Claude Lévi-Strauss, *Structural Anthropology II.*

32. Propp, *Die historischen Wurzeln des Zaubermärchens*, pp. 137–144 and 173–181.

33. See Susan Reid, "Myth as Metastructure of the Fairytale," p. 157: "In the fairytale, the hero may remain in the foreign kingdom where he marries the princess and rules as king. In the myth, which stands in the context of the ritual, this would mean a failure of the hero's expedition, because the goal of the myth (which is really the ritual goal) is the invigoration or enrichment of the community. The hero's return and reintegration are therefore of paramount importance."

34. Propp, *Die historischen Wurzeln des Zaubermärchens*, pp. 143–144.

35. Ibid., pp. 177–179.

36. Ibid., pp. 177, 181.

37. Paul Kretschmer, "Das Märchen vom Blaubart," p. 63.

38. Ibid., p. 65.

39. Ibid., p. 64.

40. Ibid.

41. Saintyves, *Les Contes de Perrault*, pp. 359–396.

42. Ibid., pp. 368–99.

43. Propp, *Die historischen Wurzeln des Zaubermärchens*, p. 36.

44. Ibid., p. 286.

45. Ibid., p. 452.

46. Ibid., p. 451.

47. Ibid., p. 285.

48. Ibid., p. 283.

49. Ibid., p. 458.

50. See Johannes Bolte, Georg Polívka, *Anmerkungen zu den Kinder- und Hausmärchen der Brüder Grimm*, p. 244.

51. Propp, *Die historischen Wurzeln des Zaubermärchens*, p. 454.

52. Ibid., pp. 454–455.

53. Ibid., p. 453.
54. Ibid., p. 458.
55. Lüthi, *The European Folktale*, p. 2.
56. See Benjamin, "Capitalism as Religion."
57. See Lévi-Strauss, "The Structural Study of Myth" and "Structure and Form: Reflections on a Work by Vladimir Propp."
58. Propp, "Study of the Folktale: Structure and History," p. 287.
59. Lévi-Strauss, "The Structural Study of Myth," p. 224.
60. Ibid.
61. Ibid., p. 226.
62. Lévi-Strauss, "Structure and Form," p. 143.
63. See A. J. Greimas, *Structural Semantics*, pp. 198–221.
64. Lévi-Strauss, "Structure and Form," p. 128.
65. Ibid., p. 130 (italics mine—W. M.).
66. See Lévi-Strauss, "The Structural Study of Myth," p. 224.
67. See Lévi-Strauss, "Structure and Form," pp. 129–131.
68. Ibid., p. 131.
69. W. v. Humboldt, letter to Goethe, Feb. 9, 1796, in *Briefe an Goethe*, vol. 1, p. 220.
70. Lévi-Strauss, "Structure and Form," p. 129.
71. See ibid., p. 130.
72. Propp, "Study of the Folktale: Structure and History," pp. 289–291.
73. Eleasar Meletinsky, S. Nekludov, E. Novik, D. Segal, "Problems of the Structural Analysis of Fairytales," p. 115. See also ibid., p. 87.
74. Meletinsky, "Marriage: Its Function and Position in the Structure of Folktales," p. 64.
75. Ibid., p. 65.
76. Meletinsky, "Problems of the Structural Analysis of Fairytales," pp. 93–94.
77. Ibid., p. 93: "In myths, the contrasts are characterized by their correlation with other mythical oppositions [. . .] In tales, however, each member of the opposition is assigned a constant positive or negative value (often of the ethical order): 'our kingdom,' is characterized as positive while 'foreign kingdom,' from where the dragon is flying, is negative."
78. The opposition high—low can in turn be further differentiated into numerous other oppositions: older—younger, king—peasant, beautiful—ugly, clever—dumb (ibid., p. 96). All these oppositional pairs in turn interact with other structural-definitional opposites like true—false and evident—concealed (appearance and being).

79. Ibid., p. 101.

80. Meletinsky, "Structural-Typological Study of Folktales," p. 48.

81. Meletinsky, "Problems of the Structural Analysis of Fairytales," p. 129.

82. The positive mediating function of myths as well as the compensatory "justice" of fairy tales, that (more than) balances a negative beginning with a positive conclusion, can be subsumed under the concept of balance only if that concept is already invested with evaluative associations (that then would need to be justified).

83. See ibid., p. 84 and "Structural-Typological Study of Folktales," p. 49.

84. Ibid., p. 31.

85. Propp, "Study of the Folktale: Structure and History," p. 289.

86. Propp, *Morphology of the Folktale*, p. 113.

87. Propp, "Study of the Folktale: Structure and History," p. 289.

88. Propp, *Morphology of the Folktale*, p. 113.

89. To be sure, some criticisms of Lüthi's analysis rehabilitate Propp's locating the style problem beyond the level of morphological constants against Lüthi's universalization of style: Lüthi, the criticism runs, took specific stylistic qualities of the "Grimm genre," that is, of editorially homogenized and (pseudo-) popularly stylized texts, essentialized them into qualities of the fairy tale *tout court*, and thus ultimately fell a victim to the confusion, very rich in tradition, of fairy tales in general with Grimms' fairy tales, of constant essence and variable accidents. See Moser, "Theorie- und Methodenprobleme der Märchenforschung," p. 47.

90. Lüthi, *The European Folktale*, pp. 10–11. Translation modified.

91. Ibid., pp. 11–12. Translation modified.

92. Ibid., p. 13.

93. Ibid., pp. 11 and 22.

94. Ibid., p. 22.

95. Ibid., p. 17.

96. Ibid., p. 24.

97. Ibid., pp. 26–28.

98. Ibid., p. 35.

99. Ibid., p. 45. Translation modified.

100. Ibid., pp. 59, 45, and 61. Translation modified.

101. Ibid., pp. 43–44. Translation modified.

102. Ibid., p. 51. Translation modified.

103. Ibid.

104. Ibid., pp. 70–71.

105. Ibid., p. 69. Translation modified.

106. See Friedrich Panzer, "Märchen," p. 120.

107. Friedrich von der Leyden, "Zum Problem der Form beim Märchen," pp. 80–81.

108. Wolfgang Mohr, "Einfache Formen," p. 325.

109. Lüthi, *The European Folktale*, p. 82. Translation modified.

110. Benjamin, "Goethe's Elective Affinities," p. 351. Translation modified.

111. Lüthi, *The European Folktale*, p. 2. Translation modified.

112. Ibid., p. 81.

113. Ibid., p. 84. Translation modified.

114. Ibid., p. 81.

115. Ibid., pp. 82–83. Translation modified.

116. In a study rich in material (*Das Märchen in der deutschen Aufklärung. Vom Feemärchen zum Volksmärchen*) Manfred Grätz advanced the thesis "that 'folk-tales' (that is, fairy tales in the sense and style of Grimm's tales) did not yet exist at the outset of the 18th century in Germany." Rather, he claims, they are the effect of a later and fully "artificial" discovery of "folk character" [Volkstümlichkeit], "naiveté," and modern pedagogy. No matter how difficult this thesis is to contradict for the "genre Grimm" (even though Perrault's *Contes* approach this genre by the end of 17th century), it does not entail any definitive answer to the question of the fairy tale's form in general—which constitutes an object of ethnological study for almost all cultures.

117. Jolles, *Einfache Formen*, pp. 240–243.

118. Lüthi, *The European Folktale*, p. 89. Translation modified.

119. See also Ranke, "Betrachtungen zum Wesen und zur Funktion des Märchens," pp. 651–652.

120. Lüthi, *The European Folktale*, pp. 88–89. Translation modified.

121. Ibid., pp. 59, 84–85. Translation modified.

122. Ibid., p. 85.

123. Ibid., p. 80.

124. Ibid., p. 84.

125. Karl Voretzsch, "Blaubart." (All citations from this article come from pages 268 and 269.)

126. Hartwig Suhrbier, "Blaubart—Leitbild und Leidfigur," p. 55.

127. One exception is Anatole France's narrative "Les Sept Femmes de la Barbe-Bleue."

128. Katalin Horn, "Motivationen und Funktionen der tödlichen Bedrohung in den Kinder- und Hausmärchen der Brüder Grimm," pp. 36–37.

129. Ibid., p. 33.

130. Perrault, *Contes*, p. 128.

131. In an interesting article, Ulrike Kindl has claimed that the avoidance of children is even the motif whose fundamental displacement underlies the Bluebeard fairy tale. Like those mythical figures who are prophesied to die at the hand of their children, so Bluebeard in killing his wives is above all trying to kill his own children and hence avoid a matrilineal succession. The mythical core of the fairy tale is thus a "classical" problem of succession. In fact, at the conclusion of several Bluebeard variations, the happy inheritance of the last wife is underlined. However, why should the fairy tale have so thoroughly suppressed the motif of child-killing, where it elsewhere never spares parents' cruelty to their own children? In any case, Kindl's interpretation basically follows types of arguments that are laid down in Propp's theory of the fairy tale. She also clearly states that the narrators of Bluebeard fairy tales could have been "completely disinterested" as to "which meaning-contexts might have originally underlain certain motifs." See Ulrike Kindl, "Blaubarts Mord-Motiv oder: Wie neugierig darf Märchendeutung sein?"

132. Grimm, *Kinder- und Hausmärchen*, p. 772 ("Das Meerhäschen").

133. See Röhrich, *Märchen und Wirklichkeit*, p. 142.

134. See Verena Kast, "Der Blaubart. Zum Problem des destruktiven Animus," p. 98.

135. See Helmut Barz, *Blaubart. Wenn einer vernichtet, was er liebt.*

136. His introductory remark betrays considerable confusion vis-à-vis the genre's general characteristics: "Actually this story [Bluebeard] is not a fairy tale, because with the single exception of the indelible blood on the key [. . .] there is nothing magical or supernatural in the story. More important, there is no development of any of the characters." (Bruno Bettelheim, *The Uses of Enchantment*, p. 299). Just as the mere occurrence of magical elements by no means allows for a positive determination of a narrative's belonging or not-belonging to the genre of the fairy tale—numerous examples demonstrate that fairy tales do not need magic at all—so too does the lack of the supernatural not permit a negative exclusion from the realm of the fairy tale. This is notwithstanding the fact that the magic key does in fact play a significant role in the Bluebeard tale. The absence of character development Bettelheim blames the narrative for is widely considered to be precisely a definiens of the fairy tale as opposed to "realistic" narratives.

137. Ibid., p. 300.

138. Ibid., p. 301.

139. Ibid., p. 302.

140. Ibid.

141. Tatar, *The Hard Facts of the Grimm's Fairy Tales*, p. 52.

142. Meletinsky, "Problems of the Structural Analysis of the Fairy-tales," p. 131.

143. Ibid., p. 130.

144. Tatar, *The Hard Facts of the Grimm's Fairy Tales*, p. 169.

145. German fairy tales traditionally end with the formulaic: "And if they have not died, then they are still alive today."—Trans.

146. Ibid., p. 166.

147. Ibid., p. 171.

148. A. W. Schlegel, *Sämmtliche Werke*, vol. 11, p. 140.

Bibliography

Adelung, Johann Christoph. *Versuch eines vollständigen grammatisch-kritischen Wörterbuchs der hochdeutschen Mundart.* Leipzig: J. G. Breitkopf und Comp., 1774–1786.

Barry III, Herbert. "The Evolutionary Significance of Adolescent Initiation Ceremonies." *American Ethnologist* 7 (1980): pp. 696–715.

Barz, Helmut. *Blaubart. Wenn einer vernichtet, was er liebt.* Zürich: Kreuz, 1987.

Bauer, Hermann. *Rocaille. Zur Herkunft und zum Wesen eines Ornament-Motivs.* Berlin: de Gruyter, 1962.

Benjamin, Walter. "Goethe's Elective Affinities;" "Fate and Character;" "The Concept of Criticism in German Romanticism;" "Capitalism as Religion." All in Benjamin, *Selected Writings*, vol. 1 (1913–1926), ed. Marcus Bullock and Michael W. Jennings. Cambridge, Mass: Belknap Press, 1996.

———. "Franz Kafka;" "The Storyteller. Reflections on the Works of Nikolai Leskov." Both in Benjamin, *Illuminations*, ed. Hanna Arendt, trans. Harry Zohn. New York: Schocken, 1968.

———. *The Origin of German Tragic Drama*, trans. John Osborne. Cambridge, Mass: Belknap Press, Verso, 1977.

Berefelt, Gunnar. "Verzierungen mit Einsicht und Sinn - Notizen um Ph. O. Runge." *Kunsthistorisk Tidschrift* 41 (1972): pp. 81–94.

Bergk, J. A. *Die Kunst zu denken. Ein Seitenstück zur Kunst, Bücher zu lesen.* Leipzig: Hempel, 1802.

Bettelheim, Bruno. *The Uses of Enchantment.* New York: Vintage, 1989.

Bloch, Ernst. *Heritage of Our Time*, trans. Neville and Steven Plaice. Berkeley: University of California Press, 1991.

Blumenberg, Hans. "Wirklichkeitsbegriff und Möglichkeit des Romans." In H. R. Jauß (ed.), *Poetik und Hermeneutik I (Nachahmung und Illusion)*. München: Fink, 1969 (2nd ed.), pp. 9–27.

Blumenfeld, Walter. *Sinn und Unsinn*. München: Ernst Reinhardt, 1933.

Bolte, Johannes and Polívka, Georg. *Anmerkungen zu den Kinder- und Hausmärchen der Brüder Grimm*. Leipzig: Dieterich, 1932, vol. 5.

Bosse, Heinrich. "The Marvellous and Romantic Semiotics." *Studies in Romanticism* 14 (1975): pp. 211–234.

Bottigheimer, Ruth B. *Grimm's Bad Girls and Bold Boys. The Moral and Social Vision of the "Tales."* New Haven: Yale University Press, 1987.

Brecht, Christoph. *Die gefährliche Rede. Sprachreflexion und Erzählstruktur in der Prosa Ludwig Tiecks*. Tübingen: Niemeyer, 1993.

Brodnitz, Käthe. *Die vier Märchenkomödien von Ludwig Tieck*. Erlangen: Junge & Sohn, 1912 (Phil. Diss. München, 1912).

Bruhns, Wolfgang. "A la grecque." In Otto Schmitt (ed.), *Reallexikon zur deutschen Kunstgeschichte*. Stuttgart: Metzler, 1937, vol. 1, pp. 323–324.

Busch, Werner. *Die notwendige Arabeske. Wirklichkeitsaneigung und Stilisierung in der deutschen Kunst des 19. Jahrhunderts*. Berlin: Gebr. Mann, 1985.

Cammaerts, Émile. *The Poetry of Nonsense*. New York: Folcrofft Library Editions, 1925.

Chesterton, Gilbert Keith. "A Defense of Nonsense." In Chesterton, *A Defense of Nonsense*. New York: Dodd, Mead & Company, 1911, pp. 1–11.

Carroll, Lewis. *Through the Looking Glass*. London: Penguin, 1984.

Crousaz, Jean Pierre de. *Traité du Beau*. Amsterdam: François L'Honoré, 1715 (reprint Genève: Slatkine Reprints, 1970).

Delarue, Paul. "L'œuvre d'un enfant de Paris: Les Contes merveilleux de Perrault et la tradition populaire." In *Bulletin Folklorique de L'Ile de France* 1951, pp. 195–201, 221–228, 251–260, 283–291 and 1952, pp. 348–357, 511–517.

———. *Le Conte Populaire Français*. Paris: Éditions Érasme, 1957.

Deleuze, Gilles. *Logique du sens*. Paris: Minuit, 1969.

———. "Woran erkennt man den Strukturalismus." In *Geschichte der Philosophie, Ideen, Lehren*, ed. François Châtelet. Berlin: Ullstein, 1975, vol. 8, pp. 269–302.

Derrida, Jacques. "Parergon." In Derrida, *The Truth in Painting*, trans.

Geoff Bennington and Ian McLoyd. Chicago: University of Chicago Press, 1987, pp. 15–147.

———. "Survivre." In Derrida, *Parages.* Paris: Galilée, 1986, pp. 117–218.

Dick, Manfred. *Die Entwicklung des Gedankens der Poesie in den Fragmenten des Novalis.* Bonn: Bouvier, 1967.

Dünkelsbühler, Ulrike. *Kritik der Rahmen-Vernunft. Parergon-Versionen nach Kant und Derrida.* München: Fink, 1991.

Eastman, Max. *Enjoyment of Laughter.* London: Hamish Hamilton, 1937.

Ede, Lisa S. *The Nonsense Literature of Edward Lear and Lewis Carroll.* Phil. Diss., Ohio State University, 1975.

———. "An Introduction to the Nonsense Literature of Edward Lear and Lewis Carroll." In Wim Tigges (ed.), *Explorations in the Field of Nonsense.* Amsterdam: Rodopi, 1987, pp. 47–60.

Falke, Jacob. *Die deutsche Trachten- und Modenwelt. Ein Beitrag zur deutschen Culturgeschichte.* 2nd part. (*Die Neuzeit*). Leipzig: Gustav Meyer, 1858.

Fichte, Johann Gottlieb. *Grundlage der gesamten Wissenschaftslehre.* In *Fichtes sämtliche Werke,* ed. I. H. Fichte. Berlin: Veit & Comp., 1845/1846 (reprint Berlin: de Gruyter, 1971), vol. 1.

Fink, Gonthier-Louis. *Naissance et apogée du conte merveilleux en Allemagne 1740–1800.* Paris: Les Belles Lettres, 1966 (= Annales littéraires de l'Université de Besançon, vol. 80).

Flescher, Jacqueline. "The Language of Nonsense." *Yale French Studies* 43 (1969/1970): pp. 128–144.

Foucault, Michel. *The Archaeology of Knowledge,* trans. A. M. Sheridan Smith. New York: Pantheon, 1972.

———. *The Order of Things,* New York: Vintage, 1994.

———. *The History of Sexuality,* trans. Robert Hurley. New York: Vintage, 1990, vol. 1 (*An Introduction*).

France, Anatole. "Les Sept Femmes de la Barbe-Bleue." In France, *Œuvres complètes.* Paris: Calmann-Lévy Éditeurs, 1930, vol. XIX, pp. 125–163.

Frank, Manfred and Kurz, Gerhard. "'*ordo inversus.*' Zu einer Reflexionsfigur bei Novalis, Hölderlin, Kleist und Kafka." In Herbert Anton, Bernhard Gajek, Peter Pfaff (eds.), *Geist und Zeichen. Festschrift für Arthur Henkel.* Heidelberg: Carl Winter, 1977, pp. 75–97.

Frege, Gottlob. "[Ausführungen über Sinn und Bedeutung]," in Frege, *Nachgelassene Schriften,* ed. Hans Hermes, Friedrich Kambartel, Friedrich Kaulbach. Hamburg: Meiner 1969, pp. 128–136.

———. "Über Sinn und Bedeutung." In Frege, *Funktion, Begriff, Bedeutung*, ed. Günther Patzig. Göttingen: Vandenhoeck & Ruprecht, 1975 (4th ed.), pp. 40–65.

Freud, Sigmund. *Jokes and the Unconscious.* In *The Standard Edition of the Complete Psychological Works of Sigmund Freud*, ed. James Stratchey. London: The Hogarth Press, 1953–1974, vol. VIII, pp. 9–236.

———. "Project for a Scientific Psychology." In *The Standard Edition of the Complete Psychological Works of Sigmund Freud*, vol. I, pp. 295–397.

———. *Totem and Taboo.* In *The Standard Edition of the Complete Psychological Works of Sigmund Freud*, vol. XIII, pp. 1–161.

———. "The Uncanny." In *The Standard Edition of the Complete Psychological Works of Sigmund Freud*, vol. XVII, pp. 217–252.

Garte, Hansjörg. *Kunstform Schauerroman. Eine morphologische Begriffsbestimmung des Sensationsromans im 18. Jahrhundert von Walpoles 'Castle of Otranto' bis Jean Pauls 'Titan'.* Leipzig: Carl Garte, 1935.

Gervinus, Georg Gottfried. *Geschichte der deutschen Dichtung.* Leipzig: Wilhelm Engelmann, 1853 (4th ed.).

Goethe, Johann Wolfgang von. "Von Arabesken." In Goethe, *Berliner Ausgabe.* Berlin und Weimar: Aufbau-Verlag, 1973, vol. 19 (*Schriften zur bildenden Kunst I*), pp. 83–87.

———. "Das Märchen." In *Goethes Werke. Hamburger Ausgabe*, ed. Erich Trunz. München: C. H. Beck, 1981, vol. 6, pp. 209–241.

———. *Goethe's Fairy Tale of the Green Snake and the Beautiful Lily*, trans. Donald MacLean. Grand Rapids: Phane Press, 1993.

———. "Xenien." In *Goethes Werke. Hamburger Ausgabe*, ed. Erich Trunz. München: C. H. Beck, 1981, vol. 1, pp. 208–234.

———. *Goethes Tagebücher*, vol. 1–10 (= Sect. III of *Goethes Werke*, herausgegeben im Auftrag der Grossherzogin Sophie von Sachsen). Weimar: Böhlau, 1887–1889.

———. *Goethe's Briefe*, vol 1–21 (= Sect. IV of *Goethes Werke*, herausgegeben im Auftrag der Grossherzogin Sophie von Sachsen). Weimar: Böhlau, 1887–1889.

———. *Briefe an Goethe. Hamburger Ausgabe*, ed. Karl Robert Mandelkow. Hamburg: Wegener, 1965, vol. 1.

———. *Briefwechsel zwischen Goethe und Marianne v. Willemer*, ed. Th. Creizenach. Stuttgart: Cotta, 1878.

———. *Goethe's und Carlyle's Briefwechsel.* Berlin: Hertz, 1887.

Grätz, Manfred. *Das Märchen in der deutschen Aufklärung. Vom Feenmärchen zum Volksmärchen.* Stuttgart: Metzler, 1988.

Gray, Donald J. "The Uses of Victorian Laughter." *Victorian Studies* 10 (1966): pp. 145–176.

Greimas, A. J. *Structural Semantics. An Attempt at a Method,* trans. Daniele McDowell. Lincoln, Nebr.: University of Nebraska Press, 1983.

Greiner, Bernhard. *Die Komödie. Eine theatralische Sendung: Grundlagen und Interpretationen.* Tübingen: Francke, 1992.

Grimm, Jacob, and Wilhelm Grimm. *Deutsches Wörterbuch.* Leipzig: S. Hirzel, 1854–1960 (reprint München: dtv, 1984).

———. *Kinder- und Hausmärchen.* München: Winkler, 1977.

Groth, Paul. *Die ethische Haltung des deutschen Volksmärchens.* Leipzig: Eichblatt, 1930.

Grün, Karl. *Über Goethe vom menschlichen Standpuncte.* Darmstadt: Leske, 1846.

Gumbrecht, Hans Ulrich and Pfeiffer, K. Ludwig (eds.). *Materialität der Kommunikation.* Frankfurt am Main: Suhrkamp, 1988.

Harries, Karsten. *The Broken Frame. Three Lectures.* Washington: The Catholic University of America Press, 1989.

———. "Laubwerk auf Tapeten." In Hans-Jürgen Gawoll and Christoph Jamme (eds.), *Idealismus mit Folgen. Die Epochenschwelle um 1800 in Kunst und Geisteswissenschaften. Festschrift zum 65. Geburtstag vom Otto Pöggeler.* München: Fink, 1994, pp. 87–96.

Hegel, Georg Wilhelm Friedrich. *Aesthetics. Lectures on Fine Art,* trans. T. M. Knox. Oxford: Clarendon Press, 1975.

Herder, Johann Gottfried. *Briefe zur Beförderung der Humanität.* In Herder, *Sämtliche Werke,* ed. Bernhard Suphan. Berlin: Weidmannsche Buchhandlung, 1883, vol. 18.

———. *Adrastea.* In Herder, *Sämtliche Werke,* ed. Bernhard Suphan. Berlin: Weidmannsche Buchhandlung, 1883, vol. 23.

Hildebrandt, Rolf. *Nonsense-Aspekte der englischen Kinderliteratur.* Diss. Hamburg 1962.

———. *Nonsense-Aspekte der englischen Kinderliteratur.* Weinheim: Beltz, 1970.

Hoffmann, Karl. *Die Umbildung der Kantischen Lehre vom Genie in Schellings System des transzendentalen Idealismus.* Bern: Scheitlin, Spring & Cie., 1907.

Hofstadter, Douglas R. "Metamagical Themes." *The Scientific American* 6, vol. 247 (Dec. 1982): pp. 19–25.

Holbek, Bengt. "Interpretation of Fairytales. Danish Folklore in a European Perspective." *FF Communications* 239 (1987): pp. 235–242.

Holquist, Michael. "What is a Boojum? Nonsense and Modernism." *Yale French Studies* 43 (1969/1970): pp. 145–164.

Hölter, Achim. "'Die sieben Weiber.' Ein handschriftlicher Entwurf zur Neufassung des 'Blaubart.'" *Wirkendes Wort* 36 (1986): pp. 251–258.

———. *Ludwig Tieck. Literaturgeschichte als Poesie.* Heidelberg: Carl Winter, 1989.

Hörisch, Jochen. *Die Wut des Verstehens.* Frankfurt am Main: Suhrkamp, 1988.

Horn, Katalin. "Motivationen und Funktionen der tödlichen Bedrohung in den Kinder- und Hausmärchen der Brüder Grimm." *Schweizerisches Archiv für Volkskunde* 74 (1978): pp. 20–45.

Husserl, Edmund. *Logische Untersuchungen,* vol. 2, ed. Ursula Panzer. The Hague: Martinus Nijhoff, 1984.

———. *Logical Investigations,* trans. J. N. Findlay. London: Routledge & Kegan Paul, 1970.

Immerwahr, Raymond. "Die symbolische Form des 'Briefs über den Roman.'" *Zeitschrift für deutsche Philologie* 88 (1969): pp. 41–60.

Jolles, André. *Einfache Formen.* Tübingen: Max Niemeyer, 1930.

Journal des Luxus und der Moden, ed. F. J. Bertuch and G. M. Kraus. Weimar: Verlag des Industrie-Comptoirs, March 1796, vol. 11.

Kafka, Franz. *Erzählungen,* ed. Max Brod. Frankfurt am Main: S. Fischer, 1965.

Kant, Immanuel. *Anthropologie in pragmatischer Hinsicht.* In *Kant's gesammelte Schriften,* ed. Königlich Preußische Akademie der Wissenschaften. Berlin: Georg Reimer, 1907 sqq., vol. 7.

———. *Anthropology from a Pragmatic Point of View,* trans. Victor L. Dowdell. Carbondale, Ill.: Southern Illinois University Press, 1996.

———. *Kritik der Urtheilskraft.* In *Kant's gesammelte Schriften,* vol. 5.

———. *Critique of Judgement,* trans. Werner S. Pluhar. Indianapolis: Hackett, 1976–1977.

———. *Critique of Pure Reason,* ed. Vasilis Politis. Carbondale. Ill.: Southern Illinois University Press, 1994.

———. *Reflexionen zur Anthropologie.* In *Kant's gesammelte Schriften,* vol. 15.

———. *The Metaphysics of Morals,* trans. Mary Gregor. Cambridge, Mass.: Cambridge University Press, 1996.

Kast, Verena. "Der Blaubart. Zum Problem des destruktiven Animus." In Mario Jacoby, Verena Kast, Ingrid Riedel (eds.), *Das Böse im Märchen.* Fellbach: Bonz, 1978, pp. 90–108.

Kindl, Ulrike. "Blaubarts Mord-Motiv oder: Wie neugierig darf Märchendeutung sein?" *Lendemains* 53 (1989): pp. 111–117.

Kittler, Friedrich A. *Discourse Networks 1800–1900*, trans. Michael Metteer and Chris Cullens. Stanford: Stanford University Press, 1990.

———. "Autorschaft und Liebe." In Kittler (ed.), *Austreibung des Geistes aus den Geisteswissenschaften.* Paderborn: Schöningh, 1980, pp. 142–173.

———. "Vergessen." In Ulrich Nassen (ed.), *Texthermeneutik, Aktualität, Geschichte, Kritik.* Paderborn: Schöningh, 1979, pp. 195–221.

Kretschmer, Paul. "Das Märchen vom Blaubart." *Mitteilungen der Anthropologischen Gesellschaft in Wien* 31 (1901): pp. 62–70.

Lang, Peter Christian. *Literarischer Unsinn im späten 19. und frühen 20. Jahrhundert. Systematische Begründung und historische Rekonstruktion.* Frankfurt: Peter Lang, 1982.

Lankheit, Klaus. "Die Frühromantik und die Grundlagen der 'gegendstandslosen Malerei.'" *Neue Heidelberger Jahrbücher* (1951): pp. 55–90.

Lévi-Strauss, Claude. *Structural Anthropology II*, trans. Monique Layton. London: Penguin, 1994.

———. "The Structural Study of Myth." In Lévi-Strauss, *Structural Anthropology*, trans. Claire Jacobson. New York: Basic, 1963, pp. 206–231.

———. "Structure and Form: Reflections on a Work by Vladimir Propp." In Lévi-Strauss, *Structural Anthropology II*, pp. 115–145.

Leyden, Friedrich von der. "Zum Problem der Form beim Märchen." In Felix Karlinger (ed.), *Wege der Märchenforschung.* Darmstadt: Wissenschaftliche Buchgesellschaft, 1973, pp. 74–83.

Liede, Alfred. *Dichtung als Spiel. Studien zur Unsinnspoesie an den Grenzen der Sprache.* Berlin: de Gruyter, 1992 (2nd ed.).

Lugowski, Clemens. *Die Form der Individualität im Roman. Studien zur inneren Struktur der frühen deutschen Prosaerzählung.* Berlin: Junker und Dünnhaupt, 1932 (reprint Hildesheim/New York: Olms, 1970).

Lüthi, Max. *The European Folktale: Form and Nature*, trans. John D. Niles. Bloomington, Ind.: Indiana University Press, 1986.

———. *Das Volksmärchen als Dichtung. Ästhetik und Anthropologie.* Göttingen: Vandenhoeck & Ruprecht, 1990 (2nd ed.).

Luhmann, Niklas. *Die Kunst der Gesellschaft.* Frankfurt am Main: Suhrkamp, 1995.

Mackensen, Lutz. "Das deutsche Volksmärchen." In W. Preßler (ed.), *Handbuch der deutschen Volkskunde.* Potsdam: Athenaion, 1936, vol. 2, pp. 305–325.

Marelli, Adriana. *Ludwig Tiecks frühe Märchenspiele und die Gozzische*

Manier. Eine vergleichende Studie. Phil. Diss., Köln: Wasmund-Bothmann, 1968.

Marin, Louis. *Études Sémiologiques.* Paris: Klincksieck, 1971.

Meletinsky, Eleasar. "Marriage: Its Function and Position in the Structure of Folktales." In *Soviet Structural Folkloristics,* ed. P. Maranda. The Hague: Mouton, 1974, vol. I, pp. 61–72.

———. "Structural-Typological Study of Folktales." In *Soviet Structural Folkloristics,* pp. 19–51.

Meletinsky, Eleasar, Nekludov, S., Novik, E., Segal, D. "Problems of the Structural Analysis of Fairytales." In *Soviet Structural Folkloristics,* pp. 73–193.

Menninghaus, Winfried. *Unendliche Verdopplung. Die frühromantische Grundlegung der Kunsttheorie im Begriff absoluter Selbstreflexion.* Frankfurt am Main: Suhrkamp, 1987.

———. "Kant über 'Unsinn,' 'Lachen' und 'Laune.'" In *Deutsche Vierteljahresschrift für Literaturwissenschaft und Geistesgeschichte* 68 (1994), Sonderheft *Figur und Stimme. Kritik und Restitution in der Literaturwissenschaft,* ed. Aleida Assmann and Anselm Haverkamp. Stuttgart: Metzler, 1994, pp. 263–286.

Michel, Willy. *Ästhetische Hermeneutik und frühromantische Kritik. Friedrich Schlegels fragmentarische Entwürfe, Rezensionen, Charakteristiken und Kritiken.* Göttingen: Vandenhoeck & Ruprecht, 1982.

Mohr, Wolfgang. "Einfache Formen." In Merker-Stammler, *Reallexikon der deutschen Literaturgeschichte.* Berlin: de Gruyter, 1958 (2nd ed.), vol. 1, pp. 321–328.

Moritz, Karl Philipp. "Arabesken;" "Spielarten des Geschmacks;" "Die Säule. Sind die architektonischen Zierathen in den verschiedenen Säulenordnungen willkürlich oder wesentlich?" "Einfachheit und Klarheit." All in Moritz, *Schriften zur Ästhetik und Poetik,* ed. H. J. Schrimpf. Tübingen: Niemeyer, 1962.

Moser, Dietz-Rüdiger. "Theorie- und Methodenprobleme der Märchenforschung. Zugleich der Versuch einer Definition des 'Märchens.'" *Jahrbuch für Volkskunde* 3 (1980): pp. 47–64.

Naumann, Barbara. "*Musikalisches Ideen-Instrument.*" *Das Musikalische in Poetik und Sprachtheorie der Frühromantik.* Stuttgart: Metzler, 1990.

Nietzsche, Friedrich. *Sämtliche Werke. Kritische Studienausgabe,* ed. Giorgio Colli and Mazzino Montinari. München: dtv, 1980.

Novalis. *Schriften,* ed. Richard Samuel in cooperation with Hans-Joachim Mähl and Gerhard Schulz. Stuttgart: Kohlhammer, 1960 sqq.

Oesterle, Günter. "Arabeske und Roman. Eine poetikgeschichtliche Rekonstruktion von Friedrich Schlegels 'Brief über den Roman.'" In Dirk Grathoff (ed.), *Studien zur Ästhetik und Literaturgeschichte der Kunstperiode.* Frankfurt am Main: Peter Lang, 1985, pp. 233–292.

———. "'Vorbegriffe zu einer Theorie der Ornamente.' Kontroverse Formprobleme zwischen Aufklärung, Klassizismus und Romantik am Beispiel der Arabeske." In Herbert Beck, Peter C. Bol, Eva Mack-Gérard (eds.), *Ideal und Wirklichkeit der bildenden Kunst im späten 18. Jahrhundert.* Berlin: Gebr. Mann, 1984, pp. 119–139.

———. "Arabeske, Schrift und Poesie in E. T. A. Hoffmanns Kunstmärchen 'Der goldne Topf.'" *Athenäum. Jahrbuch für Romantik* 1 (1991): pp. 69–107.

Paetzold, Heinz. *Ästhetik des deutschen Idealismus. Zur Idee ästhetischer Rationalität bei Baumgarten, Kant, Schelling, Hegel und Schopenhauer.* Wiesbaden: Franz Steiner, 1983.

Panzer, Friedrich. "Märchen." In Felix Karlinger (ed.), *Wege der Märchenforschung.* Darmstadt: Wissenschaftliche Buchgesellschaft, 1973, pp. 84–128.

Paul, Jean. *Hesperus oder 45 Hundposttage.* In *Jean Pauls Sämtliche Werke,* Historisch-kritische Ausgabe, ed. Preußische Akademie der Wissenschaften. Weimar: Böhlau, 1929, vol. 3 (ed. Hans Bach and Eduard Berend).

———. *Das Lob der Dumheit.* In Jean Paul, *Sämtliche Werke,* ed. Norbert Miller. München: Carl Hanser, 1974, sect. II, vol. I, pp. 307–368.

Penther, Joh. Fr. *Ausführliche Anleitung zur bürgerlichen Bau-Kunst, Erster Theil, Enthaltend ein Lexicum Architectonicum oder Erklärung der üblichsten Deutschen, Französischen, Italienischen Kunstwörter.* Augspurg: Pfeffel, 1744.

Perrault, Charles. *Contes,* ed. Gilbert Rouger. Paris: Garnier, 1967.

———. *The Complete Fairy Tales of Charles Perrault,* ed. and trans. Neil Philip. New York: Clarion, 1993.

Petzold, Dieter. *Formen und Funktionen der englischen Nonsense-Dichtung im 19. Jahrhundert.* Nürnberg: Hans Carl, 1972.

Piel, Friedrich. *Die Ornament-Groteske in der italienischen Renaissance. Zu ihrer kategorialen Struktur und Entstehung.* Berlin: de Gruyter, 1962.

Pohlheim, Karl Konrad. *Die Arabeske. Ansichten und Ideen aus Schlegels Poetik.* Paderborn: Schöningh, 1966.

Propp, Vladimir. *Morphology of the Folktale,* trans. Laurence Scott. Austin, Tex.: University of Texas Press, 1968.

———. *Die historischen Wurzeln des Zaubermärchens.* München: Hanser, 1987.

———. "Study of the Folktale: Structure and History." *Dispositio. Revista Hispánica de Semiótica Literaria* 3 (1976): pp. 277–292.

———. "Folklore and Reality." In Propp, *Theory and History of Folklore,* ed. Anatoly Liberman. Minneapolis: University of Minnesota Press, 1984, pp. 16–38.

Ranke, Kurt. "Betrachtungen zum Wesen und zur Funktion des Märchens." *Studium Generale* 11 (1958): pp. 647–664.

Reichardt, Johann Friedrich. "Notiz von Deutschen Journalen—Die Horen, erstes Stück." In *Deutschland,* ed. J. F. Reichardt. Berlin: Unger, 1796 (reprint Nedeln: Kraus, 1971), vol. 1, pp. 55–90.

Reichert, Klaus. *Lewis Carroll: Studien zum literarischen Unsinn.* München: Hanser, 1974.

Reid, Susan. "Myth as Metastructure of the Fairytale." In *Soviet Structural Folkloristics,* ed. P. Maranda. The Hague: Mouton, 1974, vol. I, pp. 151–172.

Ribbat, Ernst. *Studien zur Konzeption und Praxis romantischer Poesie.* Königstein: Athenäum, 1978.

Riegl, Alois. *Die spätrömische Kunstindustrie.* Darmstadt: Wissenschaftliche Buchgesellschaft, 1992.

Riem, Adolf. "Ueber die Arabeske." *Monatsschrift der Akademie der Künste und Wissenschaften zu Berlin* (1788), no. I, pp. 276–285; no. II, pp. 22–37 and 119–136.

Röhrich, Lutz. *Märchen und Wirklichkeit.* Wiesbaden: Franz Steiner, 1964.

———. "Mensch und Tier im Märchen." *Schweizerisches Archiv für Volkskunde* 49 (1953): 188–193.

Rotermund, Erwin. "Musikalische und dichterische 'Arabeske' bei E. T. A. Hoffmann." *Poetica* 2 (1968): pp. 48–69.

Saintyves, Pierre. *Les Contes de Perrault et les Récits Parallèlles. Leurs Origines (Coutumes Primitives et Liturgies Populaires).* Paris: Librairie Critique Émile Nourry, 1923.

Schiller, Friedrich. *Schillers Werke. Nationalausgabe,* begründet von Julius Petersen. Weimar: Böhlaus Nachfolger, 1943 sqq.

———. *Kallias oder Über die Schönheit.* In Schiller, *Sämtliche Werke,* ed. Gerhard Fricke und Herbert G. Göpfert. München: Hanser, 1975 (5th ed.), vol. V., pp. 394–433.

———. *Schillers Briefwechsel mit Körner,* 2nd rev. edition, ed. Karl Goedeke, part 1 and 2. Leipzig: Veit & Comp., 1878.

———. *Briefwechsel zwischen Schiller und Wilhelm v. Humboldt*, ed. Albert Leitzmann. Stuttgart: Cotta, 1900.

Schlaffer, Heinz. "Exoterik und Esoterik in Goethes Romanen." *Goethe-Jahrbuch* 95 (1978): pp. 212–226.

———. "Roman und Märchen. Ein formtheoretischer Versuch über Tiecks 'Blonden Eckbert.'" In Wulf Segebrecht (ed.), *Ludwig Tieck* (= Wege der Forschung, vol. 386). Darmstadt: Wissenschaftliche Buchgesellschaft, 1976, pp. 444–464.

Schlapp, Otto. *Kants Lehre vom Genie und die Entstehung der 'Kritik der Urteilskraft.'* Göttingen: Vandenhoeck & Ruprecht, 1901.

Schlegel, Alice. "Adolescent Initiation Ceremonies: A Cross-Cultural Code." *Ethnology* 18 (1979): pp. 199–210.

Schlegel, August Wilhelm. *Sämmtliche Werke*, ed. Eduard Böcking. Leipzig: Weidmannsche Buchhandlung, 1846 (reprint Hildesheim/New York: Olms, 1971).

Schlegel, Friedrich. *Kritische Friedrich-Schlegel-Ausgabe*, ed. Ernst Behler with the cooperation of Jean-Jacques Anstett and Hans Eichner. Paderborn: Schöningh, 1958 sqq.

———. *Literarische Notizen 1797–1801. Literary Notebooks*, ed. Hans Eichner. Berlin: Ullstein, 1980.

Schleiermacher, F. D. E. *Hermeneutik und Kritik*, ed. Manfred Frank. Frankfurt am Main: Suhrkamp, 1977.

Schmidt, Arno. "'Funfzehn.' Vom Wunderkind der Sinnlosigkeit." In Schmidt, *Die Ritter vom Geist. Von vergessenen Kollegen*. Karlsruhe: Stahlberg, 1965, pp. 209–281.

———. "Die 10 Kammern des Blaubart." In Schmidt, *Trommler beim Zaren*. Karlsruhe: Stahlberg, 1966.

Schmidt, Jochen. *Die Geschichte des Genie-Gedankens in der deutschen Literatur, Philosophie und Politik 1750–1945*. Darmstadt: Wissenschaftliche Buchgesellschaft, 1985.

Schöne, Annemarie. "Humor und Komik in 'Alice's Adventures in Wonderland' und 'Through the Looking-Glass'." *Deutsche Vierteljahresschrift für Literaturwissenschaft und Geistesgeschichte* 28 (1954): pp. 102–114.

Sedlmayr, Hans. *Die Revolution der modernen Kunst*. Hamburg: Rowohlt, 1955.

Sewell, Elizabeth. *The Field of Nonsense*. London: Chatto and Windus, 1952.

Simonsen, Michèle. *Perrault. Contes*. Paris: Presses Universitaires de France, 1992.

Solger, Karl Wilhelm Ferdinand. *Nachgelassene Schriften und Briefwechsel*, ed. Ludwig Tieck and Friedrich von Raumer. Leipzig: F. A. Brockhaus, 1826 (reprint Heidelberg: Lambert Schneider, 1973).

Soriano, Marc. *Les Contes de Perrault. Culture savante et traditions populaires.* Paris: Gallimard, 1968.

Stewart, Susan. *Nonsense. Aspects of Intertextuality in Folklore and Literature.* Baltimore: Johns Hopkins University Press, 1978.

Stockhammer, Robert. *Leseerzählungen. Alternativen zum hermeneutischen Verfahren.* Stuttgart: Metzler, 1991.

Strasser, Ingrid. *Bedeutungswandel und strukturelle Semantik. 'Marotte, Laune, Tick' im literarischen Deutsch der Gegenwart und der Frühen Goethezeit.* Wien: Karl M. Halosar, 1976.

Suhrbier, Hartwig. "Blaubart - Leitbild und Leidfigur." In Suhrbier (ed.), *Blaubarts Geheimnis. Märchen und Erzählungen, Gedichte und Stücke.* Berlin: Ullstein, 1987, pp. 11–79.

Tatar, Maria. *The Hard Facts of the Grimm's Fairy Tales.* Princeton: Princeton University Press, 1987.

Thalmann, Marianne. *Der Trivialroman des 18. Jahrhunderts und der romantische Roman. Ein Beitrag zur Entwicklungsgeschichte der Geheimbundmystik.* Berlin 1923 (reprint Neendeln: Kraus, 1967).

Tieck, Ludwig. *Frühe Erzählungen und Romane*, ed. Marianne Thalmann. München: Winkler, (no year).

———. *Phantasus*, ed. Manfred Frank. Frankfurt am Main: Deutscher Klassiker Verlag, 1985.

———. *Kritische Schriften.* Leipzig: F. A. Brockhaus, 1848 (reprint Berlin: de Gruyter, 1974).

———. *Schriften in 28 Bänden.* Berlin: Georg Reimer, 1828 (reprint Berlin: de Gruyter, 1974).

———. *Volksmärchen*, ed. Peter Leberecht. Berlin: Nicolai, 1797.

———. *Letters of Ludwig Tieck. Hitherto Unpublished*, ed. Edwin H. Zeydel, Perey Matenko, Robert H. Fife. New York/London: Modern Language Association of America/Oxford University Press, 1937.

———. *Ludwig Tieck*, ed. Hermann Kasack und Alfred Mohrhenn. Berlin: Suhrkamp, 1943.

Tigges, Wim. *An Anatomy of Literary Nonsense.* Amsterdam: Rodopi, 1988.

———. "An Anatomy of Nonsense." In Tigges (ed.), *Explorations in the Field of Nonsense.* Amsterdam: Rodopi, 1987, pp. 23–46.

Todorov, Tzvetan. *The Fantastic. A Structural Approach to a Literary*

Genre, trans. Richard Howard. Ithaca: Cornell University Press, 1975.

Tonelli, Giorgio. "Kant's Early Theory of Genius (1770–1779)." *Journal of the History of Philosophy* 4 (1966): pp. 108–131.

Traeger, Jörg. *Philipp Otto Runge oder die Geburt einer neuen Kunst.* München: Prestel, 1977.

Vax, Louis. *La séduction de l'étrange. Étude sur la littérature fantastique.* Paris: Quadrige Presses Universitaires de France, 1987 (2nd ed.).

Voges, Michael. *Aufklärung und Geheimnis. Untersuchungen zur Vermittlung von Literatur- und Sozialgeschichte am Beispiel der Aneignung des Geheimbundmaterials im Roman des späten 18. Jahrhunderts.* Tübingen: Niemeyer, 1987.

Voretzsch, Karl. "Blaubart." In *Handwörterbuch des deutschen Märchens*, ed. Lutz Mackensen. Berlin: de Gruyter, 1930/1933, vol. 1, pp. 266–270.

Vosskamp, Wilhelm. *Romantheorie in Deutschland. Von Martin Opitz bis Friedrich von Blanckenburg.* Stuttgart: Metzler, 1973.

Wieland, Christoph Martin. *Sämtliche Werke.* Leipzig: Göschen, 1794 (reprint Hamburg: Hamburger Stiftung zur Förderung von Wissenschaft und Kultur, 1984).

Winckelmann, Johann Joachim. *Gedanken über die Nachahmung der griechischen Werke in der Malerei und Bildhauerkunst*, ed. Ludwig Uhlig. Stuttgart: Reclam, 1969.

MERIDIAN

Crossing Aesthetics

Aris Fioretos, *The Gray Book*

Deborah Esch, *In the Event: Reading Journalism, Reading Theory*

Winfried Menninghaus, *In Praise of Nonsense: Kant and Bluebeard*

Giorgio Agamben, *The Man Without Content*

Giorgio Agamben, *The End of the Poem: Essays in Poetics*

Theodor W. Adorno, *Sound Figures*

Louis Marin, *Sublime Poussin*

Philippe Lacoue-Labarthe, *Poetry as Experience*

Jacques Derrida, *Resistances of Psychoanalysis*

Ernst Bloch, *Literary Essays*

Marc Froment-Meurice, *That Is to Say: Heidegger's Poetics*

Francis Ponge, *Soap*

Philippe Lacoue-Labarthe, *Typography: Mimesis, Philosophy, Politics*

Giorgio Agamben, *Homo Sacer: Sovereign Power and Bare Life*

Emmanuel Levinas, *Of God Who Comes to Mind*

Bernard Stiegler, *Technics and Time, 1: The Fault of Epimetheus*

Werner Hamacher, *pleroma—Reading in Hegel*

Serge Leclaire, *Psychoanalyzing: On the Order of the Unconscious and the Practice of the Letter*

Serge Leclaire, *A Child Is Being Killed: On Primary Narcissism and the Death Drive*

Sigmund Freud, *Writings on Art and Literature*

Cornelius Castoriadis, *World in Fragments: Writings on Politics, Society, Psychoanalysis, and the Imagination*

Thomas Keenan, *Fables of Responsibility: Aberrations and Predicaments in Ethics and Politics*

Emmanuel Levinas, *Proper Names*

Alexander García Düttmann, *At Odds with AIDS: Thinking and Talking About a Virus*

Maurice Blanchot, *Friendship*

Jean-Luc Nancy, *The Muses*

Massimo Cacciari, *Posthumous People: Vienna at the Turning Point*

David E. Wellbery, *The Specular Moment: Goethe's Early Lyric and the Beginnings of Romanticism*

Edmond Jabès, *The Little Book of Unsuspected Subversion*

Hans-Jost Frey, *Studies in Poetic Discourse: Mallarmé, Baudelaire, Rimbaud, Hölderlin*

Pierre Bourdieu, *The Rules of Art: Genesis and Structure of the Literary Field*

Nicolas Abraham, *Rhythms: On the Work, Translation, and Psychoanalysis*

Jacques Derrida, *On the Name*

David Wills, *Prosthesis*

Maurice Blanchot, *The Work of Fire*

Jacques Derrida, *Points . . . : Interviews, 1974–1994*

J. Hillis Miller, *Topographies*

Philippe Lacoue-Labarthe, *Musica Ficta (Figures of Wagner)*

Jacques Derrida, *Aporias*

Emmanuel Levinas, *Outside the Subject*

Jean-François Lyotard, *Lessons on the Analytic of the Sublime*

Peter Fenves, *"Chatter": Language and History in Kierkegaard*

Jean-Luc Nancy, *The Experience of Freedom*

Jean-Joseph Goux, *Oedipus, Philosopher*

Haun Saussy, *The Problem of a Chinese Aesthetic*

Jean-Luc Nancy, *The Birth to Presence*

Library of Congress Cataloging-in-Publication Data

Menninghaus, Winfried.
[Lob des Unsinns. English]
In praise of nonsense : Kant and Bluebeard / Winfried Menninghaus ; translated by Henry Pickford.
p. cm. — (Meridian)
Includes bibliographical references (p.) and index.
ISBN 0-8047-2951-4 (cloth : alk. paper). — ISBN 0-8047-2952-2 (pbk. : alk. paper)
1. Romanticism. 2. Fairy tales—History and criticism.
3. Kant, Immanuel, 1724–1804. Kritik der Urteilskraft.
4. Tieck, Ludwig, 1773–1853. Sieben Weiber des Blaubart.
5. Perrault, Charles, 1628–1703. Barbe-bleue. I. Title.
II. Series: Meridian (Stanford, Calif.)
PN754.M4613 1999
809'.9145—dc21 98-48247

∞ This book is printed on acid-free, archival quality paper

Original printing 1999
Last figure below indicates year of this printing:
08 07 06 05 04 03 02 01 00 99

Typeset by James P. Brommer in 10.9/13 Garamond and Lithos display